How to Preach the Prophets

"Some years ago, Andrew Thompson presented a paper—"Community Oracles; A Model for Applying and Preaching the Prophets"—at the annual meeting of the Evangelical Homiletic Society. The paper was so good I've been assigning it in my doctoral classes ever since. Needless to say, I'm delighted to see his full-orbed development of this subject in this book, *How to Preach the Prophets*. Now I'll have something even better to assign! Thompson's aim is to help readers deliver biblically faithful, theologically sound, and rhetorically effective sermons from prophetic oracles. And he succeeds. With readable text (and scholarly footnotes) Thompson takes the reader through the literary and theological features of the prophets that guide sermon construction and delivery. Biblical explanations and sermonic snippets abound. Each chapter ends with exercises and resources for further reading, and two Appendix messages fully illustrate his concepts. In every way, this is a solid, helpful and interesting book."

— **Donald R. Sunukjian**, Professor of Preaching, Talbot School of Theology, Biola University

"Preaching the prophets is a much more difficult task than most preachers want to admit. And resources on preaching the prophets are few and far between. That is, until now. In his book, *How to Preach the Prophets*, Drew Thompson provides a timely resource to help preachers faithfully preach the prophets accurately and effectively. From hermeneutical approaches regarding covenantal context to recognizing one's body language and imagery in preaching, Thompson helps the reader approach the oracles of the prophets with confidence. If you want to preach the whole counsel of God and have been avoiding the prophets, this is the book for you.

— **John C. Richards Jr.**, M.Div., J.D., Connections Pastor, Saint Mark Baptist Church, Little Rock, Arkansas

"Many preachers aren't making beelines toward the prophetical books when preparing their sermon calendars—and for legitimate reasons. In our cultural moment, however, *How to Preach the Prophets* is just what the world needs. As a seasoned and skilled pastor, preacher, teacher, and scholar, I can't think of a better guide than Andrew Thompson. He not only identifies the formidable factors and, at times, the foot-dragging of God's prophets who communicated the Word to idolatrous people long ago, but he's also given us salient tools for lovingly engaging wayward listeners today. Like the prophets of yesteryear, we need courageous preachers who will preach the prophets now. This book is a biblical, theological, pastoral, and homiletical gem that all preachers need in their library!"

— **Matthew D. Kim**, Professor of Practical Theology and holder of the Hubert H. and Gladys S. Raborn Chair of Pastoral Leadership, Truett Theological Seminary, Baylor University; author of *Preaching to People in Pain*

"Drew has created an excellent resource for preachers who are looking to bring the words of the prophets to new life within their congregations. This book has all the scholarly rigor necessitated by its topic paired with the everyday wisdom of a trusted practitioner. It is Drew's admiration for the prophets and the craft of preaching that makes this book such a welcomed and trustworthy guide."

— **Ashley Mathews**, Rector at Christ the King, Fayetteville, AR

How to Preach the Prophets

Andrew C. Thompson

Fontes

How to Preach the Prophets

Copyright © 2023 by Andrew C. Thompson

ISBN-13: 978-1-948048-97-2 (paperback)
ISBN-13: 978-1-948048-98-9 (epub)

All rights reserved. No part of this publication may be reproduced, stored in a retrieval system, or transmitted in any form or by any means—electronic, mechanical, photocopy, recording, or any other—except for brief quotations in printed reviews, without the prior permission of the publisher.

Unless otherwise noted, all Scripture quotations are from The Holy Bible, English Standard Version, Copyright © 2001, 2006, 2011, 2016 by Crossway Bibles, a division of Good News Publishers. All rights reserved.

Typeset by Monolateral™ in Minion 3 and Museo Sans.

FONTES PRESS
DALLAS, TX
www.fontespress.com

For Mandy
צַר־לִי הַמָּקוֹם
גְּשָׁה־לִּי וְאֵשֵׁבָה

Contents

Abbreviations xvii

Preface xix

Introduction: A Voice Says, Cry 1
    "Prophetic Preaching" and Terminology Trouble 3
    Preachers with Big Ideas 5
    This Is the Way, Walk in It 5

Part I: Prepare the Way: Reading the Prophets 9

1. Prepare to Meet the Prophets 11
    Getting Over a Fear of the Prophets 11
    Identifying the Prophets 15
    Israel's Covenant Enforcers 20
    Strategies for Preaching the Prophets 22
        Strategy 1: Read the Prophets 23
    For Further Reading 25
    Talk about It 25
    Dig Deeper 25
    Practice 25

2. Prepare to Interpret the Prophets 27
    Familiar Paths 27
    Covenant Context 30
        Community Oracles 32
    Two Strategies for Preaching the Prophets 33
        Strategy 2.1 Compare Audience to Audience 34
        Strategy 2.2 See How It Has Already Begun 35
    The Church's Covenant Context 36
    Using a Covenant Context to Interpret the Prophets for the Church 40
        Strategy 3.1 Their Lord Is Our Lord 41
        Strategy 3.2 Their History May (or May Not) Be Our History 42
        Strategy 3.3 Their Stipulations May (or May Not) Compel Us 44

  Strategy 3.4 Their Promises Are Our History........... 46
  Strategy 3.5 Their Promises May Be Our Promises..... 48
  Strategy 3.6 Combine as Necessary 48
 The Path of the Apostles 50
 Oracles Addressed to Foreign Nations 52
 Benefits of a Covenant Context Approach 54
 Conclusion 55
 For Further Study 56
 Talk about It 56
 Dig Deeper 56
 Practice 56

PART II: WHAT SHALL I CRY? SERMON CONSTRUCTION AND DELIVERY... 59

3. OVERLAP (I): POETRY 61
 Prophetic Poetry 62
 On Preaching Poetry... 63
 Poetic Structure 65
  Repetitive Structure 66
  Repeated Refrain.. 67
  Repeated with Variation 67
  Repeated Keywords 68
  Repeated with Symmetry.................................... 68
  Repeated Themes... 69
  Strategy 4.1 Repeat Yourself 70
  Progressive Structure......................................71
  Strategy 4.2 Structure the Sermon to Progress with the Passage 72
  Conclusion: Poetic Structure.............................. 74
 Poetic Language... 74
  Word Choice... 75
  Strategy 5.1 Choose Your Words Wisely 76
  Parallelism 78
  Strategy 5.2 Preach in Parallel?.......................... 79
  Irregular Language.. 81
  Strategy 5.3 Be Irregular 82
 Conclusion 84
 For Further Reading 85

  Talk about It 85
  Dig Deeper 86
  Practice 86

4. OVERLAP (II): PARABLE, APOCALYPSE 87
  Prophetic Parables 87
  On Preaching Parables 90
    Strategy 6.1 Explain the Joke (Carefully) 91
    Strategy 6.2 Re-Work the Joke 93
    Strategy 6.3 Just Tell the Joke 94
    Conclusion: Preaching Parables 95
  Prophetic Apocalyptic 95
    Defining Apocalyptic Literature 96
    Interpreting Apocalyptic Literature 97
  Preaching Apocalyptic Literature 99
    Strategy 7.1 Reveal 100
    Strategy 7.2 Confront 102
    Strategy 7.3 Encourage 104
  Prophetic Epistle and Narrative 105
  A Final Word on Prophetic Overlap 106
  For Further Reading 106
  Talk about It 106
  Dig Deeper 107
  Practice 107

5. IMAGE 109
  Prophetic Images 111
  Preaching with Images 114
    Strategy 8.1 Use Images Ancient and Modern 115
    Strategy 8.2 Use Images Micro and Macro 117
    Strategy 8.3 Imagistic Language 120
      Two Examples: Joel 1 and Isaiah 6 122
    Strategy 8.4 Think Carefully About Technology 124
  Conclusion 126
  For Further Study 126
  Talk about It 126
  Dig Deeper 127
  Practice 127

6. EMOTION 129
   Emotion in the Prophets 130
   Preaching with Emotion 132
      Emotional Contagion and Preaching 132
   Experiencing Emotion 134
      Strategy 9.1 Practice Emotional Steeping 134
      Strategy 9.2 Remember Who Will Drink the Tea 136
      Strategy 9.3 Learn to Drink Tea 138
   Expressing and Evoking Emotion 139
      Strategy 10.1 Watch What You Say 139
      Strategy 10.2 Watch How You Say It 142
      Strategy 10.3 Watch Someone Else Say It 144
      Strategy 10.4 Watch What You Do While You Say It ... 145
      Strategy 10.5 Watch This 146
   For Further Study 147
   Talk about It 148
   Dig Deeper 148
   Practice 148

7. CONFUSION 149
   Confusion in the Prophets 152
      Nahum: Confusion to Empathize 152
      Joel: Confusion to Instruct 153
      Ezekiel: Confusion to Undermine 154
      Confusion that Remains 155
   Confusing Preaching? 156
   Preaching with Confusion 158
      Strategy 11.1 Wander with Them 159
      Strategy 11.2 Drop It on Them 162
      Strategy 11.3 Leave It with Them 164
   Conclusion 165
   For Further Study 166
   Talk about It 166
   Dig Deeper 166
   Practice 166

8. SHOCK 169
   Shock in the Prophets 171
   Preaching with Shock 173

  Strategy 12.1 Shock from the Start 176
  Strategy 12.2 Shock Yourself 177
  Strategy 12.3 Shock with Anachronism 178
  Strategy 12.4 Shock with Delight and Disgust 180
  Strategy 12.5 Shock with Satire 182
  Strategy 12.6 Shock with the Liturgy 183
 And Yet 184
 Conclusion 185
 For Further Study 185
 Talk about It 186
 Dig Deeper 186
 Practice 186

PART III: MAKE STRAIGHT IN THE DESERT A HIGHWAY: OBSTACLES TO PREACHING THE PROPHETS 187

9. **JUSTICE** 189
 Justice as a Problem 190
  Justice in the Church 191
  Justice among the Philosophers 194
  Justice in the Pulpit 197
 Do Not Step Here 199
  Strategy 13.1 Do Not Shy Away 199
  Strategy 13.2 Do Not Split the Difference 200
  Strategy 13.3 Do Not Do It Alone 200
 Step Here 201
  Strategy 14.1 Learn About Justice 201
  Strategy 14.2 Learn About Injustice 202
  Strategy 14.3 Let Them See You Learn 203
  Strategy 14.4 One Step at a Time 204
  Example: "Worship in Justice" 204
 Conclusion 206
 For Further Study 206
 Talk about It 207
 Dig Deeper 207
 Practice 207

10. **DISTANCE** 209
 Distance in the Prophets 210

    Cultural Distance 211
    Historical Distance 211
    Theological Distance 213
  Distance in the Pulpit 215
    Strategy 15.1 Gauge the Distance 216
    Strategy 15.2 Cross the Distance 219
    Strategy 15.3 Ignore the Distance 221
    Strategy 15.4 Use the Distance 223
  Conclusion 224
  For Further Study 224
  Talk about It 225
  Dig Deeper 225
  Practice 225

11. MONOTONY 227
  Monotony vs. Boredom 228
  Monotony in the Prophets: What, Why and How 229
  Monotony in the Pulpit 233
    Strategy 16.1 Develop Variations on a Theme 234
    Strategy 16.2 Cultivate Grit 236
    Strategy 16.3 Recognize Your Own Boredom 238
  Preaching Through a Major Prophet 240
    Strategy 17.1 Preach in Themes 241
    Strategy 17.2 Preach as You Read 241
    Strategy 17.3 Take Breaks 242
    Strategy 17.4 Take Laps 242
    Strategy 17.5 Spend Time on Titles 242
  Conclusion 243
  For Further Study 243
  Talk about It 244
  Dig Deeper 244
  Practice 244

CONCLUSION 245

APPENDIX 1: SAMPLE SERMON 247
  THE FAVOR OF FOCUS (ISAIAH 5:8–24)
  Andrew Thompson 247

Appendix 2: Sample Sermon 259
    Walking in the Ruins (Micah 4:1–5)
    Heather Joy Zimmerman 259

Bibliography 271

Index 283

Abbreviations

BHS	*Biblia Hebraica Stuttgartensia*
BibSac	*Bibliotheca Sacra*
BW	*Biblical World*
CJ	*Concordia Journal*
CT	*Christianity Today*
CTJ	*Calvin Theological Journal*
CTM	*Concordia Theological Monthly*
EBC	Expositor's Bible Commentary
ECNT	Exegetical Commentary on the New Testament
ERT	*Evangelical Review of Theology*
FOTL	The Forms of Old Testament Literature
GL	*Gospel in Life*
HALOT	*The Hebrew and Aramaic Lexicon of the Old Testament*
JBL	*Journal of Biblical Literature*
JEHS	*The Journal of the Evangelical Homiletics Society*
JETS	*The Journal of the Evangelical Theological Society*
JP	*Journal for Preachers*
JSOT	*Journal for the Study of the Old Testament*
LNTS	Library of New Testament Studies
NA27	*Novum Testamentum Graece*, 27th edition
NIB	New Interpreter's Bible
NICOT	New International Commentary on the Old Testament
NIDOTTE	*New International Dictionary of Old Testament Theology and Exegesis*

NIGTC	New International Greek Testament Commentary
PBL	Preaching Biblical Literature
PT	*Preaching Today*
ResQ	*Restoration Quarterly*
RevExp	*Review and Expositor*
SBL	Society of Biblical Literature
SJT	*Southwestern Journal of Theology*
SMR	*St. Mark's Review*
SR	*Sewanee Review*
TOTL	The Old Testament Library
WBC	Word Biblical Commentary

Preface

Oversize projects like planting churches, loving cities, and writing books require the love and sacrifice of a host of people. If the pages that follow can serve the church, then these people are largely responsible. The errors and oversights are my own contribution.

Thank you to the EHS study group for inviting me to join the discussion about preaching biblical genres. Your ideas and enthusiasm have been contagious. Todd Scacewater and the crew at Fontes provided valuable feedback and advice, and the book is better for it.

Thank you also to the wonderful people of Brunswick, who continue to teach me about walking in the ways that the prophets commend and demand. Rachael, DeWayne, Tom, Rita, Craig, Beth, Kate, John, and all the members of Glynn Clergy for Equity: your companionship has been a gift, and your example an inspiration. I'm proud to walk with you. Thank you to Abra, for the lunch and the wisdom, and for never being too busy to cheer me on. Thank you to Tres, for demonstrating humble, courageous leadership in our town. And thank you to the amazing people of Union City Church. You gave me time and space to write, but more importantly, you give me hope that the prophets were telling the truth.

Thank you to my friends and brothers: Bret, Madhur, Kory, Kris, and Gareth. I love you. Thanks to the professor-mentor-friend, super-editor, and disc-golf master Jeff. I have been riding your coattails for years and see no reason to stop now.

My love and thanks to Ben and Tonya. Ride or die.

And of course, Ava, Eva, and Mandy. All the days.

Introduction:
A Voice Says, Cry

PAUL ORDERED HIS PROTEGEE Timothy to "preach the word" (2 Tim 4:2). Although preachers believe that the same charge is laid on us, we find that some words are easier to preach than others. The prophets, especially, give us trouble, and that for two reasons.

First, the oracles of the Old Testament (OT) Prophets span a dizzying array of forms and content. The prophets lament, warn, comfort, proclaim, narrate, emote, and shock.[1] They sing dirges; they see visions; they tell parables; they rhyme and pun as kingdoms totter. They intrigue, haunt, delight and confuse. Occasionally they bore. What a "prophetic" passage looks like can be hard to nail down.

Moreover, sermons on the Prophets are as varied as the oracles themselves. Consider the following examples. First is a sermon from Martin Luther based on Isaiah 60:1–6, expounding the phrase, "Arise, shine; for your light has come":

> Undoubtedly, Christ is the light of which Isaiah here speaks, and which, through the Gospel, shines in all the world.... So Isaiah says, in effect: "Permit yourself to be enlightened; or, Let there be light. Allow the light to fall upon you. Thou dead one, crawl not into the grave of thy filthy life; that is, cease to love and to follow thine evil course of conduct that the light of

---

[1] This book will often discuss "the prophets," who were people, and "the Prophets," which is a section of the canon. Lowercase or capital letters will clarify which entity is being referenced.

the Gospel may fall upon thee and abide in thee.... Let the true light have some claim upon thee."[2]

Luther says that Isaiah's light is the light of Christ, fulfilled at his coming, and is also the light that wakes the unbelieving sleeper from spiritual death (see Eph 5:14). Isaiah was in some way talking about Jesus.

Now listen to Luther's namesake, Martin Luther King, Jr., who also preaches from Isaiah—this time from chapter 40—and who offers a different take on Isaiah's song:

> Then I can hear Isaiah again, because it has profound meaning to me, that somehow "every valley shall be exalted, and every hill shall be made low; the crooked places shall be made straight, and the rough places plain...." That's the beauty of this thing: all flesh shall see it together. Not some from the heights of Park Street and others from the dungeons of slum areas.... Not some white and not some black, not some yellow and not some brown, but all flesh shall see it together.... And God grant that we will get on board and start marching with God because we got orders now to break down the bondage and the walls of colonialism, exploitation, and imperialism...[3]

For King, Isaiah's promise involves sweeping social change and a call to action against specific political threats.

Sometimes prophets' words in preachers' mouths give spiritual lessons or reveal his character. Leonard Ravenhill, in a sermon on Habakkuk 1:5 ("Look among the nations, and see; wonder and be astounded. For I am doing a work in your days that you would not believe if told") confesses:

> Sometimes it looks as though God is indifferent! Why doesn't he intervene? Because he is working to his divine timetable. As

---

[2] Martin Luther, "The True Light," in *The Sermons of Martin Luther*, accessed October 9, 2020, https://www.monergism.com/sermons-martin-luther-8-volumes.

[3] Martin Luther King, Jr., "Birth of a New Nation," April 7, 1957, Dexter Avenue Baptist Church, http://www.mlkonline.net/nation.html.

I've told you, neither in your affairs, nor in the affairs of your church or nation—God will hear your prayer but he won't take advice. He works everything after the counsel of his own will. Why therefore should we be afraid?[4]

Ravenhill understands the prophets as men and women who knew God, spoke for God, and who can unravel the mysteries of divine providence for his people.[5]

Finally, prophetic words can eventuate in sermons about the future: the prophets' predictions are coming to pass in our day. Denny Kenaston gives a sermon on Habakkuk 2:1–4. He argues, "Our days of peace and prosperity are numbered.... This is a message the Spirit of God is speaking to the American church.... Our own days are numbered.... It is on its way."[6] Habakkuk, according to Kenaston, warns of imminent persecution for the contemporary American church.

These are remarkably different approaches to preaching from the Prophets. Which of these can we admire and emulate? Which should we avoid? And more importantly—why?

A voice says, "Cry!" but preachers often have no idea what to say. This book is meant to help those preachers who want to fulfill Paul's charge but could use some help when it comes to the Prophets.

"Prophetic Preaching" and Terminology Trouble

One could say that this is a book about "prophetic preaching." Unfortunately, that term has proved to be rather plastic: it can mean

---

[4] Leonard Ravenhill, "I Will Work a Work Not Believed," accessed October 29, 2020, http://ia800301.us.archive.org/27/items/SERMONINDEX_SID20816/SID20816.mp3.

[5] I use inclusive terminology intentionally. Although most prophets were men (and almost all the prophetic oracles in Scripture are attributed to men), prophetesses such as Huldah also operated in Israel (2 Kgs 22), and a strong case can be made that the songs sung by Hannah (1 Sam 2) and Deborah (Judg 5), Miriam (Exod 15) and Mary (Luke 1) are examples of prophetic speech.

[6] Denny Kenaston, "The Approaching Wave of Persecution," accessed October 29, 2020, https://www.sermonindex.net/modules/mydownloads/scr_index.php?act=bookSermons&book=Habakkuk&page=0.

anything from preaching about social issues to eschatological preaching, from taking a certain theological stance to being ornery in the pulpit.[7] As such, it seems best to avoid the term "prophetic preaching" as too prone to misunderstanding.

I will instead use the term "preaching the Prophets." Though a little cumbersome and perhaps liable to its own misinterpretation, it more clearly indicates the focus of this work: *preaching sermons that are based on or derive their theological content from prophetic oracles.* The prophets themselves often use the word "oracle" (Hebrew *massa'*) to describe a message they have received from Yahweh.[8] For the most part, those oracles are found in the Major and Minor Prophets of the OT.[9]

However, even that definition requires sharpening. Some prophetic oracles occur outside of the Prophets (for instance, Num 23–24) and even outside of the OT (Rev 1:3). Additionally, not everything in the prophetic books is a prophetic oracle: there is also narrative (for example, Isa 7–8) and a good bit of biographical material (Jonah and portions of Jeremiah).[10] Thus, in this book "preaching the prophets" means preaching sermons based on the oracles of the prophets—understanding that these will normally be found in the OT prophetic corpus.[11] When Ezekiel describes

---

7 A small sample of such variety: Chang-Hoon Kim, "Prophetic Preaching as Social Preaching," *ERT* 30 (2006): 141–151; Timothy R. Sensing, "A Call to Prophetic Preaching," *ResQ* 41 (1999): 139–154; Sangyil Park, "Speaking of Hope: Prophetic Preaching," *RevExp* 109 (2012): 413–428.

8 Even the term "oracle" is not without complications. Apparently, in Jeremiah's context, it had become so abused by false prophets as a term for prophetic speech that Yahweh told Israel to stop using it (Jer 23).

9 The canonical division of the English OT into Law, History, and Prophets is based on the arrangement of the Septuagint. The Hebrew Tanak instead categorizes what we call "Prophets" as "Latter Prophets," with the historical books (Joshua, Judges, Samuel, and Kings) labeled "Former Prophets." For details, see Karen H. Jobes and Moises Silva, *Invitation to the Septuagint* (Baker Academic, 2000), 79–85. These issues notwithstanding, we will continue to use the term "prophetic corpus" and "Prophets" to indicate what in the English Bible are the Major and Minor Prophets.

10 Most of Jonah, in fact, is biographical narrative, the exceptions being his song in 2:2–10 and his warning in 3:4 ("Yet forty days and Ninevah shall be overthrown!"). The large amount of narrative material is probably why the book of Jonah appears in the pulpit with more frequency than most other prophetic books.

11 Daniel forms an interesting borderline case: The Hebrew Bible categorizes

God lifted up on his mighty wheeled throne (Ezek 1), when Nahum predicts the fall of Ninevah (Nah 2), when Malachi confronts the corrupt priests and their offerings (Mal 1), these are prophetic oracles. "Preaching the Prophets" means preaching sermons based on such oracles.

Preachers with Big Ideas

Readers should also note that this book uses the "Big Idea" approach to biblical preaching, developed and popularized in large part by Haddon Robinson.[12] Big Idea preaching seeks to derive a single biblical concept from a passage that captures the ideational content and rhetorical force of that passage.[13] The sermon is then structured around that central idea.

Of course, other approaches exist to the development of sermons from the Scripture, and the material here can easily be adapted to each reader's homiletical practice.[14]

This Is the Way, Walk in It

The goal of this book is to equip readers to preach biblically faithful, theologically sound, and rhetorically effective sermons from prophetic oracles.[15] Here is how I propose to do that.

---

it under *kethubim* (Writings), along with the Psalms, Chronicles, and other miscellaneous books. However, much of the material in Daniel, especially in chapters 7 through 12, are prophetic oracles and apocalyptic visions. For a discussion of Daniel's place in the canon, and the logic of the arrangement of the Prophets and the Writings, see Christopher R. Seitz, *The Goodly Fellowship of the Prophets: The Achievement of Association in Canon Formation* (Baker Academic, 2009).

12 Robinson, *Biblical Preaching: The Development and Delivery of Expository Messages*, 3rd ed. (Baker Academic, 2014).

13 Ibid., 21. There have been developments and discussions of his basic approach, but if the reader does not have a clear and consistent way to move from text to sermon, Robinson's scheme is a great place to begin.

14 See, for instance, Paul Scott Wilson, *The Practice of Preaching*, rev. ed. (Abingdon, 1995); Thomas G. Long, *The Witness of Preaching*, 2nd ed. (Westminster John Knox, 2005); Eugene L. Lowry, *The Homiletical Plot: The Sermon as Narrative Art Form*, exp. ed. (Westminster John Knox, 2001).

15 This book, and the others in this series, take their cue from Thomas Long's seminal *Preaching and the Literary Forms of the Bible* (Fortress, 1989).

Part I introduces us to the OT prophets. It describes these strange men and women as Israel's covenant enforcers and addresses common fears about preaching from their oracles. Part I also familiarizes preachers with the prophetic corpus of the OT and provides a theological framework for interpreting prophetic speech.

Part II, the body of the book, handles literary and theological features of the prophets that guide sermon construction and delivery. Part II discusses prophetic genres and literary devices, describes how they worked in their original context, and explores how preachers can craft sermons that function like the prophetic oracles originally did.

Part III confronts obstacles to preaching from the Prophets: the prophetic focus on justice, the vast distance between their world and ours, and the potential monotony of delivering what is essentially the same message of warning and hope time and again.

Finally, the appendix offers two complete sermon manuscripts from prophetic oracles to illustrate the homiletical variety open to those who seek to share the Prophets with God's people.

This book is not a comprehensive introduction to homiletics and as such will pass by large areas in that discipline. Throughout, I will focus on those features unique to or characteristic of OT prophetic oracles: the challenges they bring and the strategies that can be used to preach them. I will engage theological questions mainly in chapters 2, 9, and 10, and hermeneutical issues as they arise.

This book is written primarily for preachers and theological students who desire to develop and deliver sermons from the Prophets that are faithful to the content and form of the text. The book is formatted for learners, with exercises and resources for further reading at the end of each chapter. A knowledge of Hebrew and Greek will not be required, though I will occasionally make exegetical points from the original languages. I will also place most of the technical jargon and ancillary issues in the footnotes; readers who are interested in pursuing such questions will find further direction there.

There, Long began the work of analyzing biblical genres through a homiletical and rhetorical lens. The present book aims to do roughly the same for the OT Prophets.

Isaiah wrote of a time in the future when God would speak to and guide his people in the way of the LORD. If I may anticipate some of our discussion in Part I, that time was inaugurated when Christ poured out the Holy Spirit upon his people at Pentecost. May that same Spirit, then, guide us in the way as we approach his word with reverence and love.

Let's start walking.

Part I

Prepare the Way:
Reading the Prophets

P ROFOUND AND FAITHFUL PREACHING always grows out of immersion in the biblical text. This holds for the prophetic oracles as much as for any other section of Scripture; thus, preachers who want to preach from the Prophets must first learn to read the Prophets. Part I introduces the OT writing prophets, situates them within God's redemptive work, and constructs a framework for interpreting their oracles in preparation for sermon construction.

1

Prepare to Meet the Prophets

> *Then the reverence of the law is praised in song,*
> *and the grace of the prophets is recognized,*
> *and the faith of the gospels is established,*
> *and the tradition of the apostles is preserved,*
> *and the joy of the church exults.*
> —Epistle to Diognetus[1]

You are more likely to meet someone named John than someone named Malachi, and with good reason. The prophets and their writings are less familiar to contemporary Christians than other authors and sections of the Bible. This initial chapter will introduce the men and women who dared to frame their words with the declaration, "Thus says Yahweh." It will first argue for the necessity of preaching from the Prophets, then offer a general orientation to the prophets and their writings.

Getting Over a Fear of the Prophets

Unfamiliarity with the prophetic literature breeds fear, and fear keeps preachers on the well-marked roads of the Gospels and epistles and away from the trackless forests of the Prophets. Let us begin, then, by naming our fears, and asking what may be said in response.

To begin with, the Prophets make people nervous because they predict quite specific events in ways that sermons usually

---

1 Diogn. 11:6, in *Apostolic Fathers,* 3rd ed., ed. and trans. Michael W. Holmes (Baker, 2007).

do not. Joel, for instance, foretells that "the sun shall be turned to darkness and the moon to blood" (2:31), and if the Israelites trembled to hear his words, preachers today tremble yet more to think of preaching them.[2] The Prophets also disturb: Obadiah, in rage against the Edomites who watched complacently as Jerusalem was sacked, tells them that Israel "shall burn them and consume them, and there shall be no survivor for the house of Esau" (v. 18). Preachers will be hard put to bring comfort and encouragement from such a text.

Furthermore, the Prophets confuse, using such obscure wording or images that today's readers are left scratching their heads. Zechariah's woman in a basket (Zech 5:5–11) appears in pulpits much less often than John's woman at the well (John 4:1–45), not because she is less compelling but because she is less comprehensible. Finally, the Prophets shock. They were driven to desperate measures to rouse hardened sinners. Thus, they speak of dung, nakedness, harlotry, weeping, locust armies, earthquakes that split mountains, and fire riddled with undying worms. To try to tame them would be faithless; to turn them loose in the church, reckless.

Why, then, even preach from the Prophets? I suggest three reasons—one historical, one theological, and one homiletical. The historical reason has to do with Abraham Heschel's notion that prophecy is "exegesis of existence from a divine perspective."[3] The writing prophets from Isaiah to Malachi give readers a way to view history from God's point of view. Their writings coincide with the histories narrated in Kings and Chronicles, but their words provide needed perspective on that history as Israel descended from the heights of David and Solomon to the depths of exile and beyond.[4] We understand Israel—and therefore ourselves—when the

---

2 Unless otherwise noted, I use the English versification where it differs from the Hebrew, as it does here. If needed, the Hebrew versification will appear in brackets.

3 Abraham Heschel, *The Prophets*, vol. 1 (Harper Colophon Books, 1962), xiv.

4 This is not, of course, to relegate the historical books to mere reports. But the prophets' position of commenting on that history from within contrasts with the authors of later history who narrate in retrospect.

Prepare to Meet the Prophets 13

Prophets speak.[5] If the church ignores divine commentary on that history, it will mean a loss to the people of God.

Theologically, the church has always held these oracles to be God's word, and therefore "useful for teaching, for reproof, for correction, and for training in righteousness" (2 Tim 3:16). This comes home with even more force when one remembers that Paul's assertion referred to the OT, so that the prophetic words comprised an even more significant percentage of the Bible for Paul than it does for the church today.

This is why the early church time and again declared that the Prophets speak directly to NT believers. Christ, who came to fulfill the Prophets (Matt 5:17) cited the Prophets to proclaim his mission (Matt 11:5), explain his parables (Matt 13:14–15), and critique his opponents (Matt 9:13). Paul was intimately familiar with prophetic oracles, drawing upon them as a lens through which to view everything from universal sin (Rom 2:24) to freedom in Christ (Gal 4:27) to glossolalia (1 Cor 14:21). Phrases which are now theological touchstones—new covenant, gospel, righteousness by faith—were bequeathed to the church by Israel's prophets. In short, we do not understand our faith if we do not hear the Prophets. And how can people hear without someone preaching?

Finally, the homiletical reason for sermons from the Prophets is that prophetic oracles are already sermons. The prophetic corpus, in all its wild variety, is a record of the preaching of the prophets.[6] Their sermons are passionate, convicting, inspiring, and unpredictable. They preached to persuade the people of God.[7] Isaiah's

---

5 Different theological positions will posit several views on the relationship between Israel and the church. See ch. 2 for discussion.

6 See Robert Carlson, *Preaching Like the Prophets: The Hebrew Prophets as Examples for the Practice of Pastoral Preaching* (Wipf & Stock, 2017); Gary V. Smith, *The Prophets as Preachers: An Introduction to the Hebrew Prophets* (Broadman and Holman, 1984).

7 Throughout this chapter several ancillary issues will be noted, all of which to some degree bear on preaching from the Prophets, but which lie outside the scope of this work. I will therefore note them and refer interested readers to some beginning resources. A discussion of preaching's (rather complex) relation to persuasion is the first such side trail. While it seems clear to me that the prophets, Peter, Paul, and other preachers did seek to persuade, others disagree that preaching should be persuasive. For an exploration, see Duane Litfin, *Paul's Theology of*

song of the vineyard (5:1-7) lulls listeners into seeing themselves as the beloved vineyard of the Yahweh—then rounds on them to expose the rotten fruit they bore.[8] Haggai gives what amounts to a sermon series, encouraging the remnant returned from exile to make the temple of Yahweh its priority. And preachers will empathize with Micah's complaint that his audience is completely unreceptive to God's words: "'Do not preach'—thus they preach—'one should not preach of such things; disgrace will not overtake us.'... If a man should go about and utter wind and lies, saying, 'I will preach to you of wine and strong drink,' he would be the preacher for this people!" (Mic 2:6,11). The prophets are preachers. Therefore, the question is not whether the prophetic oracles can be preached; they already have been. The question is how their words can be faithfully proclaimed now.[9]

If these arguments are well-founded, today's preachers must learn to preach from the Prophets. Biblical and homiletical scholars have already called for more frequent preaching from the Prophets and provided some guidance for doing so.[10] But there has been no extended exploration for how to construct and deliver sermons from this portion of Scripture.[11] The present work seeks

---

Preaching (IVP Academic: 2015).

8 Readers will recognize this song as the likely source of Christ's parable of the vineyard (Mark 12:1-12 parr.).

9 Most scholars agree that prophetic oracles were oral at some point, though their exact historical connection to their written forms can rarely be traced with confidence. For a traditional view, see Willem A. VanGemeren, *Interpreting the Prophetic Word* (Zondervan, 1990), 43. On recognizing the mixed oral and written characters of the Prophets, see John H. Sailhamer, "Preaching from the Prophets," in *Preaching the Old Testament*, ed. Scott M. Gibson (Baker, 2006), 119-120; R. Reed Lessing, "Orality in the Prophets," *Concordia Journal* 29 (2003): 152-165.

10 Andrew Blackwood, "Servants of the Word: How to Preach from the Prophets," *Interpretation* 2 (1948): 158-71; Donald A. Leggett, *Loving God and Disturbing Men: Preaching from the Prophets* (Clements Publishing, 1990); Sensing, "A Call to Prophetic Preaching," *Restoration Quarterly* 41 (1999):139-154; Timothy M. Pierce, "Micah as a Case Study for Preaching and Teaching the Prophets," *Southwestern Journal of Theology* 46 (2003): 77-94.

11 The works referenced in n. 10 spend the bulk of their time either making a case for preaching from the Prophets or else giving extended introductions to each of the prophetic books. I should also mention Andrew Hamilton's *How to Preach the Prophets for All Their Worth: A Hermeneutical, Homiletical, and*

Prepare to Meet the Prophets

to fill that gap to serve preachers and the church.[12]

Before moving on, perhaps we should pause here and, in the spirit of the prophets who pictured for God's people a new reality, take time to wonder. Imagine a pulpit ministry unafraid of the prophetic oracles. Imagine sermons charged with the intensity of prophetic speech and the power of their daring images. Imagine a church taught by the prophets' words, reproved by their accusations, corrected by their teaching, and trained in hope by their visions. And imagine a preacher with a complete Bible, able to bring these oracles to bear in building up the people of God. What sermons may come? And what might the Spirit do in your own context, if more of his Word resounded in the worship of his church?

Identifying the Prophets

The next two sections will build a biblical case for identifying the prophets as spokespersons of Yahweh. The final section will introduce their writings.[13]

The main OT terms for the people who speak for Yahweh are "seer"[14] and "prophet."[15] The former appears to be the older term, and simply indicates one who sees—presumably seeing what Yahweh has shown in visions and dreams.[16] The far more frequent

---

Theological Guide to Unleash the Power of the Prophets (Wipf and Stock, 2022), which appeared too late for substantial interaction.

This work will focus on the homiletical aspects of the task.

12 Other works in this series will do the same for different genres of Scripture. They stand squarely in the tradition of homileticians like Thomas Long and Jeffrey Arthurs. Thomas G. Long, *Preaching and the Literary Forms of the Bible* (Fortress, 1989); Jeffrey D. Arthurs, *Preaching with Variety: How to Re-create the Dynamics of Biblical Genres* (Kregel, 2007).

13 Side trail number two that we pass by would outline the content and context of each prophetic book in the OT. Those who want to familiarize themselves with one prophetic book in depth should consult the resources at the end of the chapter.

14 Heb. רֹאֶה, a participle from רָאָה, to see.

15 Heb. נָבִיא.

16 See 1 Sam 9:9. For visions and dreams associated with prophets, see the early reference in Num 12:6. Eichrodt makes some speculative claims about the differences between earlier "seers" and later "prophets," although the late book

term "prophet" probably derives from an Akkadian verb meaning "to call," and (if the form is passive, as some suggest) would have originally meant "one who is called."[17] Across the Ancient Near East there were figures who had a similar function, though Israel's prophets had unique features that set them apart.[18]

The term "prophet" is used in two ways in the Bible. One finds first a broad use that covers a variety of people who represented God. In this loose sense, Abel (Luke 11:49–51), Enoch (Jude 14), and Abraham (Gen 20:7) are all prophets. The Bible recounts several unnamed prophets (Judg 6:8; 1 Kgs 13), as well as prophets whose works are lost to us (2 Chr 13:22). The NT has its share of prophets, like Agabus (Acts 21:10), Philip's daughters (Acts 21:8–9), and unnamed Christians who have the spiritual gift of prophecy (1 Cor 12:10).[19] And Christ himself is sometimes called a prophet,[20] the church recognizing his prophetic offices alongside his priestly and kingly roles.[21]

Within the broad stream of "prophets" one also finds a narrow use of the term that indicates a specific line of chosen Israelite men and women. Both Testaments refer to a succession of official prophets, stemming Moses and culminating in John the Baptist.[22] Moses stands before and above the biblical prophets: he is superior

---

Chronicles uses the term "seer" several times. Walther Eichrodt, *Theology of the Old Testament*, trans. J. A. Baker, 2 vols. (The Westminster Press, 1961), 1:296–303.

17 P. A. Verhoef, "Prophecy," *New International Dictionary of Old Testament Theology and Exegesis*, ed. Willem A. VanGemeren (Zondervan 1997), 4:1067–1079.

18 See VanGemeren, *Interpreting*, 19–27; O. Palmer Robertson, *The Christ of the Prophets* (P&R Publishing, 2004), 21.

19 A third path which we must decline to follow addresses the relation between OT prophets and prophets in the NT church. Interested readers may consult Richard B. Gaffin, Jr., *Perspectives on Pentecost: New Testament Teaching on the Gifts of the Holy Spirit* (P&R Publishing, 1979); Wayne Grudem, *The Gift of Prophecy in the New Testament and Today*, rev. ed., (Crossway, 2000).

20 See Deut 18:15–19; Matt 16:14 parr.; Luke 24:19; John 6:14. See also Robertson, *Christ of the Prophets*, 18.

21 E.g., John Calvin, *Institutes of the Christian Religion*, ed. John T. McNeill, trans. Ford Lewis Battles, 2 vols. (Westminster John Knox, 1960), 1:494–496.

22 For discussion of the succession of official prophets from Moses to John the Baptist, see VanGemeren, *Interpreting*, 27–38; Robertson, *Christ of the Prophets*, 24–39.

to them in his unmediated access to Yahweh (Num 12:6–8). Yet Moses also describes the ministry of the prophets to come after his death (Deut 18:15–22).[23] That ministry begins with Samuel, who is said to be the first of the official line of prophets.[24] Samuel occupies a transitional place between the judges of Israel and the kings, so that prophecy comes into existence alongside royal power.[25] He is called a "seer" (1 Chr 9:22; 26:28) and begins his ministry when he hears and delivers God's word to Eli the priest (1 Sam 3). Samuel is Yahweh's official spokesperson who sees what others cannot see.

The line of prophets continues from Samuel, reaching a high-water mark in the ministry of Elijah. He declares the word of Yahweh to king Ahab, performing signs and wonders, and stands forth in the Bible as the prototypical prophet.[26] The line of prophets carries on, and includes all the writing prophets whose words have been preserved in Scripture. The chain of succession terminates in John the Baptist, who prepared the way for Christ: "A prophet? Yes, I tell you, and more than a prophet.... Among those born of women none has arisen greater than John the Baptist" (Matt 11:9,11). Thus, the term "prophet" can be employed loosely or formally. We will focus on the formal usage, as it encompasses those who wrote the prophetic books in the OT.

What is immediately clear from the biblical evidence is the prophet's role as a spokesperson for God.[27] Among their favorite

---

23 For a discussion of how this passage may address both a line of coming prophets and an eschatological prophet "like Moses," see Norman C. Habel, "Deuteronomy 18—God's Chosen Prophet," *Concordia Theological Monthly* 35 (1964): 575–582.

24 See 1 Chr 29:29; 2 Chr 35:18; Acts 3:24; 13:20; Heb 11:32.

25 The relation of prophets to kings is explored below.

26 Elijah's greatness is manifest in his miracles, his political impact, and in his being carried directly to heaven in a chariot of fire. Perhaps this last fact led to expectations of his return before the day of Yahweh (Mal 4:5–6). In the NT that expectation is fulfilled by John the Baptist, who appears dressed like Elijah and prepares the way for the coming of the Lord (Matt 3:4). When Christ is transfigured (Mark 9:2–13 parr.), only the two figures of Moses and Elijah appear with him on the mountain.

27 VanGemeren, *Interpreting*, 42–46; Robertson, *Christ of the Prophets*, 27.

refrains are "Thus says Yahweh," and "... declares Yahweh."[28] When they spoke and wrote, they did so with the understanding that they were speaking on behalf of Yahweh himself.[29] But beyond the general role of spokesperson, can we be more specific?

The prophet's identity does not come from his or her social location. Prophets were sometimes associated with the royal court (1 Sam 7:1–3) but were often independent of it (2 Kgs 17–19). They could be anyone from a shepherd (Amos 1:1; 7:14) to a priest (Ezek 1:3).[30]

The prophets instead shared other characteristics. They were first intensely concerned with the current state of affairs, local and international. Although the word "prophecy" in contemporary parlance connotes a prediction of the future, the prophets normally addressed current events in Israel and abroad. Their predictions of the future were responses to the behaviors and events they saw in the present. To take one example among many: Zephaniah predicts imminent judgment on Judah. He declares, "The great day of the LORD is near, near and hastening fast; the sound of the day of the LORD is bitter; the mighty man cries aloud there" (1:14), but Zephaniah predicts future disaster because of present behavior. He reacts to "the remnant of Baal and the name of the idolatrous priests ... those who have turned back from following the LORD ... all who array themselves in foreign attire ... everyone who leaps over the threshold, and those who fill their master's house with violence and fraud" (1:4, 6, 8, 9). Like all the prophets, Zephaniah predicts the future with his eye on the present.

---

28 The phrase כֹּה אָמַר יְהוָה appears 291 times in the OT, 226 of which occur from Isaiah to Malachi. The phrase נְאֻם יְהוָה appears 254 times in the OT, 246 of which occur from Isaiah to Malachi.

29 Yet a fourth side trail branches off here: in what manner can prophets claim that their words are the very words of Yahweh? To act as a spokesperson for someone may involve anything from delivering that person's exact words to representing their interests generally, as an ambassador does for a head of state. For a discussion, see Nicholas Wolterstorff, *Divine Discourse: Philosophical Reflections on the Idea that God Speaks* (Cambridge University Press, 1995).

30 One finds some evidence that earlier prophets were more closely affiliated with the royal courts, and later (as kings drifted yet further from God) became more independent. See VanGemeren, *Interpreting*, 48.

Second, the prophets' words draw heavily on the law of Moses. Robertson states, "From the earliest era of prophetism to the last, the law is applied to the people as an explanation for the judgment or blessing they may expect."[31] The prophets do not invent new moral standards or dream up new blessings and curses. They remind people of what everyone already knows from Moses. Micah 6:8 famously declares, "He has told you, O man, what is good." Similarly, Isaiah calls on his hearers to "remember the former things of old" (46:8), and Jeremiah commands the people to "ask for the ancient paths, where the good way is; and walk in it, and find rest for your souls" (6:16). The prophets address such basic issues as idolatry (Ezek 36:25), Sabbath-keeping (Isa 58:13–14), concern for the poor (Amos 8:4–6), adultery (Jer 23:14), sacrifice (Mal 1:6–14), and compromise with foreign nations (Isa 31). All of these are central concerns in the Law of Moses.[32]

More broadly, the prophets draw from all of God's covenants with Israel. Though most oracles are based on the covenant with Moses, the prophets also refer to God's covenant with Abraham (Mic 7:20), Noah (Jer 31:35–36), and David (Ezek 34:20–24). No surprise, then, that when they wish to speak of Israel's restoration and God's future glory, they refer to that hope as a new or everlasting covenant (Isa 55:3; Jer 31:31; Ezek 16:60).

Finally, prophetic oracles nearly all fall into two categories: woe (warning) and weal (comfort). The prophets predict disaster or deliverance: they warn of consequences for breaking the covenant, and they predict salvation because of God's faithfulness to

---

31 *Christ of the Prophets*, 144. See also his extensive citations of how the Prophets apply the Decalogue (144–161).

32 The final side trail: Traditional historical-critical OT scholarship reverses this order and contends that Israel's prophets were the originators of covenant and legal demands, which later authors used to compile a (largely fictional) "Deuteronomistic history" of Deuteronomy–2 Kings, and in the post-exilic period, what we now know of as the Pentateuch. Such historical-critical scholarship is rightly being called into question, with serious attention being paid to the canonical form of the text that indicates the exact opposite historical order. For a representative critical view, see Ronald E. Clements, "Deuteronomy," in *The New Interpreter's Bible*, vol. 2 (Abingdon Press, 1998), 273–280. For a rejoinder: T. D. Alexander, *From Paradise to Promised Land: An Introduction to the Pentateuch*, 2nd ed. (Baker Academic, 2002), 3–94.

that same covenant.[33] Two brief examples from Micah will suffice. First, Micah delivers an oracle of judgment in Mic 2:1–5. The accusation is that the upper class in Israel use their power to take others' land, against the laws of inheritance (2:1–2). Micah thus draws attention to provisions in the Mosaic law against these very acts (Lev 25:10, 24; Deut 19:14). In consequence, those who have gathered land illegitimately will themselves lose their inheritance, and "will have none to cast the line by lot in the assembly of the LORD" (Mic 2:5). Casting the line here refers to stretching out a line to mark the boundaries of property. In other words, they themselves will lose their ancestral property. This is nothing more than what Moses promised (Deut 28:63).

Later in Micah, the prophet offers hope: he predicts that shame will cover the enemies of Israel (7:10, 16–17) and that she will be restored to greatness (7:11, 14). This is all because of God's "steadfast love to Abraham, as you have sworn to our fathers from days of old" (7:20). God's covenants with Israel provide stern warning and blessed hope for Israel.

To sum up the discussion thus far: Israel's prophets were spokespersons of God, in the traditions of Moses, Samuel and Elijah. They addressed the current events of their time with requirements from the Law and other covenants and gave warnings and promises based on those traditions.

Israel's Covenant Enforcers

Douglas Stuart offers the helpful term "covenant enforcers" to encompass all the above.[34] By this term he means someone appointed by Yahweh to announce his evaluation of Israel's covenant faithfulness. The prophets stand, as it were, in the divine council of Yahweh as he pronounces judgment and deliverance to Israel based on

---

33 In fact, some prophetic books like Isaiah, Amos, and Joel appear to be organized by placing oracles of judgment in the first half, with oracles of salvation in the second.

34 Douglas Stuart, *Hosea–Jonah*, WBC (Word Books, 1987), xxxii. Robertson (*Christ of the Prophets*, 23) uses the term "covenant mediators." VanGemeren calls Elijah the "covenant prosecutor" (*Interpreting*, 36).

existing covenant arrangements.[35] They then declare this message as Yahweh's spokesperson. In doing so they remind Israel of the existing covenant arrangements, and announce the consequences of those covenants, both disastrous and delightful. As Stuart writes, "Nearly all of the content of the classical (writing) prophets' oracles revolve around the announcement of the near-time fulfillment of covenantal curses and the end-time fulfillment of covenantal restoration blessings. They speak of little else than these two topics: how and why God's people may expect to be punished by a variety of disasters soon, and how and why they may expect to be rescued and restored eventually."[36] Prophets take standing covenant requirements and consequences and apply them to Israel and the nations.[37]

In this sense, the prophets were truly unoriginal. They created no new requirements for God's people and delivered no new consequences; everything was straight from the book. Stuart goes so far as to catalogue prophetic oracles according to Mosaic blessings and curses in Leviticus 26 and Deuteronomy 28–30.[38] The prophets thus had the difficult task of declaring to Israel what they already knew (Mic 6:8). Their reputation as creative or inventive or visionary should be understood as referring to their style, not their substance.[39]

This explains why issues like idolatry, social injustice, exile, and restoration appear so frequently in the Prophets: they are paramount issues in the Mosaic law. Israel knew that making idols or worshipping other gods was forbidden (Exod 20:3–6); they knew

---

35 See the intriguing description of how Micaiah the prophet participates in Yahweh's divine council in 1 Kgs 22:19–23.

36 Stuart, *Hosea–Jonah,* xxxii.

37 Oracles to or about foreign nations (with whom Yahweh was not in covenant) will receive treatment in later chapters.

38 Ibid., xxxii–xlii.

39 Brueggemann makes a persuasive case that the prophets were able to imagine the world from God's point of view, and that it was strikingly different than the worldly view of current affairs. He is correct, and their imagination was a sharp tool in God's hands. Yet they never imagined new content; they imagined theological (Mosaic) realities above and behind current circumstances and imagined vivid ways to declare their message. See chap. 11 for discussion. Walter Brueggemann, *The Prophetic Imagination,* 2nd ed. (Fortress Press, 2001).

that social justice was required (Exod 21:1–32); they knew that the land was a covenant gift (Gen 15:18–21); and they knew that exile was a possibility (Deut 28:36).

In this light, one may consider the book of Deuteronomy as a kind of prophetic primer. Set at the end of Israel's 40 years of wilderness wandering, after a stubborn and rebellious generation had died, Deuteronomy addresses the children of those who left Egypt, who may not have been alive at Mt. Sinai (1:34–40).[40] Yet when Moses repeats key portions of the Law found in Exodus and Leviticus, he states, "The LORD our God made a covenant with us in Horeb. Not with our fathers did the LORD make this covenant, but with us, who are all of us here alive today" (5:2–3). Moses takes standing covenant regulations from decades ago and applies them to a new generation. In fact, he makes provision for this process to be repeated each generation (27:1–8), because this covenant is with "whoever is standing with us here today before the LORD our God, and with whoever is not here with us today [i.e., future generations]" (29:15). Already, then, the Mosaic law contained provisions for applying existing covenants to new generations. The Prophets sit squarely in this tradition.

Thus, in this book I define an OT writing prophet as a covenant enforcer: an inspired spokesperson from God who brings existing covenants to bear on God's people.

Already, then, we are on our way to being able to preach the Prophets. For what do we as preachers do, if not apply existing covenant material to God's people in our contemporary context? We see a strong theological continuity between their ministry and ours.

Strategies for Preaching the Prophets

This book's aim is to help readers deliver biblically faithful, theologically sound, and rhetorically effective sermons from prophetic oracles. Each chapter will offer strategies for doing so. Let us, then, begin at the beginning.

---

[40] The book is thus appropriately named "*deutero-nomos*" or "second law" in the Septuagint translation.

Strategy 1: Read the Prophets

A conceptual understanding of who the prophets were cannot replace a close familiarity with what they wrote. In other words, the best way to prepare to preach the Prophets is to study their words. Nothing can replace slow, repeated, thoughtful, and prayerful reading of their oracles. Secondary material such as commentaries will only be of service to one whose time and attention is first given to the Scriptures. This section will orient the preacher in preparation for such careful reading.[41]

As preachers carefully read the Prophets, they will notice three things. First, the prophetic books have shape. They have been intentionally edited and organized, though not necessarily in chronological order.[42] Their structure, rather, is thematic and theological. Isaiah, for instance, apparently places great weight on the Assyrian attack against Jerusalem narrated in chapters 36–39. Chapters 1–12 look ahead to it; chapters 13–23 address mostly foreign nations; chapters 24–35 return to the theme; and then the historical account of the attack and deliverance is given—with a foreshadowing of Babylonian threat to come (chapter 39). The latter half of the book is addressed to those who have gone into exile and need a word of hope for the future.[43]

Ezekiel likewise has a macro-structure that pivots around the fall of Jerusalem in chapter 33. Before this, the prophet is all dire warning; afterward he begins to speak of a future covenant of peace and the restoration of Israel to their land. Likewise, the Minor Prophets have their own structures, which often end on notes

---

41 It may also be helpful to consult an OT introduction on specific prophetic books, such as R. K. Harrison, *Introduction to the Old Testament* (Hendrickson, 2004).

42 The details of this process are mostly irretrievable. See Brevard S. Childs, *Biblical Theology of the Old and New Testaments* (Fortress, 1993), 170–171; Robertson, *Christ of the Prophets*, 189–199.

43 There exists significant debate on the historical relationship of chs. 40–66 with the rest of the book. For a theological exploration that takes the final form of the book seriously, see Christopher R. Seitz, "How Is the Prophet Isaiah Present in the Latter Half of the Book?" in *Word Without End: The Old Testament as Abiding Theological Witness* (Eerdmans, 1998), 168–193.

of deliverance (e.g., Amos, Zephaniah). The Minor Prophets also show some evidence of having been shaped into one collective work. For instance, the Twelve, as it is called in the Hebrew Bible, begins and ends with oracles about marriage and divorce (Hosea, Malachi); Joel ends and Amos begins with the LORD roaring; Amos ends with a prediction of Edom's downfall (9:12), which Obadiah addresses; Jonah and Nahum provide contrasting evaluations of Assyria; and the Twelve ends with the three postexilic prophets.[44] Noting the shape of each book and collection will guide preachers' reading and interpretation.

Second, the prophetic books have variety. They contain historical accounts, prayers, and prophetic oracles. The last of these makes up most of the material, which is why the present work is focused on preaching oracles. The oracles themselves fall into several categories: they can address Israel or the nations; they can address an individual or a whole group; and they can hold forth either judgment or salvation.[45] Preachers who familiarize themselves with the basic categories of oracles will be able to use these as a rough guide to contemporary application, as the next chapter will show.

Third, preachers will note that the prophetic oracles all have a historical and theological context. They were given to particular people in a specific situation. Sometimes (as in Haggai) we have precise dates and locations; at other times (as in Joel) we know little of the historical circumstances. In any case, preachers must use what they know of the theological context (Abrahamic, Noahic, Mosaic, and Davidic covenants), as well as the historical context (Israel or Judah, pre-exilic, exilic, post-exilic, whose reign, etc.) to understand why the prophet says what he does.

---

44 For discussion on the unity of the twelve, see Paul R. House, *The Unity of the Twelve* (Almond Press, 1990); Christopher R. Seitz, *The Goodly Fellowship of the Prophets: The Achievement of Association in Canon Formation* (Baker Academic, 2009); Jeanette Mathews, "Preaching from the Minor Prophets," *SMR* 223 (2013): 1–12.

45 Claus Westermann wrote the classic work on the forms of prophetic oracles. Claus Westermann, *Basic Forms of Prophetic Speech*, trans. Hugh Clayton White (Westminster John Knox, 1991), 90–98.

The more familiar one is with the prophetic corpus, with the shape of a particular book, with the type of oracle one is reading, and with the context of that oracle, the shorter and straighter will be the path from prophet to pulpit.

The next chapter will turn to the task of developing an interpretive method for prophetic oracles. And then, on to sermons.

For Further Reading

Carlson, Robert A. *Preaching Like the Prophets: The Hebrew Prophets as Examples for the Practice of Pastoral Preaching.* Wipf & Stock, 2017. 1–56.

Harrison, R. K. *Introduction to the Old Testament.* Hendrickson, 2004.

Robertson, O. Palmer. *The Christ of the Prophets.* P&R Publishing, 2004.

Smith, Gary V. *The Prophets as Preachers: An Introduction to the Hebrew Prophets.* Broadman & Holman, 1994.

Talk about It

In a group, see if participants can remember any sermons they have heard or given from a prophetic oracle. Now, get rid of the Advent sermons from Isaiah and the sermons on Jonah, and see if anyone can remember any. What do you remember about those sermons?

Dig Deeper

See if you can find any macro-structures in a short book like Zephaniah or Amos. Are there clear breaks in the topics? Why do you think the oracles have been arranged this way?

Practice

Try this: open your Bible to a random page in the Prophets, and find an oracle addressed to Israel or Judah (rather than to a foreign nation). Jot down some notes about what kind of a sermon might come from this oracle:

- What is the oracle's tone? Is this woe or weal?

- What might this oracle have to do with the church?

- What is unclear to you?

- What in this passage could make for a vivid preaching moment?

2

Prepare to Interpret the Prophets[1]

> *Again and again you called us into covenant with you,*
> *and through the prophets you taught us to hope for salvation.*
> —The Book of Common Prayer (1979)[2]

THE LAST CHAPTER helped preachers to read the OT Prophets on their own terms; this chapter will assist them in bringing the prophets' words to bear on the church.[3] It turns out that the prophets' role as "covenant enforcers" is just as helpful here as it was there. After surveying two common approaches to interpreting the prophetic oracles, this chapter will introduce an interpretive framework for the prophets based on their role as covenant enforcers.

Familiar Paths

Two standard techniques are available to anyone who preaches the Prophets. First, the preacher can trace a predictive prophecy and indicate its fulfillment (Figure 2.1). (That fulfillment may be past,

---

1 This chapter is a modified and expanded version of my article, "Community Oracles: A Model for Applying and Preaching the Old Testament Prophets," *JEHS* 10 (March 2010): 31–57. A popular version appeared in Craig Brian Larson, ed., *Prophetic Preaching* (Hendrickson, 2012), 119-130.

2 *The (Online) Book of Common Prayer* (The Church Hymnal Corporation), Eucharistic Prayer C, 373, https://www.bcponline.org.

3 This will be the most technical in the book and will engage hermeneutical and theological issues surrounding the Prophets. Footnotes will be ample for those readers interested in digging deeper.

present, or future from our point of view.) The lesson is usually that the Bible is true, or that God knows all things and can be trusted. But theological guesswork and speculative end-times scenarios haunt this road. Besides, one often wonders, "Where is my parishioner in this sermon? How does this word address them?"

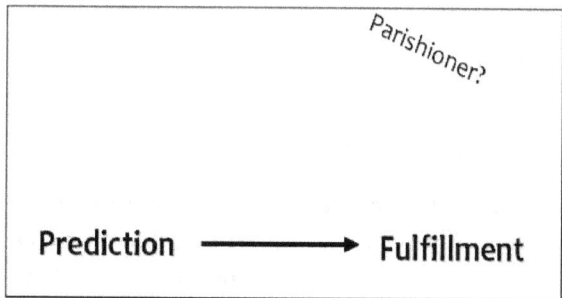

Figure 2.1: Prophecy as Prediction

In a second method, preachers limit themselves to narrative material in the Prophets like Daniel in the lion's den or Jonah in the belly of the fish. Now we are back in the familiar terrain of story, and all that remains is to draw parallels between the life of the prophet and the life of the parishioner (Figure 2.2): "Be like Daniel!" and "Don't be like Jonah!"[4]

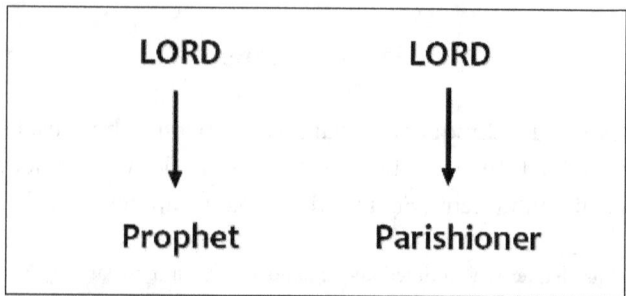

Figure 2.2: Prophets as Moral Exemplars

---

4 For examples of this type of sermon from the Prophets, see Walter Brueggemann, "The Secret of Survival: Jeremiah 20:7–13, Matthew 6:1–8," JP 26 (2003): 42–47; Beau Hughes, "Into the Storm," The Village Church (podcast), June 22, 2008; John Ortberg, "Resisting God," Menlo Park Presbyterian Church (podcast), November 8, 2008.

This second approach also has serious drawbacks. In the first place, it puts congregants in the center of the story rather than God. Consider Isaiah 6, where Isaiah relates a glorious account of his calling in Yahweh's temple. Did God do this just to provide a blueprint for how he might call Joe Smith to a new job in Cincinnati? Isaiah can of course serve as an example for modern lives, but this passage probably has a grander purpose.

In the second place, preachers can use this technique inconsistently, even thoughtlessly: they connect some details of the narrative (such as Jonah's running from God) to modern lives, but omit others (huge storms, giant fish, Assyrian hostility, God's care for livestock, predicted disaster, and miraculous vines and worms). Why would some aspects be normative today and not others? Finally, this approach drastically limits preaching material in the Prophets because, as we saw in chapter 1, most prophetic material is not narrative but prophetic speech—oracles from Yahweh to his people Israel, through the mouth of an inspired prophet.

Of course, at times one can and should preach OT figures as examples. Paul does so with Abraham and David in Romans 4, and Jesus does the same with Lot's wife (Luke 17:32). The question of when and how to preach moral exemplar sermons (which involve questions of authorial intent and a reader's agency) lies beyond the scope of this book. There may be appropriate times to preach on Jeremiah's weeping or Amos's agricultural occupation. My point here is simply that making this one's *primary* approach to the Prophets has significant cost, in that it centers parishioners instead of God, risks inconsistency, raises thorny hermeneutical issues, and does all of that while eliminating over 95% of the prophetic material for preaching. In view of the disadvantages of "prophecy as prediction" and "prophecy as narrative," intrepid preachers must seek a new path from prophet to pulpit.

This chapter will map out such a path: a way forward for applying and preaching the prophetic oracles of the OT. The path begins with the previous chapter's identification of prophets as covenant enforcers. By focusing on the *covenant context* of a prophetic speech, preachers can consistently and faithfully apply prophetic oracles to the church in richly textured ways. I will first develop the notion of "covenant context" and then use that idea to show how prophetic oracles can speak to the church today. I will also give examples so that preachers can see the approach at work.

Covenant Context

As Walter Brueggemann notes, "The task of prophetic ministry is to nurture, nourish, and evoke a consciousness and perception alternative to the consciousness and perception of the dominant culture around us."[5] The prophet sees his nation and his countrymen through God's eyes, and it moves him to speech. He declares Yahweh's word, setting before his audience Yahweh's view of the situation in sharp contrast to their own. Israel may feel secure, but Yahweh warns of destruction. They may be hopeless, but Yahweh offers comfort.

But this revelation from God does not take place in a vacuum. These are not just any people to whom the prophet speaks. They are Israel—Yahweh's own nation by covenant—and the prophets are his covenant enforcers. Therefore, OT prophecies always take place within a *covenant context*. The hearers are bound to him and to one another in an intricate web of relationships, to which the Prophets refer again and again. Figure 2.3 illustrates the main features of those connections.

Prophets speak about Israel's *covenant Lord* whose character forms a basis for their relationship. They write about Israel's

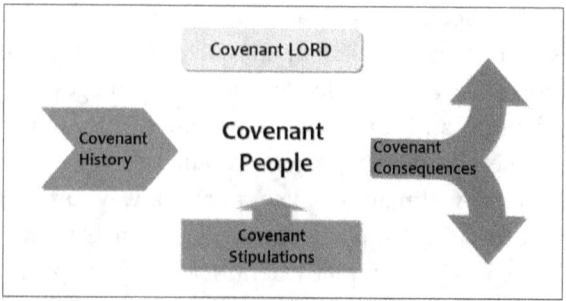

Figure 2.3: Israel's Covenant Context

---

5 Walter Brueggemann, *The Prophetic Imagination*, 2nd ed. (Fortress Press, 2001), 3.

Covenant LORD	"I am the first and the last, besides me there is no God." Isa 44:6–8
Covenant History	"It was I who brought you up out of the land of Egypt and redeemed you from the house of slavery." Amos 2:10
Covenant Stipulations	"Why then are we faithless, profaning the covenant of our fathers? …Judah has profaned the sanctuary of the LORD." Mal 2:10–11
Covenant Consequences	"If you are willing and obedient, you shall eat the good of the land; but if you refuse and rebel, you shall be eaten by the sword." Isa 1:19–20

Table 2.1: Aspects of Covenant Context

covenant history with Yahweh and his faithfulness in the past. They remind Israel of the *covenant stipulations* and how they have or have not kept them. And they repeat the dual *covenant consequences* of blessings for obedience and curses for rebellion. See Table 2.1 for examples.

Often a single oracle walks hearers through several aspects of the covenant context. Micah 6, for instance, reminds Judah of how Yahweh brought them into the Promised Land (vv. 3–5), discusses the type of response he requires (vv. 6–8), rebukes their faithlessness (vv. 9–12), and warns of curses to come (vv. 13–16).

Figure 2.3 can apply to any of the several covenant arrangements that were in effect during Israel's history. The Abrahamic, Noachian, Mosaic, and Davidic covenants were the primary arrangements depicted in the OT.[6] Each covenant between Yahweh and his people had its own historical background, unique demands, and specific consequences.[7] Because Israel is under all these arrangements at once, prophets can draw on these as appropriate to the situation.

The Mosaic covenant features most prominently in the

---

6 Malachi 2 also includes an allusion to God's covenant with Levi, referring most likely to Yahweh's promise of priesthood to Phinehas and his descendants in Num 25.

7 This raises the issue of the overlap of the covenants in the OT. See below for discussion.

Prophets, probably because the biblical material on this covenant (Exodus–Deuteronomy) is more extensive than the material on other covenants. The prophet reminds Israel of God's mighty acts of deliverance in Egypt and his faithfulness in the conquest of the Promised Land (Jer 34:13). Or he recalls the Mosaic commandments that they had broken (Hos 14:8) and warns of covenant curses like foreign conquest (Hab 1:5–11, from Deut 28:49), or promises covenant blessings like peace and agricultural prosperity (Ezek 34:25–31, from Lev 26:3–5).

Most prophetic oracles follow this standard pattern, highlighting one or more covenant elements. Covenant context is the Prophets' normal frame of reference.[8]

Community Oracles

Critical for our discussion is the fact that covenant context is always *communal*. Prophets do call individuals to respond and bring them comfort; yet the scope of the warnings and promises are national. These are community oracles, directed to an entire people, and based on a common heritage. Interpreting them accurately requires a corporate mindset.

Therefore, each aspect of Figure 2.3 relates to Israel as a community: The covenant Lord is a communal Lord. God did not make a direct covenant with each Israelite; he instead made it with Abraham and his descendants, with Moses and the people under his authority, and with David and his subjects. Individual Israelites participated in the covenant only as part of the community.

Similarly, covenant history is a communal history. Yahweh brought an entire people into existence; he rescued that people out of slavery and forged them into a nation. Even when the prophets note the personal histories of Moses or Abraham or David, those histories are significant because of their broader repercussions (e.g., Isa 51:1–3).

Likewise, covenant demands are communal demands. As OT scholars have noted, God's requirements in the prophetic texts

---

8 See below for a discussion of how prophetic oracles against other nations also fit this framework.

focus on communal relationships.[9] The prophets habitually address corporate idolatrous worship (Isa 2:8), oppression (Isa 3:5), unrighteous wealth (Isa 57:17), deceit (Isa 28:17), selfish leadership (Isa 3:12), murder, and adultery (Isa 57:5).

Finally, covenant consequences are communal consequences. Through his prophets Yahweh promises good to his people if they repent and judgment if they rebel (Isa 1:19–20). As it turned out, they did not repent, and were judged at the fall of Samaria (722 B.C.) and Jerusalem (586 B.C.). Of course, not every wicked person died a violent death during the Assyrian and Babylonian conquests, and not every obedient man or woman was spared and sent into exile. Rather, God views his people as a body, and their corporate sins come home to roost in their corporate lives.

Of course, prophets do address individuals at times (Jer 45:1–5), and of course each individual Israelite had to choose whether to heed the prophet's message. But the only people the prophets spoke to were those already in the covenant:

> Hear this, O house of Jacob,
> who are called by the name of Israel,
> and who came from the waters of Judah,
> who swear by the name of the LORD
> and confess the God of Israel,
> but not in truth or right. (Isa 48:1)

The prophets called people who lived in the bonds of communal covenant. When one reads the Prophets from this perspective, the path from then to now becomes easier to find.

Two Strategies for Preaching the Prophets

Covenant context and its corporate nature lead to two major strategies for interpreting and preaching the Prophets. Together they indicate a way forward from text to sermon.[10]

---

9 See, e.g., Abraham Heschel, *The Prophets* (Harper Colophon Books, 1962), 1:195–220, and Brueggemann, *Prophetic Imagination*, 1–37.

10 Here we must mention in passing the thorny issue of biblical

Strategy 2.1 Compare Audience to Audience

The first comes from Sidney Greidanus, who observes that preachers often make a comparison between the biblical character and the modern audience, drawing life lessons as the main interpretive thrust of a passage.[11] I have addressed the drawbacks of that approach above.

Greidanus suggests that a more fruitful comparison can be made between the prophet's ancient audience and a preacher's contemporary audience. In other words, the wise preacher will not ask, "How are my people like Hosea?" but will instead ask, "How are my people like the people to whom Hosea preached?"

Take Hosea as an example. He was an exceptional person, called by Yahweh to speak his word to Israel. The preacher who wants to use Hosea as an exemplar will face the difficult task of sorting out what was true only about Hosea and what is true about modern hearers. Often these choices tend to be arbitrary, based on what preachers already know or want to say anyway. So, one might use Hosea to encourage marital fidelity, but not to justify marriage to prostitutes.

However, Hosea spoke to people who were (for lack of a more flattering term) common. Hosea's audience and the church are alike: they both hear the word of God and are both called to respond. Neither group is necessarily gifted, prophetic, bold, winsome, or persecuted. More to the point, they are both recipients of God's word *as people who live in covenant with him*.[12] When

---

hermeneutics—the art and science of what a text *meant*, what it now *means*, and how a reader *comprehends* that meaning. Most of these difficult issues we will leave to the side. For works that deal with biblical hermeneutics and preaching, see Craig G. Bartholomew, *Introducing Biblical Hermeneutics: A Comprehensive Framework for Hearing God in Scripture* (Baker Academic, 2015); Andrew C. Thompson, *Projection Interpretation: Toward a New Hermeneutic for Homiletics* (PhD diss., London School of Theology, 2020).

11 Sidney Greidanus, *The Modern Preacher and the Ancient Text* (William B. Eerdmans, 1988), 169–172.

12 Hosea was in the covenant, too, of course. But Hosea did not marry Gomer, have children, give them bizarre names, and preach to Israel because he was in covenant with God. He did those things in his office as a prophet. That office is the theologically significant difference between Hosea and us.

preaching from the Prophets, then, unless the text clearly indicates otherwise, preachers should take a default approach of comparing audience to audience in application.

Strategy 2.2 See How It Has Already Begun

A second insight: scholars have observed that applying the Prophets to a different audience is an ancient practice. Recent canonical approaches to biblical interpretation pay attention to the way in which the Scriptures were arranged for the benefit of later readers.[13] Amos, for example, did not give all his recorded oracles at one moment in time, nor did he necessarily give them in the order they appear in his book. Either Amos himself or a group of his disciples wrote down a selection of his oracles and arranged them in the form in which they appear in Scripture for the benefit of a later audience.[14] The book presents oracles designed for readers ten, 100, or 1000 years after Amos lived. This is why most prophetic books end on a note of redemption and promise. That uplifting arrangement is not coincidental but is part of a contextualization process meant to encourage later readers who had seen Yahweh's judgment and were awaiting his favor and forgiveness. An audience in the Babylonian exile or among the returners after exile could read these books, gain an understanding of why judgment came upon Israel, and harbor a future hope in God's promises. The selection and arrangement of their oracles indicates that although a prophet's message was delivered in one time to one people, it already had a trajectory aimed beyond its immediate context.[15]

This shared covenant with God gave the oracle a continuing relevance for later readers. Because those readers were also in covenant with the same God on the same terms, God's words through

---

13 For two recent treatments of this idea in relation to OT Prophets, see Sailhamer, "Preaching from the Prophets," in *Preaching the Old Testament*, ed. Scott M. Gibson (Baker, 2006), 115-136, and Christopher R. Seitz, *Prophecy and Hermeneutics: Toward a New Introduction to the Prophets* (Baker Academic, 2007). I rely heavily on their insights in the following discussion.

14 Gary V. Smith, *Amos* (Mentor, 1998), 25-27; Shalom M. Paul, *Amos*, Hermeneia (Fortress, 1991), 5-6.

15 See also the discussion in chapter 1 of this phenomenon in Deuteronomy.

Amos to a pre-exilic community remained helpful for those living during or even after the exile. Covenant context was (already) the key to applying the Prophets to later hearers. Therefore, interpreting and preaching the Prophets requires asking how these oracles resounded through the years as God's people went into exile, suffered in strange lands, returned home, and struggled to establish their nation anew.

The Church's Covenant Context

When preachers compare the ancient and contemporary audiences and follow the trail of editors who reapplied prophetic oracles to God's people in different (covenant) contexts, the way forward becomes clear. If one follows the trail long enough, one reaches the New Testament, where a comparable covenant context obtains.

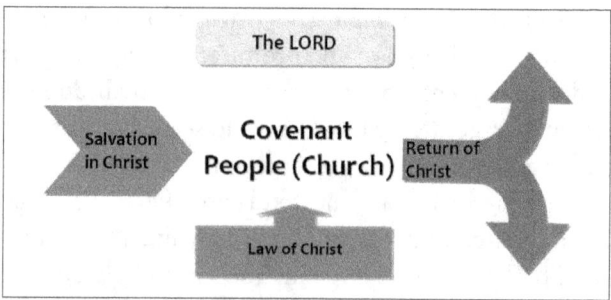

Figure 2.4: The New Covenant Context

As Figure 2.4 indicates, NT believers live in covenant with God—what Jeremiah (31:31) calls a "new covenant" and Isaiah (54:10) and Ezekiel (37:26) a "covenant of peace." The church is in covenant with the Triune God, who has provided redemption in the death and resurrection of Christ and the outpouring of the Holy Spirit. He holds out covenant demands that his people love God and neighbor and has promised that he will return to bring salvation and judgment to the world.

Thus, Israel and the church live under parallel covenant structures. Both groups live under the same covenant Lord, whose character does not change. They both live in the light of his deliverance in the past. They both live under his demands for love and obedience, and they both live in hope of God's promises of salvation and judgment. The church's covenant situation is remarkably like Israel's.

And just like Israel's covenant, the church's covenant is a communal arrangement. Just as each element in Figure 2.3 was corporate, so also in Figure 2.4. God is Father over the entire family of faith. The salvation Jesus accomplished redeemed an entire people for his possession. The Law of Christ is for the whole church, as are his warnings and promises. The blood of Christ, the words of Christ, and the presence of Christ, apply to each person only as she or he is in the body of Christ. Thus, prophetic oracles to the OT community are best applied to the NT community.

Of course, differences also exist between Israel and the church, and preachers must make room for them. Greidanus, for instance, notes three kinds of "distance" that preachers should consider in applying ancient Scripture to modern people: culture, levels of revelation, and kingdom history.[16] Cultural differences between then and now are present in every text of Scripture, and they need not detain us here. As for levels of revelation, Greidanus notes that OT prophets did not always see the full picture of God's work. Preachers now have the benefit of God's definitive self-revelation in Christ, and as such, have insight into the events to which the prophets were looking forward. This may change how they preach a prophetic text. For example, in Amos 9:11–15 the prophet speaks of God restoring David's fallen "tent" (i.e., his dynasty) and foreign nations like Edom being called by God's name. Yet in Acts 15 James declares this prophecy to be fulfilled by the exaltation of Christ, the Davidic King, and by the church's mission to the Gentiles.[17] The text gives no indication that the prophet had this degree of awareness; but preachers do and should make use of it.

Most important for preachers are the kingdom history differences. The church is in a later stage in the history of redemption, and wise preachers will think hard on the historical-theological

---

16 Greidanus, *Modern Preacher*, 167–168.
17 Of course, views differ on whether prophecies such as these still await further fulfillment(s). See below on different theological systems.

distance between the OT audience and their own. Israel's Exodus was physical while the church's is spiritual. Israel's law is of Moses, and the church's law is of Christ. Many of Israel's promises of judgment and restoration have already come to pass, while the church awaits a great deal to come.

What preachers make of these differences will depend upon the theological system in which they operate and how that system connects Israel to the church.[18] Some will posit more discontinuity between the covenants, for instance, by drawing a sharp distinction between Israel and the church or labeling the old covenant "conditional" (a ministry that produced death) and the new "unconditional" (producing life by the Spirit). Some forms of dispensational theology fall here, as well as some Lutheran perspectives that posit a radical distinction between law and grace, and some mainline theologies.[19]

For example, I remember sitting with a preacher shortly after 9/11. He said to a gathering that we should not see the terrorist attack as warning or discipline or punishment from God, because all punishment had been absorbed by the cross and God no longer deals with his people that way. Whatever one makes of that statement, it posits significant discontinuity between Israel and the church.

Others will find more continuity between the two covenant eras. Reformed and Presbyterian denominations tend to fall here, as do some Wesleyan thinkers. For example, Robertson (a Reformed, covenant theologian) argues, "The cumulative evidence of the Scriptures points definitively toward the unified character

---

18 The literature on this topic is vast. For an extended comparison between systems of continuity and discontinuity, see John S. Feinberg, ed., *Continuity and Discontinuity: Perspectives on the Relationship Between the Old and New Testaments* (Crossway, 1988). For a recent treatment that attempts to find a middle ground, see Peter J. Gentry and Stephen J. Wellum, *Kingdom Through Covenant* (Crossway, 2012).

19 The Lutheran case is complex because the law/grace distinction is not perfectly aligned with the Israel/church distinction. Mainline theologies are also complicated: Some Protestant theologians' view of Scripture allows for moral and theological error on the part of biblical authors, and as such, when prophets preach judgment there may be a blanket refusal to countenance such ideas from a loving God.

of the biblical covenants."[20] He views events like the restoration of Israel as having been fulfilled in the coming of Christ and the birth of the church.[21] Again, I recall a discussion with a Presbyterian pastor who, in conversations about the Old Testament, told me, "When I read about Israel, I see myself." The examples below show that how one understands the respective situations in Israel and the church will guide one's interpretation and application by finding similarities or differences in covenant context.

A caveat: no matter how much some want it to be the case, no contemporary nation state is in covenant with God.[22] There exists no theological framework for taking prophetic oracles to the covenant people of *Israel* and applying them to a modern *country*.[23] To take my own country as an example: America, as expressed in its founding documents, has no covenant Lord, no covenant promises. Therefore we have no biblical license for taking oracles addressed to Israel and pasting them onto a non-theological corporate entity like America.[24] When, for example, Isaiah says, "The nations shall see your righteousness, and all the kings your glory, and you shall be called by a new name that the mouth of the LORD will give" (Isa 62:2), this is no prediction of American hegemony. The words are a promise to the people of God. Some of God's people are Americans, but most are not. And how we find them (and relate this promise to them) is not to cross a border, but to cross the

---

20 O. Palmer Robertson, *The Christ of the Covenants* (P&R, 1980), 28.

21 Ibid., 486–498.

22 This includes the United Stated of America. As an American I am acutely aware of how the church can hijack oracles to apply them to my country. But no modern nation has the covenant status of ancient Israel. This even applies, I believe, to the modern nation-state of Israel. This is a controversial claim for some, and space permits only a bald assertion here. For more, see O. Palmer Robertson, *The Israel of God: Yesterday, Today, and Tomorrow* (P&R, 2000).

23 For two examples of this approach, see Walter Brueggemann, "Bragging About the Right Stuff," *JP* 26 (2003): 27–32; and Donald Ackland, "Preaching from Hosea to a Nation in Crisis," *SJT* 18:1 (1975): 43–55.

24 Elizabeth Achtemeier argues that prophecies condemning foreign nations most directly apply to modern-day nations like the United States! Elizabeth Achtemeier, *Preaching from the Old Testament* (Westminster John Knox, 1989), 135.

threshold of the church as it gathers for worship. Only the church has a parallel covenant context, and to the church these oracles speak.[25]

Using a Covenant Context to Interpret the Prophets for the Church

Now that we have set prophets and preachers (and those who hear their words) in their respective covenant contexts, we will outline ways those contexts connect to one another.

First, note that covenants in Scripture come in a series and build on one another. The Bible depicts a chain of overlapping covenant arrangements between God and his people stretching from the patriarchs to the present (see Figure 2.5).[26]

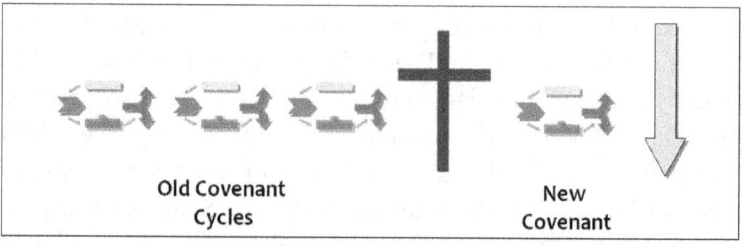

Figure 2.5: Covenants in Scripture

The covenant context approach takes each part of the covenant arrangement in a prophetic oracle (Lord, history, stipulations and consequences) and asks how that relates to the corresponding

---

25 Of course, politicians and parties and policies are subject to critique or praise based on biblical values, because "Righteousness exalts a nation, but sin is a disgrace to any people" (Prov 14:34). But moral critique of society generally is a far cry from taking specific covenant promises and applying them to a modern secular political entity.

26 This diagram is simplified because it depicts the OT covenants seriatim. For a more nuanced discussion of how OT covenants overlap and intersect, see Roy E. Ciampa, "The History of Redemption," in *Central Themes in Biblical Theology: Mapping Unity in Diversity*, ed. Scott J. Hafemann and Paul R. House (Baker Academic, 2007), 254–308.

entity (Lord, history, stipulations and consequences) in the church's new covenant context. The resulting sermon will address that corresponding part of the new covenant relationship.

In some cases, the preacher will discern a basic similarity in our respective contexts. Thus, the sermon will not only address the same part as the oracle, but make the same point as the oracle. Their history or their stipulations are similar to our own, and therefore the sermon will seek to perform the same function as the oracle; if a prophet convicts or inspires or reassures, so will the sermon.[27]

In other cases, the preacher will find significant differences between their covenant context and ours. Their stipulations and ours are not the same, or their future promises are a part of our past history. This scenario requires a less direct approach, where the sermon will either have to stretch to find similarities, or else end making an entirely different point than the oracle.[28]

Let us break down this broad strategy into specific cases. The examples below show how each element of Israel's covenant context connects with the corresponding element of the present-day church.

Strategy 3.1 Their Lord Is Our Lord

In the most straightforward case, a prophet describes the character of God, who remains the same in Israel's context and our own. For example, Isa 40:12–31 speaks of Yahweh's tremendous wisdom and power, displayed in creation and in his sovereign rule over the nations. He is not to be compared with idols or with any power of men. In this case the strategy is simply to preach about our covenant Lord, just as the prophet did.

A contemporary sermon on Isaiah 40 will also stay true to Isaiah's reason for focusing on God's character. Because Yahweh

---

27 This distinction (between the content of a text and its point or illocutionary force) is explored in my "Projection Interpretation: Toward a Hermeneutic for Homiletics" (PhD diss., London School of Theology, 2020), 23–31, and in Abraham Kuruvilla, *Text to Praxis: Hermeneutics and Homiletics in Dialogue*, LNTS 393 (T&T Clark, 2009), 11–36.

28 See below for examples. Sailhamer, "Preaching from the Prophets," 122–124, is particularly strong on this point.

knows all and can do all, he is not ignorant of Israel's situation (v. 27) and can be trusted to deliver them (v. 29). Believers now serve the same God, and long for a kingdom that cannot be shaken (Heb 12:28). Since we too are God's people, we can trust God to restore us. So, a big idea for that sermon might be, "We can trust the Almighty God for our future."

Strategy 3.2 Their History May (or May Not) Be Our History

The prophets often recite covenant history: God's salvific acts on behalf of his people. I will first describe cases where the application is direct and straightforward, and then tackle more complex examples.

In Jer 33:20–22, God recalls his covenant with Noah and the whole earth (Gen 8:22), establishing a firm pattern of day and night, and reasons from that faithfulness to his faithfulness in Jeremiah's day to have a king and a priest stand before him. At first glance, this promise to Jeremiah may seem discontinuous with our day. But in fact, their history is our history, because the world continues under the same covenant order of day and night established in Genesis. Christians today can take comfort in God's faithful ordering of nature, seeing it as a proof of his constancy.

The point of Jeremiah's historical recital is to assure Israel that God will take just as much care to have a king on the throne as he does to make sure day and night endure. As long as the sun is rising, God will make sure that a ruler sits the throne. Because their history is our history, we too share in these promises. We can rely on him to provide a great King and High Priest in Jesus Christ. God in Christ keeps his promises. In preaching a sermon on this oracle, we would, like Jeremiah compare the reliability of the sunrise with the reliability of God's promises. And we now know the way he fulfills that promise: by his installment of Jesus on the throne forever.

Or consider Mic 7:18–20, where Micah recites God's promises to show steadfast love to Abraham and Jacob. These promises provide the basis of assurance that Israel's sins will be forgiven.[29]

---

29 In this case we have a "cheat sheet" in the NT: there Paul affirms that the

Israel's history is in this case the church's history; along with Micah and his audience, the church can count on God's forgiveness. A sermon on this oracle would take their history as our history and could draw the same conclusions.

The two examples above trade on similarity in covenant context: God's covenant with Noah endures for all people now, and the covenant promises to Abraham are fulfilled in Christ. Thus, their history is our history, and application is direct. However, if the covenant in question is the Mosaic covenant (as it most commonly is in the Prophets), some theological frameworks would see that as the church's own history, while others would not.

For example, the prophets often recall God's deliverance of Israel from Egypt through the Red Sea to Sinai and the Promised Land. Hosea 11:1–4 repeats this history and then rebukes Israel for her unfaithfulness and foretells judgment. Is the Exodus history our history, or does it belong to Israel and not to us? Is this a case of similarity or difference?

Contrasting answers lead to different sermons. On the one hand, preachers who see a sharp difference between the old covenant of law and the new covenant of grace will highlight the discontinuity between then and now. They will say something like, "We too have been unfaithful like Israel, and we too have deserved to judgment and abandonment. But because of Jesus, we are no longer under law but under grace. Our story has a different ending. In our case, where sin increased, grace increased all the more (Rom 5:20)." A "discontinuity" sermon on Hos 11:1–4 would replace warning with gratitude: the OT judgment has been transformed into NT forgiveness, and all of us who fall short of God's standards can take comfort in Christ.

On the other hand, some preachers posit more continuity between Israel and the church. To them, the Exodus is our history, too. When we read about Israel, we see ourselves. Hosea's words were a warning then and they still warn now. Do not take the grace of God lightly! Those who think that their covenant with God is a license to rebellion will find the same fate as Israel: "Though they

---

promises to Abraham do indeed belong to those who are in Christ (Gal 3:29). Instances like this let us know that we are on the right track in our approach.

call out to the Most High, he shall not raise them up at all" (Hos 11:7). Hosea's warning is not transmuted into anything else. It remains a stark admonition for the church.

If those sound like two radically different sermons, that is because they are. Which is the right one? That is up to preachers to decide, based on how they understand our new covenant situation. The covenant context model asks the question rather than answering it. It asks us to get clear on how we understand the relationship between old and new covenants and uses that understanding as a lens through which the prophetic oracle is refracted in the pulpit.

Strategy 3.3 Their Stipulations May (or May Not) Compel Us

The prophets regularly remind Israel of what Yahweh demands from them in covenant obedience. As with the last strategy, when we ask whether those demands apply to us, we discover simple cases of similarity and more complex cases of difference.

In simple cases, the stipulations for righteous behavior are so general that they obviously address all of God's people, past and present. Murder is always wrong; fairness is always right. Micah calls people (6:8) to do justice, love mercy, and walk humbly with God. Hosea (4:1-14) rails against those guilty of murder, lying, stealing, cursing, and adultery. Jeremiah (22:13-30) condemns King Jehoiachin for injustice and hoarding wealth. Zephaniah (2:1-3) encourages people to seek the LORD, seek righteousness, and seek humility, and "perhaps you may be hidden on the day of the anger of the LORD." All these passages find clear parallels in the lives of our parishioners who are still under the injunction to "be holy, for I am holy" (Lev 11:44; 1 Pet 1:14-16).[30] Sermons from passages like these will be relatively clear echoes of the

---

30 In many cases, such commands are repeated or affirmed in the NT. Yet not always: for instance, some forms of predatory lending condemned in the OT (Exo 22:25) are not condemned in the NT. If a preacher is doubtful about whether a command is truly universal, then the command in question becomes a more complex case, which I address next.

oracles. For instance, in preaching on Mic 6:6–8, a big idea I have used is, "You already know what God wants from you." Rather than extravagant expressions of worship, God desires mercy, justice, and faith. Micah's words need very little tuning to be on key in the church.

On the other hand, Malachi demands tithing, Hosea rebukes the nation for its political alliances, and Haggai exhorts the people to build a temple. As in the discussion of covenant history, some preachers will see continuity (i.e., Christians should tithe), while others will see discontinuity (i.e., a separation of church and state in our country, implying that political alliances are not something Christians need concern themselves with).

In cases where preachers find discontinuity, they can take an indirect route, finding NT stipulations loosely analogous to the Prophets'. Haddon Robinson says that preachers can move up a "ladder of abstraction," deriving increasingly general principles from specific demands.[31] Climbing the ladder of abstraction, Malachi's tithing may translate to a general exhortation for sacrificial and joyful giving (2 Cor 8). Or Hosea's political oracle may challenge us more generally to be careful with whom we associate (2 Cor 6:14–18).

Careful thought and some NT study can often help us climb the ladder. For instance, in reading Haggai's command to build the temple, we may note that temple language in the OT was appropriated by Jesus (who implied that he is the true temple, John 2:18–21), and by Paul (who said as the body of Christ that we are the temple, 1 Cor 3:16), and by Peter (who envisioned the building of that temple as our growth into spiritual maturity, 1 Pet 2:4–5). Therefore, the NT version of "building the Temple" in Jerusalem is to build up the church by making disciples. A sermon on Haggai about making the temple the top priority would urge believers to make discipleship and spiritual formation one of the great goals of their lives. Every commandment in the OT is an expression of love for God or love for neighbor; climb the ladder high enough and we can cross the gap from OT to NT.

---

31 Haddon Robinson, "The Heresy of Application: An Interview with Haddon Robinson," *Leadership* 18 (Fall 1997): 20–27.

Thus, even when prophetic demands are not directly transferable, a more general theological principle that applies to both covenant situations may offer a way forward.[32]

Strategy 3.4 Their Promises Are Our History

Now we examine a case of difference, where temporal distance complicates the connection between then and now. Here, what was future for the original audience is in the past for us. When modern preachers see God threaten to destroy Jerusalem in Amos 3:11–15, that word is not directly a threat for the church, because ancient Jerusalem was destroyed long ago. It would be foolish to stand up and predict the coming invasion of Jerusalem (or Chicago, or Oslo). Israel's promise is our history, and therefore a more indirect approach is called for. Amos 3 performs a different function for us: it explains why God's people have suffered, highlights the seriousness of God's wrath, and reminds us that he keeps his word.

Likewise, when Isaiah writes of a future restoration from exile (43:1–7), which is now behind us, preachers can thank God for how he cared for a faithful remnant after the exile and reflect on how God continues to protect his people amid suffering.[33]

Messianic oracles fall in this category: Israel's future is our past, and we can take comfort and rejoice in Jesus' advent. Yet the point of these prophecies was not just accurate prediction but the person and work of the coming deliverer. So, one should of course marvel that Jesus was born in Bethlehem, as Micah 5 foretells. But more important than accurate forecasting is the peaceful and royal character of his presence: the Messiah is a Shepherd over God's

---

32 The reader will note that in this section I cite NT texts to support the theological conclusions drawn. This is not to say that sermons on OT material must use NT texts for legitimacy. Rather, I cite these NT texts to indicate the theological stances that NT texts take and that explain why an interpretation along these lines would be legitimate.

33 Yet another path we must forego is a discussion about whether and how the promises of return from exile were or were not fulfilled in Ezra's time, in the time of Christ, in our present age as the Kingdom expands, or whether we still await a completion of this promise. See below on partial fulfillment, and on this issue specifically, see N.T. Wright, *The New Testament and the People of God* (Fortress, 1992).

people. A sermon I preached on Micah 5 had the big idea, "He is our peace." Of course, part of it addressed Micah's prediction and Jesus' fulfillment. But the bulk of the sermon focused on the way that Micah predicted what this Shepherd would *do* in his capacity as ruler. And we know this now because we are looking back to Christ, rather than forward to an unclear hope.

To complicate matters further, here is another wrinkle in time: an oracle may have been only partially fulfilled, as today the church lives in the tension between the resurrection and the parousia.[34] Isaiah 2, for instance, foretells a time when Mt. Zion will become the highest of mountains and all nations will stream to it to know the LORD. Today, of course, Mt. Zion remains a humble hill among higher neighbors. Yet this tiny nation and its worship have been exalted through Jesus and the worldwide church, and that the nations are streaming in. A partial-fulfillment scheme would affirm that God's people can rejoice in the spiritual exaltation of the people of God, even though that elevation is not yet realized physically. Or one might preach from Joel 2:28–32, where God says he will pour out his Spirit freely on his people and celebrate this happening at Pentecost in Acts 2. However, the latter part of the oracle, that "the sun shall be turned to darkness, and the moon to blood, before the great and awesome day of the LORD comes," has not yet come to pass—the church awaits the final judgment.[35] A sermon on Joel 2:28–32 could therefore proceed in two halves: the first half would celebrate God's gift of the Holy Spirit not just to anointed leaders but to all of God's people, while the second half would link the presence of the Spirit with the inbreaking Kingdom of God, that shakes thrones and powers and will culminate in God's complete rule on earth. A big idea could be, "God pours out his Spirit as a down payment of his power."

---

34 The possibility of multiple fulfillments of prophecy is yet another theological mare's nest. Interested readers can find a helpful and nuanced introductory discussion in VanGemeren, *Interpreting*, 70-99.

35 Even here we find controversy! A Preterist interpretation would understand that these cosmic signs were indeed fulfilled at Pentecost. The point of this discussion is not to map out every possible take on prophecy and fulfillment, but to bear in mind that, whatever one's interpretive position, that position can be used to take Israel's covenant context and connect it to our own.

Strategy 3.5 Their Promises May Be Our Promises

Finally, what was future to Israel may be future to present-day readers. One could preach from Zechariah 14 about a future time when God will visit his people, splitting the Mount of Olives in two, saving them from their enemies, and making the entire land "holy to the LORD" (14:20). Or one may hope for the day when God's glory and presence return to his people in a rebuilt temple in Ezekiel 40–48. Of course, both passages require preachers to settle on an interpretive position first. Are these oracles still awaiting a physical fulfilment in the land of Israel? Are they being initiated now in the church? Are they adumbrations of our glorious future with Christ?

My own perspective on a passage like Zechariah 14 is that it describes (in highly charged OT apocalyptic terms) a grand deliverance on the day of Yahweh. That deliverance comes amid suffering and apparent abandonment by God. The same reality is depicted in different terms in NT contexts like the Olivet discourse, Romans 8, 1 Peter 1, and Revelation. In preaching on this text, I would say that in our present sufferings, we can know that God has a glorious vindication in store for his church. Like Zechariah, I cannot give a literal description, but can tell my people that it will be beyond anything we have seen or heard before. Grand redemption is surely coming.

However one reads passages like these, the future from Zechariah's point of view is still future for us. We look ahead with the prophets to God's future work.

Strategy 3.6 Combine as Necessary

Prophetic oracles are complex. Interpreting a single oracle may involve several aspects of the respective covenant contexts. For instance, a passage like Zeph 3:1–13 calls for a skillful application of the various themes: Yahweh's unchanging character (v. 5), his past acts of judging other nations (v. 6), his demand for obedience (v. 7a), the people's rebellion (vv. 1–4, 7b), Yahweh's threatened judgment (v. 8), and his future restoration of all nations (vv. 9–13). As Zephaniah walks through each part of the covenant relationship, so could a sermon. Preachers could highlight God's righteousness, his power, his expectations, the people's response to those demands, and the consequences for sin. They can also assure people that God's final plan (to have a humble, obedient people from all nations) will come to pass. Each of the covenant elements could form a move in the sermon.

Furthermore, each element may be past or future from our own perspective. Consider the book of Joel, which is oriented around the idea of disaster and how it fits into God's purposes. The prophet depicts a locust invasion (past for both Israel and the church), an actual invasion of an army (future for Israel and past for the church), the outpouring of his Spirit (future for Israel and past for the church), and the valley of judgment on the day of Yahweh (future for Israel and future for the church). Some of Joel's words point backward, some to his present, some to his near future, some to the new covenant mission, and some to the final rule of God on earth (see Figure 2.6).

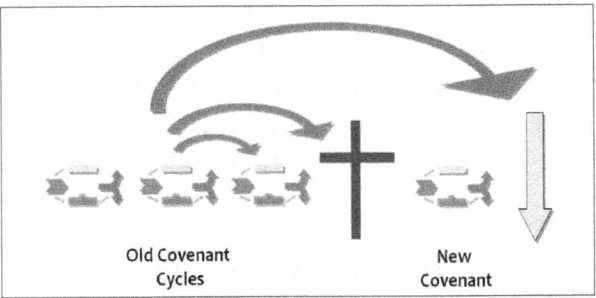

Figure 2.6: The Prophets' Words Point to Different Moments in Redemptive History

Preachers can consider how each of these elements applies to the church's current situation. Perhaps a sermon series might be appropriate here, where each sermon resembles a single arrow in the figure, pointing to a particular moment in sacred history. See Table 2.2 for an example of a series outline on the book of Joel.

To sum up: the covenant context approach relies on the similarities and differences between Israel's relationship to God and our own as a bridge between then and now. Just like ancient Israel,

Passage	Big Idea
Joel 1:1–20	Disaster disciplines us
Joel 2:1–27	Disaster warns us
Joel 2:28–32	Disaster surrounds us
Joel 3: 1–16	Disaster rescues us
Joel 3:17–21	Disaster leaves us

Table 2.2: An Outline for a Sermon Series on Joel

the church of Christ lives in a covenant relationship with a glorious God, who requires loving obedience and gives sure promises. Instead of drawing tenuous parallels between prophets and individuals in our church, or between Israel and our nation, this approach relies on the much broader base of a shared communal identity as the people of God.[36] Transferring from one to the other will then be a matter of reckoning the distance between the old covenants and the new and making appropriate distinctions.[37]

This chapter is rich in theory, whereas later chapters will be stuffed with examples. But for now, readers may consult the index for two sermons that apply prophetic oracles based on covenant context. They do so from different theological perspectives, one favoring more continuity and one more discontinuity. They show how one's understanding of covenant arrangements guides sermon construction.

The Path of the Apostles

It may be helpful to see here that when NT authors cite prophetic oracles, their approach dovetails with the model of interpretation

---

36 The following are two homiletical models that follow this basic approach: Al Fasol, "Preaching from Malachi," *SJT* 30 (1987): 32–34; Pierce, "Micah as a Case Study."

37 Sidney Greidanus offers an interpretive system that reaches similar conclusions from a different direction. He speaks of six different ways to preach Christ from the OT (such as analogy, longitudinal themes, and theological contrast). I find his approach fruitful but think that a covenant framework helps preachers to determine when a particular type of application should be used and why. Sydney Greidanus, *Preaching Christ from the Old Testament: A Contemporary Hermeneutical Method* (Eerdmans, 1999), 203–225.

this book recommends.[38] They take note of what I am calling "covenant contexts." In fact, the NT record shows direct approaches of continuity as well as indirect uses based on discontinuity.

First, the NT reports sermons that draw upon prophetic oracles and interpret them quite directly and with continuity between old and new. For example, in Luke 4 Jesus preaches from Isa 61:1–2 and applies those words to himself and his announcement of the good news; in Acts 2 the apostle Peter preaches from Joel 2:28–32 to explain what happened on the Day of Pentecost; and in Hebrews 8 the author expounds on Jer 31:31–34 to explain why Jesus mediates a new and better covenant. Let me zero in on just one of those examples.

In Hebrews 8 the author cites Jeremiah's words and tells his audience that *this* is *that*: the audience is currently enjoying the new covenant that the prophet predicted. The author draws a direct line from then to now, taking words addressed to Israel and saying to the church, in effect, this is for you. Continuity.

Yet even in this clear, direct case, note the subtlety of the citation: the author is aware of a temporal distance: Israel's future new covenant is the church's present heritage, because now Christ has come. The citation is more than a declaration that Jeremiah was right. The author concludes from Jeremiah that, because a new covenant has arrived, the first covenant is no longer in force. He asserts, "In speaking of a new covenant, [God] makes the first one obsolete. And what is becoming obsolete and growing old is ready to vanish away" (Heb 8:13). Thus, what was a promise for Jeremiah's audience is now a declaration to the church that the old covenant must be left behind. The NT covenant context shows how Jeremiah's words continue to speak.

The NT also uses prophetic oracles to highlight discontinuity and difference—sometimes with profound rhetorical effect. For instance, in Revelation 13 John describes a beast rising out of

---

38 Here again, the literature on NT use of Old Testament material is voluminous. For helpful introductions, see Richard B. Hays, *Echoes of Scripture in the Letters of Paul* (Yale University Press, 1989); G. K. Beale, ed., *The Right Doctrine from the Wrong Text? Essays on the Use of the Old Testament in the New* (Baker Academic, 1994).

the sea that is "allowed to make war on the saints and to conquer them" (v. 7). He then paraphrases Jer 15:2 as follows:

> If anyone is to be taken captive
> to captivity he goes;
> if anyone is to be slain with the sword,
> with the sword must he be slain.
> Here is a call for the endurance and faith of the saints. (v. 10)

John brings Jeremiah's words to bear on the church with a sharp cognizance of the differences between Jeremiah's time and John's own. In Jer 15:2 Yahweh declares judgment on *faithless* Israel's idol worship. God is withdrawing his hand of protection and allowing disaster to come. He says, in essence, "Let them go wherever they are destined to go when judgment falls!"

John's context is quite different. He addresses *faithful* saints who will not bow down to worship the beast (see Rev 14). These faithful ones would normally expect divine protection, but they will not get it. When John applies Jeremiah's words to suffering saints, he thus offers a brutally ironic commentary: faithful saints will *feel as if* they are under God's wrath, abandoned by a God who has withdrawn his care. They will experience what feels like judgment. Yet they can still hope, because if God never withdrew his covenant love even from those faithless ones he drove into exile in Jeremiah's time, how much more will he ultimately rescue faithful saints in John's time the midst of persecution? The more closely one reads how NT authors applied prophetic oracles to the church, the more useful a covenant context framework becomes.[39]

Oracles Addressed to Foreign Nations

Before we finish a description of the covenant context model, we must take note of a particular subtype of prophetic oracle: speeches that address foreign nations. Some, like Nahum and Obadiah,

---

[39] Interested readers might also study the following additional examples: Matt 13:10–17; 1 Cor 14:20–25; and the series of prophetic citations in Romans 9–10.

contain only this kind of material. These nations do not have the same covenant relationship with Yahweh as Israel does. Nonetheless, a covenant context framework still gives preachers direction for handling these passages, in two ways.[40]

First, preachers can read these oracles as messages given to the nations *because of how they treat Israel*. God tells Abraham in Gen 12:1–3 that he will bless or curse others based on the way they treat Abraham and his progeny. Similarly, in a passage on covenant blessings and curses, Moses predicts that God's chastisement will fall on Israel's enemies based on *Israel's* obedience to Yahweh (Deut 28:7–10; 30:7). Take that insight into a prophetic context: Obadiah declares that the Edomites will suffer retribution for the way they gloated over Israel's demise (vv. 10–15), not because Edom is in covenant with Yahweh, but because Israel is. Preachers can thus preach about peoples, nations, or other entities based on the way that those entities treat God's covenant people. Depending on the local context, a sermon from this text might remind hearers that state-sponsored religious persecution or cultural religious discrimination will not go unnoticed or unpunished: "Your deeds shall return on your own head" (Obad 15).

Second, preachers should remember that oracles against foreign nations were always *overheard by Israel*. Though these oracles are ostensibly addressed to Egypt or Tyre or Assyria, they were written in Hebrew by Israelites, and almost certainly proclaimed to Israelites.[41] These oracles give heart to (or warn) Yahweh's people by assuring them that God is the Lord of the nations, and that he will bring worldwide justice.[42] In a similar way, preachers who speak words of warning or accusation against nations, corporations, or individuals that flout God's rule give comfort and assurance to the church. Just as Israel overheard God's judgment on the

---

40 For evidence of specific uses of these oracles in ancient Israel, see John H. Hayes, "The Usage of Oracles Against Foreign Nations in Ancient Israel," *JBL* 87 (March 1968): 81-92.

41 The sole exception here is Jonah's message to Ninevah (Jon 3:4). Yet even here, the Jonah *narrative* is clearly intended for Israelites to remind them of God's compassion on all people.

42 Christopher R. Seitz, *Isaiah 1–39*, Interpretation (Westminster John Knox, 1993), 115–121.

nations, so we overhear what they once overheard, and we too take comfort.

So, in a sermon on Obadiah whose big idea is, "The kingdom will be the LORD's," I went through the prophet's excoriation of Edom for how they shamefully treated Israelites after they were defeated by a powerful army. Though Israel was being disciplined, God would not forget those who piled on. It always made it easier, I told them, when I was getting disciplined by my father, when he would look at my brother and say, "I haven't forgotten you, son. You're next." Obadiah's words "to Edom" are still there for God's covenant people to overhear.

Again, the key is Israel's covenant context and ours—even when the focus is how that context impacts outside entities.[43]

Benefits of a Covenant Context Approach

Although thinking through an oracle's covenant context may be a challenging path to tread, this approach offers three advantages. First, preachers will have more material from which to preach. Most OT prophetic passages are oracles, and those oracles live within a covenant framework. We have a lot of material to preach from!

Second, a covenant context approach fosters theological consistency. Rather than grabbing for perceived parallels between ancient Jeremiah and contemporary Jeremy, or between Amos and America, covenant context sermons will repeatedly highlight the core features of the church's new covenant connection to God. Over time, this method helps a church to understand where they are in God's larger narrative, what they have in common with Abraham and Moses, and how they differ. Preachers will find themselves going back, time and again, to God's faithfulness, his gracious covenant in Christ, his demands, and his promises. Nothing could be more appropriate to discipleship in the local church.

Finally, the covenant context approach helps to build a church's identity. The prophets addressed their people as a community, and their words apply to the church as a community. Too often

---

[43] Tom Nelson demonstrates such an approach in his sermon *Lord of the Nations*, Denton Bible Church (podcast), December 14, 2008.

parishioners investigate the Bible to find only themselves and to hear God's word to them alone. Of course, God's promises and warnings and declarations do affect people's daily lives, minute decisions, and inner thoughts. But (especially in the Prophets), God's words address these realities from the perspective membership in a community that is in relationship with God and therefore is bound together as a family. Sermons from the Prophets that emulate their corporate approach will help to counterbalance Western culture's hyper-individualism, because those sermons will speak to people through the grid of the church's corporate relationship with God.

Conclusion

In place of methods that focus exclusively on fulfillment of prophecies or on biographical details, the covenant context framework compares the audience of a prophetic oracle with the audience of a sermon on the basis of the respective covenants under which each group resides. This approach results in a variety of applications to a contemporary audience, all of which trace back to core theological links between Israel and the church. Such a framework can be adjusted to fit various theological views on the relation between these two groups. This approach also coheres with how the NT authors use prophetic oracles. All in all, the covenant context framework offers distinct advantages to the preacher.

The prophets were not isolated individuals, and neither are we. We are all members of a community that is bound together by thick theological cords. Those cords not only connect us to the present, but by memory they reach back into the past, where God has proven himself in mighty deeds of salvation and judgment. By hope they also stretch into the future, where God will usher in his glorious kingdom in a climactic manner, making all things new. These cords provide the bridge from their time to ours.

Now that I have laid an interpretive foundation, Part II will build on that foundation. I will use the notion of prophets as covenant enforcers and the interpretive grid of covenant context to explore sermon construction and delivery from prophetic oracles.

For Further Study

Brueggemann, Walter. *The Prophetic Imagination*. 2nd edition. Fortress, 2001.

Greidanus, Sidney. *The Modern Preacher and the Ancient Text*. Eerdmans, 1988.

_____. *Preaching Christ from the Old Testament: A Contemporary Hermeneutical Method*. Eerdmans, 1999.

Stuart, Douglas. *Hosea–Jonah*. WBC. Word Books, 1987. Xxxi–xlv.

VanGemeren, Willem A. *Interpreting the Prophetic Word*. Zondervan, 1990. 70–99.

Talk about It

This chapter highlighted significant theological differences in perspective on how Israel relates to the church, ranging along a spectrum of continuity to discontinuity. Some see them as distinct groups for whom God has different purposes; others think that the church is the new Israel, and that God has the same plans for both. Talk in a group together: do you have a perspective on this issue? If so, where did you learn it?

Dig Deeper

The way NT authors use OT texts is a fascinating area of study. Take, for example, Matthew's citation of Hos 11:1 ("Out of Egypt I called my son") in Matt 2:15. Think about how Matthew is employing this verse (where Hosea recalls the Exodus and God's "son" Israel) to explain Christ's flight to and return from Egypt when he was an infant. Obviously, Hosea was not talking about Jesus of Nazareth; so what covenant principles might illuminate Matthew's thinking here?

Practice

Read Ezek 34:1–24. This long oracle has many of the elements discussed above: God's shepherd-like care for his people (vv. 15–16), his demand for righteous rulers who care for the flock (v. 2), his rebuke of leaders who "fleece" his people for their own benefit (vv. 3–8, 18–19), and his judgment on the shepherds to save the sheep (vv. 9–17, 20–24). How might a covenant context framework help to interpret and apply this passage? The following questions may help you form your answer:

- What is the character of Yahweh portrayed in this passage?

- What event lies in the past, which Ezekiel references when he says, "So they were scattered" (34:5)? (Hint: read chapter 33.) How was this event part of the Yahweh's covenant with Israel?

- What did Yahweh require that was not done? From whom did he require it?

- What are the covenant consequences (positive and negative) portrayed here?

- How might each of the above elements fit in a new covenant context?

- What is the main thrust of this passage? How can it form the big idea of a sermon to the church?

Part 2

What Shall I Cry?
Sermon Construction and Delivery

Faithful reading and careful understanding of the Prophets lays the foundation; the house must now be framed and finished. Part 2 assumes that preachers have read, understood, and been able to apply a prophetic oracle to the contemporary church, and proceeds to sermon construction and delivery.[1] Developing sermons from the Prophets requires familiarity with the literary features of prophetic oracles in order to re-create the rhetorical effects inherent in the text. Chapters 3 through 8 therefore examine literary features of prophetic material and the possibilities for sermon construction and delivery that lie therein.

---

1 This work does not lay out a comprehensive system for sermon construction; it rather assumes that preachers already have a methodology of developing and delivering sermons and offers guidance specific to doing so from the prophets. For help here, see Haddon W. Robinson, *Biblical Preaching: The Development and Delivery of Expository Messages*, 3rd ed. (Baker Academic, 2014); Paul Scott Wilson, *The Practice of Preaching*, rev. ed. (Abingdon, 1995); Thomas G. Long, *The Witness of Preaching*, 2nd ed. (Westminster John Knox), 2005; Donald R. Sunukjian, *Invitation to Biblical Preaching: Proclaiming Truth with Clarity and Relevance* (Kregel, 2007).

3

Overlap (I): Poetry

> *Beautiful things reproach us. They also make us hope, casting a glamour over us.*
>
> William Norman Guthrie[2]

PASSION WAS THE FUEL of the Prophets, but language was their vehicle. They constructed their oracles to transport the fire of their convictions from their own soul to their listeners'. Joel does not just flatly tell people that God would usher in a glorious future. Instead, he predicts, "The mountains shall drip sweet wine, and the hills shall flow with milk" (Joel 3:18). To preach prophetic oracles, we must see how the literary features of prophetic oracles operated in the minds of the first listeners, and then learn to recreate those effects from the pulpit.

Only prophets had many tools at hand and felt free to use them as necessary. The story of Jonah, the visions of Ezekiel, the prayers of Habakkuk, and the songs of Isaiah accomplish similar theological tasks with different literary implements. As Sweeney points out, "Genres do not always define texts; they function within them as compositional tools."[3] Prophets picked up those tools from their surrounding culture, just like other authors of Scripture. Thus, we

---

[2] William Norman Guthrie, "The Poet as Prophet," *SR* 6 (1898): 406.

[3] Marvin A. Sweeney, *Isaiah 1–39*, FOTL vol. xvi (Eerdmans 1996), 14. See also his categorization (18–30) of prophetic material into narratives and speeches (with subcategories), and Westermann's division into accounts, prayers, and speeches (Claus Westermann, *Basic forms of Prophetic Speech*, trans. Hugh Clayton White [Westminster John Knox, 1991], 90).

will find a broad overlap in the devices used in the Prophets and elsewhere in the Bible.

Prophetic overlap is good news for preachers because what you already know from preaching other portions of Scripture will help you preach the Prophets. This chapter and the next describe the literary tools that the prophets had in common with other authors of Scripture. We will thus move somewhat quickly through these shared literary features. Future chapters will slow down to concentrate on aspects that are unique to the Prophets.

Prophetic Poetry

Pollard writes of the prophets, "When truth is fired with feeling, poetry is inevitable."[4] Most prophets were in fact also poets: flipping through the Bible from Isaiah to Malachi shows large blocks of material typeset in poetic form.[5] Poetry is the most common tool in the hands of a prophet because it makes for powerful persuasion.[6]

But the written form in which we now experience the prophets' material can blind us to the fact that the poetry they created was first and foremost spoken and sung. Sweeney notes that prophets "delivered their messages to their Israelite and Judean audiences in oral speeches spoken in the temple, the royal court, the streets of the city, or in other locations that might provide a suitable setting for prophetic speech."[7] Prophets were poets, but their poetry was preached. Interpreters therefore must pay close attention to the poetic, oral character of their work.

Contemporary spoken poetry can have the same profound effects. Amanda Gorman's poem "The Hill We Climb," delivered at the inauguration of President Biden, functions similarly to the words of the OT Prophets. Gorman's words stir, delight, and inspire. She declares,

---

4 Edward B. Pollard, "The Prophet as a Poet," *BW* 12 (1898): 327.

5 In fact, the Latin for poet is *vates*, from whence the verb *vaticinor* (to prophecy) derives, perhaps because poets and prophets both sang or spoke in verse.

6 It lies beyond the scope of this work to offer a formal definition of poetry. I proceed under the assumption that (with some significant exceptions) readers will know it when they see it.

7 Sweeney, *Isaiah*, 10.

> We've learned that quiet isn't always peace,
> and the norms and notions of what just is,
> isn't always justice. ...
> And, yes, we are far from polished, far from pristine, but that doesn't mean we are striving to form a union that is perfect.
> We are striving to forge our union with purpose.
> To compose a country committed to all cultures, colors, characters and conditions of man.
> And so we lift our gaze, not to what stands between us, but what stands before us.
> We close the divide because we know to put our future first, we must first put our differences aside.
> We lay down our arms so we can reach out our arms to one another.
> We seek harm to none and harmony for all.[8]

Her playful word choice, rhythmic cadence and stirring tone sweeps hearers along. The persuasive power of Gorman's poem owes much to the fact that it was heard and not read.

Of course, not all prophetic oracles are poetic. Haggai is entirely prose, as probably is Malachi. But every other prophetic book (including Jonah) includes poetry, and some (like Zephaniah) are entirely in verse. Occasionally translators have difficulty distinguishing prose from poetry. Ezekiel 21:10–17 is set out as poetry in the ESV, NASB and KJV, and as prose in the NIV and NLT.[9] But normally the first time a preacher opens the text at hand, it should be obvious whether the passage is poetry. Preachers will find that in the Prophets, it often is.

On Preaching Poetry

Poetry persuades. Long states that biblical poetry "aims at creating a shift in the basic moral perception of the reader."[10] This gives

---

8 Amanda Gorman, "The Hill We Climb," January 20, 2021, Washington, D.C., https://www.youtube.com/watch?v=LZ055illiN4.

9 The passage in *BHS* [21:15–22] is printed as poetry.

10 Thomas G. Long, *Preaching and the Literary Forms of the Bible* (Fortress, 1989), 47.

preachers a double task: we must strive to understand how the prophets' words moved, incited, inspired, and offended hearers, and we must then think through how *our* words can do something similar in our own context.[11] The two tasks are distinct.

The first task summons preachers to become familiar with devices in Hebrew poetry (many of which can be seen in English translations or accessed using a good commentary or biblical language software).[12] How, for example, does Joel evoke the total devastation—agricultural, economic, environmental, and social—wrought by a locust swarm?

> The vine dries up;
> the fig tree languishes.
> Pomegranate, palm, and apple,
> all the trees of the field are dried up,
> and gladness dries up
> from the children of man (Joel 1:12).

Here the prophet uses parallel constructions. Joel gives us two pairs of lines, each depicting agricultural death. The final pair uses the same word ("dries up"), now applied to human joy. Everything withers: what a desolate picture in just a few words! With a little patience, preachers can become familiar with techniques like Joel's. The sections below highlight some poetic devices and give examples from the Prophets, beginning with larger structural patterns and zooming in to specific language choices.

The second task for preachers (using our own words to reproduce the effects of their poetry) move beyond imitating merely their techniques to replicating their effects. After all, sermons are

---

11 For more on how we use our words to act, see J.L. Austin, *How to Do Things with Words*, 2d ed. (Harvard University Press, 1975). For some of these insights applied to preaching, see Abraham Kuruvilla, *Privilege the Text! A Theological Hermeneutic for Preaching* (Moody Publishers, 2013), 48–54.

12 Langley helpfully lists poetic devices that survive translation: refrain, inclusio, anaphora, echo, and chiasm. Others (such as alliteration, word play and acrostic) do not. Kenneth Langley, *How to Preach the Psalms* (Fontes, 2021), 59–68. These terms are discussed below. Preachers must decide how deep they are willing and able to go, and then make a secondary decision about which effects to bring to listener's attention.

not poems, and anyone who has tried to deliver a sermon entirely in verse will quickly discover the difference. Arthurs is helpful here when he advises, "The key to genre sensitive preaching is to replicate the impact of the text, not its exact techniques."[13] Thus, in a sermon on the text from Joel cited above, preachers will try to help listeners make the link between natural and human devastation. Preachers may use Joel's devices and choose a single repeated word to evoke a picture of disaster from God as both external and internal. What does it feel like when our economy withers? When our businesses wither? When our marriages wither? When our bodies wither? When our hope withers?

On the other hand, they may choose another strategy that aims at the same effect. For example, the year 2020 shoved the world into COVID-chaos that demolished social institutions, crashed economies, stalled education, and took untold lives. It also created fear, depression, and hopelessness in many. Stories, photos, and slogans from 2020 could forge the same link that Joel does with different tools.

Whatever methods preachers choose, they are obligated to do more than relay abstract content. As Langley notes, "For *pastoral* reasons we cannot afford to ignore the aesthetics of biblical poetry."[14] We do not do enough merely to convey the content of a poem; we owe our congregations an experience akin to the first hearers'.

The following sections categorize poetic devices under two broad headings: poetic structure and poetic language. In this book I use the phrase "poetic structure" to indicate the large-scale organization of a pericope, and "poetic language" to describe the choice of the words in each line. Under each heading I describe the most common devices found in the Prophets and suggest ways that preachers can capture the same effect in the pulpit.

Poetic Structure

Prophets shaped their poems with precision, so that the structure

---

13 Jeffrey D. Arthurs, *Preaching with Variety: How to Re-create the Dynamics of Biblical Genres* (Kregel, 2007), 28. See Also Langley, *Psalms*, 36, who makes a similar point about poetry specifically.

14 Langley, *Psalms*, 12. Emphasis original.

itself conveys meaning as the different sections reinforce, sharpen, or even undermine one another. These structural cues prompt listeners to pause, reflecting on what they have heard. In this way, the meaning of a prophetic poem often does not lie on the surface, but instead requires (and repays) close attention.

Nonetheless, preachers should not expect just two or three "standard" structures: Hebrew poetic form exhibits more variety and flexibility than, say, an English sonnet with its rigid 14-line form.[15] The beauty of a poem is not found in its conformity to a certain mold, but in its creative use (or violation) of the many options for form.[16] Furthermore, the structure always serves the overarching purpose of the message. As Pollard states, "The old prophet would smash a distich, if it could not worthily bear 'the burden of the LORD.'"[17] Roughly speaking, however, preachers can think about the structure of a poetic oracle as either repetitive or progressive.[18]

Repetitive Structure

Some prophetic oracles repeat themselves. Themes, words, and phrases appear again and again to reinforce or expand upon an

---

15 One structural poetic device I will pass over is meter. The quest for a standard Hebrew meter has yielded mostly frustration, though Dion can still speak of the "syntactic constraints" in lines of poetry (Paul E. Dion, *Hebrew Poetics*, 2nd ed. [Benben Publications, 1992], 4). Part of the issue may be the updating and editing of ancient Hebrew as the canon was developed (see Douglas Stuart, *Studies in Early Hebrew Meter* (Scholars Press, 1976)). Adele Berlin ("Introduction to Hebrew Poetry," *NIB* [Abingdon Press, 1996], 302) has abandoned the quest for "versification" or meter, and simply speaks of poetry as a "type of language." The takeaway for contemporary preachers is to look elsewhere for signs of poetic structure.

16 For detailed lists of Hebrew poetic devices see Douglas Stuart, *Old Testament Exegesis*, 3rd ed. (Westminster John Knox, 2001), 19–20; Langley, *Psalms*, 59–68; Berlin, "Introduction," 303–314.

17 Pollard, "The Prophet as a Poet," 327.

18 Readers may notice that I do not discuss acrostic structure. This is because while common in the Psalms, acrostic is quite rare in the prophets, though there exists a (possible) partial acrostic in Nah 1. See Tremper Longman, III, "Nahum," in *The Minor Prophets*, vol. 2, ed. Thomas Edward McComiskey (Baker, 1993), 773–775.

idea. However, the Prophets use this apparently simple device with creativity and variety.

Repeated Refrain

At its most simple, repetition occurs as a word-for-word refrain. In Isa 9:8–10:21, the prophet predicts disaster after disaster, each ending with the refrain, "For all this his anger has not turned away, and his hand is stretched out still" (9:12, 21; 10:4). In each case, as Isaiah piles grief upon grief, he alerts us of yet more to come. Repetition like this invites readers to slow down to absorb the waves of woe the Isaiah predicts. If they do, this refrain staggers the reader with the scale and scope of God's (repeated) judgment on Israel's (repeated) stubbornness.

Repeated with Variation

Like jazz or classical music, prophetic repetition can sound forth as variations on a theme. For instance, the repeated description of a locust invasion in Joel 1 and 2 is carefully designed. In chapter 1 Joel's locusts and their damage are described literally. But by chapter 2, the locust-like descriptions seem to portray an invading army:

> They do not jostle one another;
> each marches in his path;
> they burst through the weapons
> and are not halted.
> They leap upon the city,
> they run upon the walls,
> they climb up into the houses,
> they enter through the windows like a thief. (Joel 2:8–9)

If we read carefully, we will hear Joel inviting us to compare the two chapters. His repetition blends the images of locust and warfare, so that one disaster foretells and interprets another: both locusts and armies are sent from Yahweh to Israel in response to their sins.

Repeated Keywords

Prophets will sneak in repeated keywords that, though less obvious, can be quite effective. For instance, in Jeremiah 3:1–4:2 the prophet repeats the words "return" throughout (3:1 [twice], 7 [twice], 10, 12, 14, 22; 4:1). Let us take a closer look at what this repetition accomplishes. Jeremiah repeatedly draws the comparison between an unfaithful wife and Israel, asking whether a wife who left her husband and married another could possibly "return" to her first husband. "Returning" would never be accepted by any rational husband. And yet God entreats Israel multiple times to "return" to Him (3:12, 14, 22; 4:1) so that he can pardon them.

By using "returning" language as a refrain, Jeremiah subtly evokes the image of a husband who longs for his wife so deeply that he would welcome her home even after the marriage was deemed irreparable. "Return, faithless, Israel, declares the LORD. I will not look on you in anger, for I am merciful, declares the LORD" (3:12). God's longing for his people breaks the bounds of propriety. Jeremiah conveys God's passion with the repetition of a single word.

Repeated with Symmetry

Hebrew poetry often arranges lines chiastically (or symmetrically), so that the first and last lines correspond, the second and second-to-last, and so on. This is a particular kind of repetition, as the poems progresses in one direction, and then reverses course, repeating concepts it has just covered. Look at Zephaniah 1:2–18, a chiasm that declares the nature and scope of the day of Yahweh:

A: Destruction of the whole earth is coming (2–3)
B: Destruction of sinful Israelites (4–6)
C: The day of Yahweh (7–16)
B': Destruction of sinful Israelites (17–18a)
A': Destruction of the whole earth (18b)

Key words and themes appear in parallel sections (A–A' and B–B'), and the large middle section is the only one where "day" language appears (twelve times). Zephaniah's repetition here, by zooming in and then back out, offers a theological commentary on the concept of "the day of Yahweh." We start with a broad view of universal destruction (A); why is this happening? Because of the sinful conduct of Israel (B). What will it involve? The central section (C) elaborates: it will be like a sacrificial slaughter; it will reach to the richest and most powerful; it will proceed street by street through all of Jerusalem; it will involve wrath, distress, anguish, and a host of other awful descriptors. Once again, all this is due to Israel's sin (B') and it involves the whole earth (C'). The scope, the reasons, and the nature of the day of Yahweh are highlighted by Zephaniah's careful symmetry.

Repeated Themes

Sometimes repetition is quite loose, involving a string of images or phrases that are related thematically. Isaiah 2 furnishes an example, centered on the paired themes of "high" and "low." The repetition here is not organized into large blocks or around a single word or phrase. Rather, the imagery and language repeatedly cluster around the specific concepts of height and depth.

After the stunning description of Mt. Zion being elevated as the highest of all mountains (Isa 2:2–5), the prophet rails against the sinful pride of those who do not trust in God but instead rely on idols and foreign alliances. Verses 10–11 provide an apt summary:

> Enter into the rock
> and hide in the dust
> from before the terror of the LORD,
> and from the splendor of his majesty.
> The haughty looks of man shall be brought low,
> and the lofty pride of men shall be humbled,
> and the LORD alone will be exalted in that day.

The rest of the oracle (2:12–22) unfolds the contrast between the false heights of man's pride (symbolized by lofty cedars, high hills, tall towers, and ship's masts) and the caves, rocks, and cracks of the earth into which they will flee with their idols when God appears. By this loose clustering of "high and low" word-pictures and phrases, Isaiah draws a sharp line between the humble who will be raised on Mt. Zion and the prideful who will descend to the depths of the earth in fear.

Strategy 4.1 Repeat Yourself

The Hebrew poets repeated themselves. But what about modern preachers?

Repetitive oracles can be preached repetitively, though repetition should dazzle and not bore. To jump-start your own creative thinking, consider the following examples based on the oracles above.

We can repeat with a carefully chosen refrain. A sermon from Isa 9:8-10:21 (where Isaiah repeats the phrase, "For all this his anger has not turned away...") could mimic the prophet's disbelief in yet more tragedy to come. Our sinful hearts are so stubborn that God's discipline can harden us instead of causing us to repent. The repeated question, "Had enough yet?" could become a sermonic refrain, as the preacher reviews the pains that have visited us personally and corporately. The preacher might recall discipline after discipline, heartbreak after heartbreak, story after story of broken families, fractured peace, wounded consciences, languishing churches. Have we had enough yet? Then let us return to God's mercy and repent of our ways.[19]

Or we can repeat with variation, by slightly changing the phrase or story or concept with each repetition. A phrase can change from, "Have *they* had enough yet?" to "Have *we* had enough yet?" to, "Have *you* had enough yet?" Variation can also take place on a larger scale. Recall that Joel offers two different visions of disaster: a locust invasion becomes a metaphor for an impending military invasion. A story from the past shapes their understanding of

---

19 Such a sermon of course calls for theological and pastoral sensitivity. Not all suffering is discipline or warning, and preachers will need to help congregations discern between suffering as discipline, as the effects of a fallen world, and as persecution for faithfulness. See ch. 2 for more.

Overlap (I): Poetry

the present. In preaching from Joel 2 at a men's gathering, I tried to mimic that effect. I told a story (beginning with "once upon a time") of how Israel had been chosen as God's people, how they had been unfaithful, how they rebelled, how God sent disaster on them, how they repented and how God graciously forgave. Those disasters were meant to bring them back to God. Then I paused and launched into another story (also beginning with "once upon a time") about a person. What was his name? Carl? Bob? I talked of how he had been chosen by God's grace, but had been unfaithful, rebelled, and how God sent hardships on him, how he repented and how God graciously forgave. I was careful to use the same phrases and order each time, so that the repetition would be obvious. But the story was now a story of us, and the way God interacted with Israel could become a lens for our own troubles and God's call to return to him. It was obvious repetition, but the second time around was designed to hit close to home.

The ways in which we can help hearers experience repetition is limited only by our creativity. For instance, in a sermon on Isaiah 2, I started by designating one half of the church as the "high" side, and the other half as the "low" side. I asked them, as I read the full chapter, to raise their hands if they heard anything that corresponded to their side. (I had to pause once or twice to prompt them, and make sure to slow down on the right words.) The effect was wonderful: we could literally see Isaiah's cadence come to life as the church rocked back and forth between high and low. The big idea of the sermon was, "Follow God with high hope and deep dread," and like Isaiah I wanted to raise the intensity of the salvation and judgment that we can hope for on the day of the Lord.

Progressive Structure

Prophets structure their oracles not just repetitively but progressively. A theme or motif unfolds as the poem moves along. The Servant Songs of Isaiah are a classic example, but the Prophets contain others. For instance, Jeremiah 23 ends a long section about corrupt kings in Jerusalem (Jer 21–22). This final pericope (23:1–8) consists of three brief oracles contrasting the old order of kings (pictured as shepherds) with God's new order.[20] The three oracles progress: they are linked by key words in each section, and they build upon one another to progressively reveal a picture of Israel's future. In vv. 1–4 God declares that in place of the corrupt shepherds, God will "set shepherds over them who care for them" (v. 4). The next oracle (v. 5–6) crystallizes that picture of many shepherds to one specific king, a Righteous Branch, who shall "execute justice and righteousness in the land" (v. 6). The final oracle (vv. 7–8) predicts that the return from exile under Yahweh's hand will be even greater than the exodus from Egypt. Jeremiah progresses from good kings to the Great King to the grand deliverance.

Or consider the progression in Jeremiah 12, which starts with the prophet's complaint (vv. 1–4) and moves to Yahweh's answer (vv. 5–13). The prophet bemoans the fact that "all the treacherous thrive" (v.1) and asks Yahweh to punish them. He replies, incredibly, that Jeremiah is in for much worse than he has seen thus far:

> If you have raced with men on foot, and they have wearied you,
> How will you compete with horses?
> And if in a safe land you are so trusting,
> What will you do in the thicket of the Jordan? (12:5)

Yahweh is bringing far worse trouble than corrupt Israelites: he has forsaken his heritage entirely (v. 7) and is summoning foreign invaders (vv. 9–13). The final section of the chapter (vv. 14–17) progresses by offering hope in the form of a future redemption after the exile.

Strategy 4.2 Structure the Sermon to Progress with the Passage

Preaching a progressive structure is relatively straightforward because the sermon can progress as the oracle does. But replicating

---

[20] Only the middle oracle (vv. 5–6) is in verse (and not all English versions even agree on that), but the progression is obvious.

the effect of that progression requires careful planning, because oracles don't all progress in the same way. Some add one thought to another, forming a careful argument; some take readers through an emotional progression; some pose a problem and solve it; some take a thought and undermine it. Preachers must study how a pericope progresses before they can help listeners experience it for themselves.

For instance, the progression in Jeremiah 12 is not only a progression of content but is at least as much a progression of emotion. Preachers might try what Arthurs calls an "emotional outline" for a sermon on Jeremiah 12.[21] A sermon could start with indignation at the injustices that God not only seems to tolerate but even favor. How do we help listeners feel the same indignation? Examples of injustice, large and small, surround us.[22] Someone cuts us off in traffic; our health insurance claims get denied; we see videos of police shooting unarmed victims; we look at the statistics on kids in foster care or who are trafficked. In each case we see those in power thriving from acts of cruelty. Of course, we complain! Where are you, Lord?

The middle section could look ahead to God's judgment of all the earth in terms that go far beyond what we expect. The response from God will overtop even our own anger; his indignation is greater than our own. The whole earth will come under his judgment, and every sin—every single one!—will be brought into the light. God's judgment will be searching and completely thorough. Our rage is humbled as we recognize in ourselves a small, distorted reflection of God's righteous anger.

Finally, the promise of ultimate redemption would end the sermon on a high note of hope. What sort of future does God have in mind for his people? A future of justice, where all can dwell securely. My town, for example, is constructing a village of "tiny homes" (small one-room houses) to help the homeless transition to a more settled existence. What must it be like the first time they get the keys placed in their hands and step inside? To be able to close the

---

21 See Arthurs, *Preaching with Variety*, 53.
22 See ch. 9 for more on justice. Zimmerman's sermon in the Appendix also offers a helpful example.

door and sit in peace and safety? Preachers can use stories, images, and tone of voice to evoke emotions of home, of safety, of abundance, of reliable fairness under the hand of God.[23]

Preachers will need to put in the time and effort required, not just to talk about anger, dread, and hope, but to help the church grumble, shiver, and gasp at Jeremiah's words.

Conclusion: Poetic Structure

The Prophets paid attention to structure. Preachers can pay them the compliment of close study and thoughtful replication. However, sermons on structure that drone on about chiasms and refrains like paleontologists pointing out dinosaur vertebrae will fail to evoke the power of the oracles. Let listeners experience the whole shape of the animal: hear the roar of the T-Rex, see the glide of the pterodactyl. Structure serves wonder.

Poetic Language

Long states, "Poetry works to disrupt the customary ways in which we use language."[24] Linguistic "disruptions" move readers, not with argumentation but with imagination and emotion. Metaphors, for instance, work this way. Wendell Berry writes in his poem "The Wild" about an abandoned lot in which he sees a few locusts and songbirds:

> But they are the habit of this
> Wasted place. In them
> The ground is wise. They are its remembrance of what it is.[25]

Berry calls the few remaining natural features in the empty lot

---

23 The similarity here to Lowry's Homiletical Plot is patent. But note that the outline is driven here by textual structure rather than a theological grid. Eugene H. Lowry, *The Homiletical Plot: The Sermon as Narrative Art Form*, expanded ed. (Westminster John Knox, 2001).

24 Long, *Literary Forms*, 45.

25 Wendell Berry, "The Wild," in *The Selected Poems of Wendell Berry*, (Counterpoint, 2009), Kindle edition, 2.

the "wisdom" and "memory" ("remembrance") of the ground, reminding it, as it were, of its true nature as nature. The metaphor of plant and animal life as memory stirs up in readers the idea of the enduring wisdom of the earth in the fleeting bugs and flitting birds. The metaphor jars us with its comparisons, showing us new aspects of familiar objects.

Poetic language communicates by startling choices like this that violate convention. And what is true now was also true then: the poetic language of the OT Prophets yields rich homiletical rewards for preachers prepared to listen—to slow down and read with imagination. Poetic devices in the Prophets are varied and extensive; for preaching purposes we may group them into word choice, parallelism, and irregular language.

Word Choice

Words wield power to build up or tear down. On the one hand, "To make an apt answer is a joy to a man, and a word in season, how good it is!" (Prov 15:23). On the other hand, "The words of a whisperer are like delicious morsels; they go down to the inner parts of the body" (Prov 18:8). But notice that not just any words have potency: rather, people are moved by the *apt* answer in season, the *whispered* word of the gossip. We must choose our words carefully for them to have power. Langley gives examples: powerful words are specific (words like "ogle" rather than just "look"), filled with vitality (the psalmist's "he burns the shields with fire"), and appeal to all five senses.[26]

The prophets chose their words for powerful effect. For instance, the eighth chapter of Hosea is a cornucopia of well-chosen words. Rather than just accuse Israel of idolatry and forbidden foreign alliances, the prophet deploys words crafted to assault listeners' senses and to conjure violent and painful images. Verse 1 issues a ringing cry: "Set the trumpet to your lips! One like a vulture is over the house of the LORD, because they have transgressed my covenant." Sound the alarm! Rouse the sleepers! Why? Because a bird of prey—a scavenger of the dead—broods over the temple

---

26 Langley, *Psalms*, 90–95.

itself! Sound and sight combine in an arresting first scene. Image piles on image as Hosea likens Israel to farmers who sow nothing but air, to worthless vessels sitting captive in the homes of foreign nations, and to wild donkeys wandering alone (vv. 7–10). Then he plays on the concept of multiplication in vv. 11–12:

> Because Ephraim has multiplied altars for sinning,
> they have become to him altars for sinning.
> Were I to write for him my laws by the ten thousands,
> they would be regarded as a strange thing.

The proliferation of altars and sacred texts merely serve to increase their sins and elevate their confusion. Hosea has chosen powerful words to bombard his hearers: all is not well in Israel.

Strategy 5.1 Choose Your Words Wisely

Powerful words on the page can be taken up and wielded by bold preachers. One way to do this is simply to pass them on: sometimes a phrase is so poignant that it should be quoted as written, left to do its work as it always has. For instance, is there any better way to express the futility of faithlessness than Hosea's, "They sow the wind, and they shall reap the whirlwind"? That verbal sword is already sharpened and polished: take it up and wield it as it stands. Repeat it, expound upon it, drive it home.

On the other hand, sometimes one does better to update the prophet's words in ways that preserve their power. Brother Carper, an African American preacher in nineteenth-century Missouri, masterfully develops the image in Isa 32:2 of a "great rock in a weary land." Listen to his wording as he follows the lead of the great prophet:

> But against this fiery wind and this tempest of poison that withers with a breath, and mummifies whole caravans and armies in their march, there is one breastwork, one "hiding-place," one protecting "shadow" in the dreaded desert. It is "the shadow of a great rock in this weary land." ... That light is the light

of hope, and that rock is the rock of hope to the now-flying, weeping, fainting and famishing hundreds.[27]

Carper takes the pregnant image of Isaiah's great rock and gives birth to a narrative of refugees fleeing an advancing army over a poisonous desert waste. Travelers drop their possessions, drag those who have fainted on the way, and pour into the shade and shelter of a mighty rock to find respite, peace, and joy. He finishes with a desperate appeal: "Death and hell hang on your track with the swiftness of the tempest. Before you is the 'hiding place.' Fly, *fly*, I beseech you, from the wrath to come!"[28] A sermon like starts with the prophetic words but hastens to add its own carefully shaped descriptions.

Preachers today can do likewise. All preachers slip into word-ruts, repeating the same tired expressions and descriptors. But we can work to find more precise words, more effective ways to convey what we mean.[29] Active verbs (rather than added adverbs), vivid nouns (rather than added adjectives) and original images can stir, delight, and persuade.[30]

Developing your skill in word choice will take time and exposure. One way to do this is to read good literature, whether poetry or prose. Notice how authors select words and craft phrases. If reading literature for pleasure brings you no pleasure, then start by making it your business. Put time in your weekly schedule to read good books; your church will reap the rewards.[31]

---

27 J. V. Watson, *Tales and Takings, Sketches and Incidents, from the Itinerant and Editorial Budget of Rev. J. V. Watson, Editor of the Northwest Christian Advocate* (1856). Quoted in Henry Mitchell, *Black Preaching: The Recovery of a Powerful Art* (Abingdon Press, 1990), 36–37. The language here (which Rev. Watson recorded in Carper's dialect) has been updated for clarity.

28 Watson, quoted in Mitchell, *Black Preaching*, 38. Emphasis original.

29 A user-friendly work that covers language is Mark Galli and Craig Brian Larson, *Preaching that Connects* (Zondervan, 1994), 95-115. See also the sound advice of Gardner C. Taylor on pulpit eloquence in Jared Alcántara, *Learning from a Legend: What Gardner C. Taylor Can Teach Us about Preaching* (Cascade, 2016), 49-67.

30 See the helpful discussions on word choice in Arthurs *Variety*, 50–51; and Langley, *Psalms*, 87–95.

31 A particularly efficient way to do this is to read works on ministry that

A second way is to start small. Consider crafting just one paragraph of your sermon this week. Perhaps the introduction or conclusion, or a key illustration. Spend some time writing a section that has power but sounds natural when read aloud. You can develop a good habit and then expand it to other parts of the sermon.

Parallelism

The Hebrew poets did more than choose words; they arranged those words carefully. The most common way they did that was to set lines in parallel to one another, so that the second line comments in some way on the first.[32] Habakkuk 1:2 asks, "O LORD, how long shall I cry for help, and you will not hear? / Or cry to you, 'Violence!' and you will not save?" The two lines, grammatically parallel, reinforce one another, with the second adding specificity to the first. Line A has a general cry for help, but God does not hear. Line B specifies that the cry is "Violence!" and the "hearing" that the prophet hopes for is to be rescued from that violence. The first line introduces, and the second expands. Parallelism like this slows readers down and directs prolonged attention to the circumstances and thoughts of the poem.

Sometimes parallel lines contrast. Joel 3:16 declares,

---

are well-written. Good places to start: Charles Spurgeon, *Lectures to My Students* (CreateSpace, 2018); Barbara Brown Taylor, *An Altar in the World: A Geography of Faith* (HarperOne, 2010); Frederick Buechner, *Telling the Truth: The Gospel as Comedy, Tragedy, and Fairy Tale* (Harper and Row, 1977); and Eugene H. Peterson, *The Contemplative Pastor: Returning to the Art of Spiritual Direction* (Eerdmans, 1993).

32 Berlin has a helpful discussion of parallelism and the various ways it has been understood, from Lowth's synonymous/antithetic/synthetic to Alter and Kugel's continuity to his own structural approach. It is not necessary to resolve that question to appreciate and preach from parallel lines. Berlin, "Introduction," 303.

> The LORD roars from Zion,
> and utters his voice from Jerusalem,
> and the heavens and the earth quake.
> But the LORD is a refuge to his people,
> a stronghold to the people of Israel.

The first triplet proclaims universal threat to the heavens and the earth. But the second couplet alters that verdict by carving out a refuge for Israel. Parallelism in Hebrew poetry is everywhere; it often comprises the basic logic of how a passage moves forward from idea to idea.

Strategy 5.2 Preach in Parallel?

Shall we, then, speak in couplets?

Shall we repeat our lines?

Perhaps we should, but we should do so in idioms and with techniques that work in contemporary English. Robotic imitation of the Prophets' style may land no better than preaching entirely in King James English. But that does not mean that parallelism cannot make its way into the pulpit. Here are three avenues to try for yourself.

First, we can point it out. This is a good start: while it doesn't do much to recreate the rhetorical impact of the passage, it does inform listeners that parallelism exists and explains how it works. For instance, we can explain how Hab 1:2 draws out the "how long" question—extending it, mulling over it, repeating it, intensifying it—so that his complaint gains momentum before the Lord.

Even better, we can act it out. Contrasting lines can be preached from opposite side of the pulpit. Joel's prediction of universal judgment can be declared on tip toes, arms outstretched, and the refuge for his people proclaimed with bent knees and back, hands covering a small, safe space. Or we can intensify repeated lines by stepping forward, lifting hands, stomping feet, reaching out. Our bodies can help people feel parallel lines without ever having to explain the concept of parallelism.

Finally, we can sing it out. We can use our voices to restate and to elevate. If your church tradition invites cadence, singing, whooping, then so much the easier. But even in more reserved churches we can string together lines to build the depth and height of biblical ideas. I once preached a sermon on pain and providence, and I needed to help our church sit in the depths of their pain but also in the greatness of God's redemption. I've set the lines out to highlight how this section used parallelism:

> There are things that you and I have been through that cannot
>   be redeemed in the short term.
>
> They cannot be explained,
> they cannot be healed,
> they cannot be a part of something good in the short term.
>
> It was too dark,
> we lost too much,
> our heart was broken,
> we were emptied.
>
> I'm not talking about the short term,
> I'm not talking about the little picture,
> I'm talking about the big picture,
> I'm talking about your story, your destiny.
> I'm talking about God taking broken rebels like you and me,
>   people who are dead,
>   and waking us up and making us alive to him,

I'm talking about the fact that he would cleanse us from top to
 bottom,
 adopt us into his family,
 make us a part of him,
 fill us with his Spirit,
 use us for his purposes,
 use us in the redemption of all things, to the glory of his Son.
I'm talking about the big, big picture.

Let me ask you something: can you conceive of a joy that is so large, that is so deep, that it would make you sing about the faithfulness of God with reference to *this*? If you can begin to get there, then you begin to understand the scale of the gospel, and why it's called good news.

Our voices can help people experience the poetry of the Prophets.

Irregular Language

Poetic language is often irregular language. The prophets have strewn word play, alliteration, variations on root words, hyperbole, oxymoron, apostrophe, and other devices over the terrain of their work.[33] They do this to grab attention: to destabilize, to delight, even to disgust.

For instance, when Isaiah compares Israel to a vineyard, he laments that Yahweh looked for good fruit but found only wild grapes (Isa 5:2). Speaking literally a few verses later, he says that God "looked for justice (*mishpat*), but behold, bloodshed (*mispah*); for righteousness (*tsedaqah*), but behold, an outcry (*tse'qah*)!" (5:7). Though hearers do not speak Hebrew they can still appreciate a pun and can understand that (like wild and cultivated grapes) though these words pairs sound alike, they

---

33 The literature on these devices is of course vast. For brief descriptions see Stuart, *Old Testament Exegesis,* 19, Berlin, "Introduction," 303, and all of Dion, *Hebrew Poetics.* For a classification of wordplay in the prophets, see Robert B. Chisholm, Jr., "Wordplay in the Eighth-Century Prophets," *BibSac* 144 (1987): 44–52.

are diametrically opposed. Israel feigns fertility, but her fruit is futile.

Prophets also use dense language, compressing their words to let them unfold in hearers' minds.[34] Obadiah, in predicting the destruction of Edom, says that they "shall be as though they had never been" (Obad 16). Literally the phrase is, "and they will be like they were not."[35] He gives Edom a terse dismissal, the very cadence of which illustrates their sudden end. In these ways and more, prophets play with conventional language, violating the normal rules of speech to gain attention and reach their hearers.

Strategy 5.3 Be Irregular

When preachers encounter irregular wording, they sometimes stumble over them in the pulpit, either ignoring the devices or giving mini lectures on paronomasia. Instead, they can use those strange words as steppingstones to lead their people on the trail the prophets have blazed.

Preachers can find creative ways to replicate the effects of prophetic language. At a simple level, using the language tools and training available to us, we can produce deliberately awkward, literal translations. Irregular language can get our attention without the need for long explanation. I recall a sermon on Luke 8:26–39 where the preacher gave a literal rendition of the Gerasene demoniac's halting language: "What to you and to me, Jesus, Son of the Most High God?" It brought out for us (without a grammatical lecture) something Luke wanted readers to hear. Rendering Obadiah 16 in a similar way, a preacher might say, "They will like they weren't." Awkward constructions, if done intentionally and framed well, can get attention.

Or we can be a bit more polished by crafting a single phrase to make it stick in the memory.[36] Ashley Mathews, in an Advent sermon on Isaiah 9, uses the phrase "baby-sized hope" at several

---

34 Berlin, "Introduction," 303; Arthurs, *Variety*, 41–42.
35 The phrase is even more compact in Hebrew: וְהָיוּ כְּלוֹא הָיוּ.
36 See Chip Heath and Dan Heath, *Made to Stick: Why Some Ideas Survive and Others Die* (Random House, 2008), 3-62.

points throughout the sermon.[37] The phrase is unusual, but also captures the implicit contrast between the massive problems that God's people faced and the tiny, seemingly weak solution he provided in the birth of a baby.

We can also (carefully) use contemporary equivalents of poetic language. While preachers sometimes recite poetry in sermons, the choice of exactly what poetry to use can be daunting. Shakespeare or Dickinson could sound archaic; contemporary verse can be nearly impossible to understand. But written verse is not the only form of contemporary poetry available. Modern music—and rap in particular—can function in ways that are remarkably close to prophecy. Passion, poetry, and social concerns combine into contemporary art that is strikingly close to the Prophets. Toby Nwigwe's "Fye Fye Fye" is about his journey out of youthful dysfunction into a profound delight in his family:

> Yeah, I rock the slides to be humble
> I told my baby girl she gon' have more in her head than just product and bundles
> They say I'm rappin' with hunger, I tell 'em hell nah, I'm eatin'
> If you book me for a show and I can't bring my wife and my babies I'm leavin'
> ...I am a beacon for heathens, me and my hood got cohesion.[38]

Roughly, Nwigwe declares that he and his family are not going to be like a stereotypical dysfunctional family. His daughter will have education, not just money and beauty; he is not hungry for fame and fortune because his family satisfies him; they always come with him to shows; his lifestyle is a signal to others that they can have a strong, cohesive family too, no matter where they come from. Nwigwe's lyrics evoke the triumph of "making it" as a family and can bring out the kind of joy that the prophets envision (see Hos 1–2, Ezek 47, Mal 4:6). Church context will determine whether a

---

37 Ashley Mathews, "Isaiah 9:1-7," Trinity Anglican Church, December 20, 2020, https://podcast.atltrinity.org/episodes/isaiah-9-1-7-westside.
38 Toby Nwigwe, "Fye Fye Fye," (Lanell Grant, 2022).

sound clip, a slide with lyrics, or (just possibly) a recitation would be appropriate.

If rapping from the pulpit feels like too much, consider crafting a pithy, memorable big idea for your sermon that mimics the feel of the oracle. This is harder than it looks! When I prepared a sermon from Isa 4:2–6 about the restoration of God's people after severe discipline, the original idea was, "In spite of our sin, God's anger will not bring destruction but instead prepare his people for perfect communion with Him." I thought it was accurate, but I could hardly get through it without yawning. How to imitate Isaiah's wordcraft? The big idea for the sermon ended up being, "It's still on." Of course, this sentence is cryptic and needs development, but I counted on the rest of the sermon to communicate that fullness of the idea: Despite the ruin of our past, the plan of God for our redemption is still on the agenda. Sacrificing some clarity for punch felt like a worthwhile exchange to try to capture the compact power of Isaiah's oracle. In these ways we can bring out the ways that prophets bent, re-shaped, and even shattered language so that congregations can sense the power of their words.

Conclusion

The prophets were wordsmiths. They knew that to pierce the hard or despondent hearts of God's people, they would need sharp language, forged in the fire of Yahweh's character and shaped with painstaking care. We dare do no less with our own speech: to bludgeon the church with clumsy haranguing will not remove the cancer; to slather on vague platitudes will not heal the wound. Only verbal surgery will suffice. Let us then do the hard work of listening well to the Prophets, studying their songs, that we too may preach poetry.[39]

---

39 Readers will note that I have left out discussion of emotion and imagery. These features loom so large in the Prophets that a full chapter is devoted to each below.

For Further Reading

Alcántara, Jared E. *Learning from a Legend: What Gardner C. Taylor Can Teach Us about Preaching*. Cascade, 2016. 49–67.

Arthurs, Jeffrey D. *Preaching with Variety: How to Re-create the Dynamics of Biblical Genres*. Kregel, 2007.

Langley, Kenneth. *How to Preach the Psalms*. Fontes, 2021.

Long, Thomas G. *Preaching and the Literary Forms of the Bible*. Fortress, 1989.

Talk about It

Consider the following poem from Langston Hughes, "The Negro Speaks of Rivers":

> I've known rivers:
> I've known rivers ancient as the world and older than the flow of human blood in human veins.
>
> My soul has grown deep like the rivers.
>
> I bathed in the Euphrates when dawns were young.
> I built my hut near the Congo and it lulled me to sleep.
> I looked upon the Nile and raised the pyramids above it.
> I heard the singing of the Mississippi when Abe Lincoln went down to New Orleans, and I've seen its muddy bosom turn all golden in the sunset.
>
> I've known rivers:
> Ancient, dusky rivers.
>
> My soul has grown deep like the rivers.[40]

How does this poem work? What devices are there that make an impact on you as a reader?

---

[40] Langston Hughes, "The Negro Speaks of Rivers," in *Vintage Hughes*, 2nd ed. (Vintage, 2004).

Dig Deeper

What are you reading lately? List the last three books you've spent time reading. Are those choices helping you to choose words well? What book could you add that might help you to do so?

Practice

Read Micah 2 carefully and slowly. See if you can identity three poetic devices that relate to its structure or its language which enhance or alter the meaning. (There are many to choose from.) For each device, suggest a way that you could replicate the effect in a sermon on this oracle.

4

Overlap (II): Parable, Apocalypse

> *The work of art is not some alien universe into which we are magically transported for a time. Rather, we learn to understand ourselves in and through it.*
>
> —Hans-Georg Gadamer[1]

CHAPTER 3 EXPLORED the prophets' use of poetry and its implications for preaching. This chapter covers two more genres the prophets employed: parable and apocalypse.

However, these two types of literature crop up in the Prophets less frequently than poetry does, and with less clarity. One glimpses, as through a glass darkly, parabolic and apocalyptic oracles, modified to suit the prophet's purpose but still recognizable as such.[2] Astute preachers will look out for these forms and learn to preach from them in ways that replicate how they acted on their original hearers.

Prophetic Parables

When I think of parables, my mind leaps to Jesus, standing by the Sea of Galilee, telling tales about fish and seeds, fathers and sons. But Jesus was not the first to use stories, riddles, and allegories to

---

[1] Hans-Georg Gadamer, *Truth and Method*, 2nd rev. ed., trans. Joel Weinsheimer and Donald G. Marshall (Continuum, 1996), 97.

[2] In fact, the clearest examples we have of those genres comes after the prophets' time in the New Testament. It may be more accurate to say that the OT prophets used the parabolic and apocalyptic literary conventions that were available to them at the time.

make a point. Jotham did it on Mt. Gerizim (Judg 9); Samson did it at a wedding (Judg 14); Nathan did it in the court of David (2 Sam 12). Likewise, Israel's prophets used word pictures, objects, and stories as vehicles for Yahweh's message. Isaiah sang a song of a vineyard and an owner, who turn out to be Israel and Yahweh, respectively (Isa 5). Jeremiah bought a new loincloth, buried it by a river, and dug it up again to depict the sorry, ruined state of Judah and Jerusalem (Jer 13). And, as we shall see, Ezekiel's work is loaded with parabolic speeches and acts.

Nonetheless, despite its common appearance in Scripture, defining "parable" is no simple matter. Long ago Theon made a good start, calling a parable "a fictitious saying picturing truth."[3] Dodd defines a parable as "a metaphor or simile drawn from nature of common life, arresting the hearer by its vividness or strangeness, and leaving the mind in sufficient doubt about its precise application to tease it into active thought."[4] More simply, Snodgrass describes it as "an expanded analogy used to convince and persuade."[5] Though precise definition is complicated, recognizing parables when one encounters them is not too difficult.

For our purposes, it will help to cast the net a bit wider than these scholars to include cryptic sayings, moral illustrations, and symbolic gestures and events.[6] In fact, a common Hebrew term for parables, *mashal*, has just such a broad range, denoting proverbs, general comparisons, parabolic stories, and mocking songs.[7]

---

3 Theon was describing fables, a close parallel in his first century Greek world. Quoted in Klyne Snodgrass, *Stories with Intent: A Comprehensive Guide to the Parables of Jesus* (Eerdmans, 2008), 8.

4 C. H. Dodd, *The Parables of the Kingdom*, rev. ed. (Scribner's, 1961), 5.

5 Snodgrass, *Stories with Intent*, 9. My favorite definition of his is "imaginary gardens with real toads in them." His discussion on the history of the study of parables (4–17) is accessible and helpful.

6 Though brief similes and metaphors could also be classed here, I discuss them in chapter 7 under "image." Likewise, plays on words (such as Jeremiah's vision of summer fruit in Jer 1:11–12) were covered in the previous chapter under poetic devices.

7 See *HALOT* on the verb משׁל and the noun מָשָׁל. Although the most common use of the noun is as a descriptor of Solomon's proverbs (Prov 1:1), it is indicative of the word's flexibility that Long discusses the term in his chapter on parables rather than proverbs. Thomas G. Long, *Preaching and the Literary*

When Ezekiel lays on his side to symbolize the siege of Jerusalem (Ezek 4) or repeats a proverb about sour grapes (Ezek 18), these are parabolic actions and words that surprise and intrigue in order to (in Dodd's words) "tease [minds] into active thought." Our net will snag all these parabolic species.[8]

If defining parables is difficult, showing how they work presents an even greater challenge.[9] Parables are sneaky. They are simple in form but function on multiple levels. They normally operate by inviting comparisons between a symbolic character, object, or action, and a parallel entity in the world of the listener.[10] As such, they require "an unusual degree of flexibility on the reader's part."[11] So, for instance, when Assyria is called the "rod of my anger" in an extended metaphor (Isa 10:5–19), the reader understands that Yahweh is wielding this mighty empire like a stick in his hand, to bring judgment on the earth. And yet (Isaiah continues),

> Shall the axe boast over him who hews with it,
> Or the saw magnify itself against him who wields it?
> As if a rod should wield him who lifts it,
> Or as if a staff should lift him who is not wood! (Isa 10:15)

This parable requires readers to juggle the (ridiculous) image of a stick swinging a man with the notion of Assyria boasting over Yahweh when it invades Israel. The first interprets the second—and by

---

Forms of the Bible (Fortress, 1989), 89-90.

8 In particular, we will include historical events in our tally of parables. "Parabolic" in the Prophets does not always mean fictive. See, for instance, below on Jonah 4.

9 Modern hermeneutics (in particular the New Hermeneutic) has had a field day with parables. To indicate just a few of the many directions taken, see Susan Wittig, "A Theory of Multiple Meanings," *Semeia* 9 (1977): 75–103, Gerhard Ebeling, *God and Word* (Philadelphia: Fortress, 1967), Anthony Thiselton, "Reader-Response Hermeneutics, Action Models, and the Parables of Jesus," in Roger Lundin, Anthony C. Thiselton, and Clarence Walhout, *The Responsibility of Hermeneutics* (Eerdmans, 1985), 79–113.

10 See Long, *Preaching and the Literary Forms*, 91; Jeffrey D. Arthurs, *Preaching with Variety: How to Re-create the Dynamics of Biblical Genres* (Kregel, 2007), 103.

11 Long, *Literary Forms*, 89.

comparison implies that the one who wields the stick can turn and snap it over his knee.

Comparison in a parable will usually have one of two rhetorical effects.[12] First, parables can create insiders: readers who understand the symbolism or the code are certified as "insiders" who can see things for what they truly are. In Isaiah 14:4–21 the prophet sings a proleptic taunt song (Heb. *mashal*) against the king of Babylon. The song begins with parabolic language of acclamation: the cypress and cedar clap their hands, the kings in Sheol arise, the morning star outshines all others. But faithful Israelites know that his royal pretensions will not last. In fact, the praise of the trees is thanksgiving that they will no more be cut for his building projects; dead kings arise only to gloat that he is now powerless like them; the morning star is setting and falling to earth. By making this comparison, Isaiah confirms for his readers that their trust in Yahweh's power has not been misplaced: Babylon will fall.

Second (and more frequently) parables create outsiders. They undermine one's initial understanding and require reflection and repentance. Ezekiel 16 presents a tragic parable of Yahweh's faithless bride, given everything she needs in love and fidelity, who spurns it all for an adulterous and wasteful existence. "How sick is your heart, declares the LORD God, because you did all these things" (Ezek. 16:30). Readers feel the burn of betrayal but are asked to apply the label of unfaithful wife to themselves. The parable undermines their perception as a treasured bride and labels them as outsiders, faithless adulterers.

On Preaching Parables

If parables cause a spark to jump from one level to another in the minds of readers, how can we generate the same current from the pulpit? This is not as simple as it seems. Consider this joke in Spanish and English:

---

12 Ibid., 96–101, lists the function of parables as confirmation, comparison, and surprise. It seems, however that comparison is the most basic function, and confirmation/surprise as the two effects generated by that comparison.

¿Qué hace una abeja en el gimnasio? ¡Zumba!

What does a bee do in the gym? Zumba!

Not very funny unless you know that *zumbar* is Spanish for "buzz." But by the time I explain it, the joke is dead. As Arthurs notes, "We murder when we dissect."[13] Parables work like riddles and jokes; preaching them effectively demands more than just explaining (often with a scalpel) why they work—or why they once did. This leaves preachers with a few preaching options, each of which must be done cautiously to keep the joke alive.

Strategy 6.1 Explain the Joke (Carefully)

Sometimes preachers can simply point out why the parable works. If done deftly, the patient may survive. In Jeremiah 13:12–14, the prophet is sent to Jerusalem with a pithy prediction: "Every jar will be filled with wine." This sounds wonderful: agricultural bounty, plentiful harvests, overflowing vats! It coheres with the city's expectation for deliverance from the invading Babylonians. They reply, "Do we not indeed know that every jar will be filled with wine?" (v. 12). Jeremiah enjoys about five seconds of popularity, before he explains what *he* means: God will fill all the inhabitants of Judah with drunkenness and shatter them against each other like jars of wine. "I will not pity or spare or have compassion on them" (vv. 13–14). Drunkenness is a common prophetic metaphor for judgment because to make someone drunk renders them foolish, weak, sick, and overcome.[14] "Every jar will be filled with wine" means that no one will escape destruction.

Preachers can explain Jeremiah's joke, but they must take care not to kill it. For the joke to work, listeners will need to feel the glee inherent in what Jeremiah's words seemed to predict *before* they realize what the prophet was truly saying. For example, reading the entire passage at the start of the sermon will take the life out of the passage. Better to begin with Jeremiah's simple sentence, "Every jar

---

13 Arthurs, *Preaching with Variety*, 39.
14 See Isa 29:9; 49:26; 51:17; 63:6; Jer 25:27; 48:26; 51:39, 57; Rev 14:10; 16:6.

will be filled with wine." Spend time pondering God's promises of abundant life, answered prayers, inner peace—perhaps even shade into "health and wealth" theology for a moment. Only then can the rest of the passage be brought to bear with its original force. Preachers must take care not to step on the punchline.

Sometimes parables are such "inside" jokes that the only way to get them across is to explain them. Ezekiel tells a parable of two eagles and a vine which is inscrutable to most modern readers (Ezek 17:1–10). Only in the light of Judah's recent political history does the parable makes sense. In fact, even Ezekiel must explain it (17:11–24).

Briefly, here is what the parable means: Judah's current ruler (pictured as a vine) had been put on the throne as a puppet king by the Babylonian emperor (the first eagle, who planted the vine). A transplanted vine, even when planted in good soil, leads a precarious existence in the arid Near East. Whatever chance of life it has depends on the eagle dropping it in just the right spot. But the Judean king was double-crossing his overlord by making political overtures to Egypt (the other great eagle, to whom the original plant reached out with roots and branches). To abandon allegiance and turn toward another eagle—to court the wrath of a great bird of prey—is the height of folly. The betrayed eagle (Babylon) will surely rip up the plant and let it die. Judah's king is in for violent retribution from Babylon.

The parable's imagery is bizarre, the political context is unfamiliar, and the point is obscure. Any sermon on Ezekiel 17 will have to spend a significant time explaining the joke.[15] But such sermons carry a high risk of death by dissection.

Perhaps the best way to handle a parable like this is to minimize explanation to the essentials. Names of kings, lists of dates, botanical and ornithological facts should be kept to a minimum. This passage is about betrayal and its consequences. God commands submission to Babylon as discipline for Judah's sins, as Jeremiah makes clear. Rebellion against the Babylonian king is tantamount to rebellion against Yahweh. Sermons that get lost in the weeds of

---

15 For one example, see Matt Korniotes, "The Parable of Two Eagles and a Vine," August 5, 2020, https://www.youtube.com/watch?v=Vr2KAhkKVtI.

Mesopotamian politics will never find their way to listener's hearts. Explain the joke only as much as necessary to bring out its force.

Strategy 6.2 Re-Work the Joke

Some jokes can be translated, with a little work and creativity. Some parables can be updated in ways that preserve their power and surprise.

Fair warning: this is harder than it looks. I recall a preaching class in which the assignment was to create and then tell a parable. It was surprisingly difficult, and I ended up with a lame little story about gravy at the Thanksgiving table that drew some stifled yawns and taught me a sharp lesson. Too transparent and you bore your audience; too creative or cute, and you leave them in the dark. I started to read the parables of Scripture with a deeper appreciation for these little literary grenades.

Yet with practice, updating a parable is possible. In Isaiah 5:1–7 the prophet sings a song about a vineyard owner, who lovingly and at great expense, builds and plants a vineyard. When the first harvest comes in, what does he find but wild, inedible grapes? His only recourse is to uproot the entire vineyard and burn it. The song of the vineyard is about Israel's fruitlessness in reply to God's lovingkindness. It revolves around the concept of return on investment. Any investor worth her salt will abandon a project that consumes resources but does not give a return.

Modernizing this parable can be done by inventing a fictional story or using an actual event from the news. For instance, in 2006 Disney bought the Pixar company for $7.4 billion. This gem of a studio had been known for turning out some of the most original animated features in the world, like *Toy Story* and *Up*. What would the influx of cash, talent, and Disney "magic" accomplish? What fruit could the laborers produce for the owners?

Not much, apparently.[16] After the buyout, Pixar began to flounder, resorting to stereotyped storylines and tired sequels of earlier hits. What should Disney companies do? A good case could be made for chopping up Pixar and selling off the pieces. Because my

---

16 See Christopher Orr, "How Pixar Lost Its Way," *The Atlantic*, June 2017.

congregation is more familiar with Pixar films than viniculture, this story is easier than Isaiah 5 for my listeners to grasp and requires a shorter bridge to get from parable to point. Whether the sermon moves from Isaiah to Pixar to God's people, or begins with Pixar as a bridge to Isaiah, or stays on Pixar the entire time (with a reading from Isaiah before or after the sermon), the joke can be updated without losing its edge.

Once again, preachers must first understand why the parable works (in this case, it embodies the concept of return on investment). If that underlying dynamic operates in your culture today, then you can probably work up a parallel. To take another example, Ezekiel 15:1–8 compares the inhabitants of Jerusalem to a useless, charred vine. Before it was burned the stringy vine was already useless for building anything. You could not even make a wall peg from it. How much less after it has been burned? A charred bit of vine is doubly useless—about as worthless as it gets. The *a fortiori* nature of the parable can be replicated by finding doubly useless modern counterparts. For example, my family sometimes buys almond milk. If you have never tried almond milk, just imagine regular milk, only with a weird taste and a high price. Already useless, almond milk has a long shelf-life, but it will spoil eventually. How much more useless is *spoiled* almond milk! Any doubly useless item will do: a VHS tape of *Attack of the Killer Tomatoes*, a bent golf club that you cannot find, a cat who will not catch mice. We can re-work the joke.

Strategy 6.3 Just Tell the Joke

Some parables, despite the difference in time and culture, still work just fine. In this case the best advice is to tell the joke and get out of the way. For instance, the last chapter of Jonah is an enacted parable involving the prophet, a vine, a worm, and an east wind. The chapter ends as God leaves Jonah with a question ringing in his ears: "And the LORD said, 'You pity the plant, for which you did not labor, nor did you make it grow, which came into being in a night and perished in a night. And should not I pity Nineveh, that great city, in which there are more than 120,000 persons who do not know their right hand from their left, and also much cattle?'" (Jonah 4:10–11). If Jonah cares for a vine, how much more should he have compassion on this many people, even if they are his enemies?

Josh Wredberg preaches a sermon on this passage and allowed the same question to ring in listeners' ears.[17] After talking about what an incomplete ending Jonah 4 makes, he finishes like this: "I think the story ends that way because it doesn't matter what Jonah decided.... What matters is that each of us answer that question ourselves: will I repent of my arrogance, will I turn from my prejudice, will I celebrate the Father's grace? The ending is up to you." Wredberg lets the power of the story rest on us, resisting the temptation to turn a biblical interrogative into a homiletical imperative.

Other prophetic parables could also stand as they are, from Jeremiah's broken flask (Jer 19:1–13) to Ezekiel's tale of sexual promiscuity (Ezek 23). The prophets' words will hit home if we get out of the way.[18]

Conclusion: Preaching Parables

The homiletical strategies above require that preachers get the joke before they tell it. They must understand why the parable worked in the first place: how it slipped under the guard of Israelite women and men, surprising them with a word from Yahweh. For that, standard exegetical work will only take preachers so far. Literary sensitivity, experience with parables, and a good sense of humor can take preachers across the finish line to hear parables in their own setting. And if they can understand how it happened the first time, they can ponder how it might happen again.

Prophetic Apocalyptic

The boundary between parable and apocalypse is fuzzy, but we

---

17 Josh Wredberg, "The Gospel and Those People," Southeastern Seminary, October 19, 2018, https://www.youtube.com/watch?v=RgzlotbHkRA.

18 For more preaching suggestions on NT parables that will work with prophetic material, see Arthurs, *Preaching with Variety*, 118–128.

know we are crossing it when the symbols, pictures, and storylines work not so much by subversion as by shock and awe. Ezekiel sees a vast field of desiccated bones lying in the earth; at his preaching they self-assemble and grow flesh. The wind blows over these new corpses and they arise and stand to their feet, a mighty army. This is no joke.

Defining Apocalyptic Literature

Zechariah watches the Mount of Olives split in two; Joel foretells a darkened sun and a bloodied moon; Malachi depicts the day of Yahweh rising like the sun to char the wicked and enlighten the godly; Isaiah declares that death will be swallowed up forever and there will be a new heaven and a new earth.[19] The prophets are truly "seers," revealing what they have witnessed. "I saw all Israel scattered on the mountains, as sheep that have no shepherd," says Micaiah (1 Kgs 22:17). The heart of apocalyptic literature (from *apokaluptō*, to unveil) is a disclosure of the secrets of Yahweh to his people.

Nonetheless, like with the term "parable," we struggle to define "apocalypse" precisely. Perhaps the best-known description comes from John J. Collins and a SBL seminar in 1979, who say that apocalyptic literature is

> a genre of revelatory literature with a narrative framework, in which a revelation is mediated by an otherworldly being to a human recipient, disclosing a transcendent reality which is both temporal, insofar as it envisages eschatological salvation, and spatial insofar as it involves another, supernatural world.[20]

Collins's definition is perhaps too restrictive for our purposes. Though most classic apocalypse works like Revelation and 1 Enoch do have these features, the prophetic corpus has many passages which have an apocalyptic flavor, but do not conform precisely to

---

19 Zech 14:1–5; Joel 2:31; Mal 4:1–3; Isa 25:7–8; 65:17.
20 John J. Collins, "Towards the Morphology of a Genre," *Semeia* 14 (1979), 9. For another definition see Arthurs, *Preaching with Variety*, 180.

this definition. For example, Zechariah, whose visions in chapters 1–6 are perhaps the closest thing in the Prophets to classical apocalyptic, does not have the spatial dimension of Collins's definition. This is most likely because the genre itself was still in embryonic form during the time of the prophets.[21] Experts in the genre disagree on the details, but it is clear that classic apocalypses flourished beginning in the late third century B.C. and extended well after the completion of the New Testament.[22] So, while "apocalyptic" literature was in wide circulation by the time John the Baptist ate his first locust, OT examples reflect a genre still in development.[23] Scholars therefore label apocalyptic passages in the Prophets as either "proto-apocalyptic" or "full-blown." However we label them, the prophets sang and wrote oracles that had a strong apocalyptic flavor.

For present purposes, I suggest the following definition: apocalyptic literature reveals God's secret work in the readers' past, present, and future through symbolic visions, in order to encourage sufferers and warn backsliders.

Interpreting Apocalyptic Literature

If defining apocalypses was challenging, interpreting them can seem nearly impossible. I assume here that most readers feel at least some discomfort at the thought of preaching from apocalyptic oracles. I can empathize: I have pored over charts of empires and dates in the footnotes for Daniel in my study Bible; I have

---

21 Hanson is helpful here, though he posits a strong sociological split between classical prophets (representing the interests of Zadokite priests) and apocalyptic prophets (representing the disenfranchised). Paul D. Hanson, *The Dawn of Apocalyptic*, rev. ed. (Fortress Press, 1979), 1-32. See John J. Collins's critique in "From Prophecy to Apocalypticism," in John J. Collins, Bernard McGinn, and Stephen J. Stein, *Encyclopedia of Apocalypticism* (Continuum, 1998), 1:129-161. See also R. North, "Prophecy to Apocalyptic via Sechariah," *Congress Volume Uppsala 1971* (Brill, 1972), 47-71.

22 Hanson (*Dawn*, 6-16) argues that early forms ("proto-apocalyptic") appear in the late sixth century B.C. We adopt Collins's dating here. John J. Collins, *The Apocalyptic Imagination*, 2nd ed. (Eerdmans, 1998), 25.

23 Collins, *Apocalyptic Imagination*, 4, has a helpful explanation for how genres develop and wane.

felt the bewilderment of trying to navigate the idealist, preterist, futurist, and historicist approaches to Revelation.[24] Apocalyptic sometimes seems to conceal more than it reveals.

Of course, this section is too brief to untangle the interpretive knots of apocalyptic literature. But for preachers reading the Prophets, perhaps a good rule of thumb for interpretation is that *apocalyptic oracles invest readers' present circumstances with unforeseen meaning by unveiling divine realities.*[25] Let us unpack that.

Whether one reads apocalypse according to a future timeline or an abstract symbolism, all can agree that the prophets first gave these oracles not to us but to their own contemporaries. These are words to ancient Israel, and as such they impinge on ancient circumstances by depicting glorious or terrifying entities. For instance, when Ezekiel predicts a rebuilt temple in Jerusalem (Ezek 40–48), that revelation of restoration is meant to give heart to those in exile in Babylon with the prophet. God has not forgotten his people or his covenant! Their present exile has not derailed his purposes; Israelites can cling to their hope and trust God to bring them home.[26]

The way that apocalypse invests those ancient circumstances with meaning is by unveiling divine realities. God is indeed working, even if his plan cannot be seen by most. When the nations gather against Jerusalem in Joel 3, it looks like an invasion where Israel is hopelessly outnumbered. But in fact, they only gather because they are being gathered by Yahweh: "Hasten and come, all you surrounding nations, and gather yourselves there. Bring down your warriors, O LORD" (Joel 3:11). The prophet reveals that God

---

24 For the use of these approaches with respect to Revelation, see Buist M. Fanning, *Revelation*, ECNT (Zondervan, 2020), 37–40.

25 The phrase "invest with meaning" comes from N. T. Wright, *The New Testament and the People of God*, 283. Wright's dichotomy between apocalypse as predicting the end of space-time and apocalypse as solely focused on the immediate political future for Israel is perhaps too sharp, but his basic point—that readers of apocalyptic were looking for Yahweh to keep his promises to Israel, not necessarily to put an end to the whole world—is a helpful heuristic device for interpretation.

26 See Daniel I. Block, *The Book of Ezekiel Chapters 25–48*, NICOT (Eerdmans, 1998), 505–506.

is just getting them in all into one place ("the valley of [His] decision," v. 14) for the harvest-sickle of vengeance and the winepress of judgment. The nations' action is revealed to be God's secret work in alignment not with their purposes, but with his own.

Just like every genre in Scripture, apocalyptic literature acts on its readers. When prophets disclose hidden realities, hearts and minds change. The goal of the prophets is not so much to let Israel know what will happen three days or three millennia from their present (though that may be one consequence), but to do the good pastoral work of a covenant enforcer: to remind, to rebuke, to demand change, to comfort, and to inspire. Arthurs nicely summarizes the specific ways that apocalypse does this: by addressing believers in crisis, by announcing a competing interpretation of reality, by consoling and chastising, and by changing hearer's perspectives.[27]

Though Arthurs concentrates on Revelation, his list fits prophetic apocalyptic quite nicely. A prophetic apocalypse addresses believers in crises (i.e., exile or a disappointing return from exile). Its interpretation of their reality is that Yahweh, not the emperor, is all-powerful (Daniel 7–9). It consoles with hopes for the future and chastises those who stand against Yahweh (Isa 25–27). And it changes hearers' perspectives by revealing Yahweh's purposes behind current realities (Habakkuk 1–2).

Apocalyptic oracles reveal the hand of God behind current and future events, and thereby invest those events with a meaning in line with Israel's covenant.

When today's preachers interpret apocalyptic oracles, they begin by seeing how those oracles operated in the covenant context of Israel, and then look for analogous ways it can operate in our own.

Preaching Apocalyptic Literature[28]

The thrust of this book and this series is that preachers, unless they have good reason to do otherwise, should seek to reproduce the

---

27 Arthurs, *Preaching with Variety*, 181–183.
28 Aside from the volumes by Arthurs and Long, I can only interact in a limited way with three other works on preaching apocalyptic texts for the following

effects of biblical genres in their sermons.[29] As Jacobsen notes, a text's "forms can furnish us with frames for understanding how the Word would do what it does."[30] The apocalyptic form, as discussed above, performs three basic functions on readers that preachers can re-create: it reveals, it confronts, and it encourages. We can do the same.

Strategy 7.1 Reveal

When the text reveals, so can we. Zechariah's vision of a horseman (Zech 1:7–17) comes complete with an angelic guide and symbolic figures. The vision offers readers Yahweh's perspective vis-à-vis the current international political situation. Darius has just been crowned ruler of the Persian empire and established his kingdom (Zech 1:1). All the nations that oppressed Judah and helped her enemies send her into exile are "at rest" (v. 11), while Judah herself languishes under the Persian thumb. The common perception, therefore, is that Persia is mighty, Judah and her gods have been defeated, and those who sided with Persia are at ease.

Zechariah's vision in the night tells a different story. Far from being defeated, God has been sending his angelic messengers on swift horseback to patrol the nations. He is acutely aware of their "ease." Furthermore, he is filled with jealousy for his people

---

reasons: David Schnasa Jacobsen's *Preaching in the New Creation: The Promise of New Testament Apocalyptic Texts* (Westminster John Knox Press, 1999) is a valuable handbook for rhetorical interpretation of NT apocalyptic texts with a view to preaching. Yet the firm grounding of his work in the New Homiletic (12–15), his reliance throughout on Ricoeur's hermeneutic, and his orienting of interpretation around the contemporary "world in front of the text" make his work somewhat tangential to my own approach, which concentrates on the historical circumstances and the rhetorical effects in the original context. Likewise, Leah D. Schade and Jerry L. Sumney's *Apocalypse When? A Guide to Interpreting and Preaching Apocalyptic Texts* (Cascade: 2020) concentrates on the Revised Common Lectionary, and therefore omits the OT Prophets. Finally, Ryan Boys's volume in the present series appeared too late for interaction.

29 "Good reason" would include theological convictions about the connections and discontinuities between the Old Testament and the New. See ch. 2 for more on theological frameworks and how they affect interpretation.

30 Jacobsen, *New Creation*, 14.

(v. 14) and angry at the nations who are at peace (v. 15). Zechariah reveals that God has his hand firmly on the situation and that he plans drastic reversals for both the nations and Jerusalem (vv. 16–17).

Without taking up a prophetic mantle of infallibility, preachers can invite hearers to pull back the curtain on their own contexts. What does the current social and political climate suggest about God, about those who stand against him, and about the church? It would be simple to draw up a list of inaccurate conclusions, depending on circumstances: that God has been exiled from government, that the wrong people are in power, that might now makes right, that the kingdom is losing influence, that the church is headed to obscurity and dissolution. But we know that the King is on the throne! His messengers run swiftly; he is aware of every back room deal and floor vote; he is jealous for his church; his plans remain firm.[31]

Of course, we should never try to be as specific as the inspired prophet; that way lies madness.[32] We have no direct vision from God about current circumstances. But we can stand firm on what we know about God's sovereignty and his ultimate plans for his church. And we can humbly and cautiously wonder what God might be doing in the present. Joel's cry of "Who knows?" in reference to what God might do about current circumstances (Joel 2:14), seems an appropriate homiletical posture. The point is not to predict the immediate future, but to *reveal*: to lift the deistic veil of current worldviews that make God into a spectator rather than the director of the play. With apocalypse we can proclaim that somehow, this is all in the script.

Maybe you are preaching through Malachi and come to his "day of Yahweh" vision in chapter 4. As Long states, "Eschatological

---

31 Some preachers will feel uncomfortable straying into the political realm at all. I can only reply that the prophets did so regularly and that, notwithstanding the theological distinction between a prophet and a preacher addressed below, the gospel leaves no realm of life unaddressed. Be humble, but be courageous.

32 Witness the string of sermons and prophecies about Donald Trump's divinely ensured victory in 2020, or Edgar C. Whisenat's pamphlet, *88 Reasons Why the Rapture Will Be in 1988: The Feast of Trumpets (Rosh Hash–Ana) September 11–12–13* (World Bible Society, 1988).

preaching affirms that life under the providence of God has a shape, and that this shape is end-stressed; what happens in the middle is finally defined by the end."[33] The prophets' words describe the rising of the Righteous Sun, bringing flames to the wicked but light and healing to God's people, who will gambol like calves at dawn, treading the wicked down like ashes under their feet. Malachi *reveals* his listeners' future, the weight of which changes their hope in the present.

We also can help our people to end-stress their lives. Andrew Hopper, in a sermon on Malachi 4, ushers listeners into the text just so:

> We often see our present circumstances as so big that we cannot see the coming day of the LORD, we can't see the future that is out there.... Our temptation is to begin to believe things that aren't true about God because the present looms so large for us. The coming day of the LORD can snap us out of that.[34]

The future relativizes the present. The joy and beauty of carefree animals, the ashes of the wicked, the brightness of the sun: with these images we can reveal the future and harness it to right-size the present.[35]

Strategy 7.2 Confront

When the apocalyptic text confronts, so can we. At the end of Isaiah, in a long section of poetry, one prose verse stands on its own to complete an apocalyptic vision of final judgment and final glory: "And they shall go out and look on the dead bodies of the men who have rebelled against me. For their worm shall not die, their fire shall not be quenched, and they shall be an abhorrence to all flesh" (Isa 66.24). This is a brutal shock of a verse. Isaiah holds up a ghastly picture before our eyes of God's redeemed people from

---

33 Long, *Preaching and the Literary Forms*, 126.
34 Andrew Hopper, "The Sun of Righteousness (Malachi 4)," February 6, 2018, https://www.youtube.com/watch?v=wifO4aND6-M.
35 See ch. 5 for more on preaching and imagery.

all nations, at home in Zion (v. 20), who take day trips outside the city to see the burning corpses of rebels. The fire will never go out; the corrupting worms will live forever. The paradox of never-ending flames and never-ending rot *confronts* those who stand against Yahweh.

With pastoral wisdom, so can we. The preacher who wants to say what the text says and do what the text does, can think through the theological issues implicit in such visions (see chapter 2), and may conclude that this oracle speaks to hearers who are living in rebellion or are not yet believers. The shock of fire and worms can lead to pleas to come to Christ for mercy. So, we may cry with the prophets and apostles, "Save yourselves from this crooked generation!" (Acts 2:40).

Zechariah's vision in Zech 13:1–6 also confronts God's people. The fountain of mercy that cleanses God's people (v. 1) leads to a time when idol worship will be so abhorred that those who practice it will be executed by their own parents (vv. 2–3) and the man who formerly worshipped idols will be so ashamed that he lies about his past, and says that the scars of punishment on his back are "wounds I received at the house of a friend" (v. 6). Oh, how we will be ashamed of our ways on the great Day of the LORD!

Of course, Zechariah is trying to produce more than shame here: this vision is one part of his longer call to Judah to return to Yahweh (Zech 1:3). This is a call to discipleship.[36]

And so it can be for preachers now. We can pastorally evoke feelings of shame that we have experienced or witnessed. We know what it feels like to be disgraced, and in those moments we long for a chance to go back and do things differently, or unsay those words, or change our minds. Zechariah invites us to anticipate standing before God. Of what will we then be ashamed? What would we give to be able to go back to right now, and make changes? We have that chance now. Zechariah's vision of the future functions like the final ghost in *A Christmas Carol*. Prophetic confrontation is still a call to find mercy in time of need.

---

36 Arthurs, *Preaching with Variety*, 192–93, rightly points out this function of apocalyptic.

Strategy 7.3 Encourage

Finally, when apocalyptic texts encourage, so can we. Apocalyptic literature (written for the persecuted and oppressed) offers more than commiseration and rebuke. It straightens the spine and strengthens the knees. It equips one to keep walking. Isaiah does this with his vision of a new heavens and a new earth (Isa 65:17–25). He shows readers a series of scenes, the cumulative effect of which overcomes us with glory and joy: new creation (v. 17), gladness without sorrow (vv. 18–19), long and safe lives (v. 20), success and abundance in work (vv. 21–23), the immediate presence of God (v. 24), and the transformation of nature itself (v. 25). The concreteness of the images (hundred-year-old men who are still young, flourishing vineyards, wolves and lambs at peace) give one a sense of certainty. *This* is what it will be like for us (even if the imagery is only a shadow of the true reality). Certainty encourages.

We can give certainty and thereby encourage when we preach passages like this one. Daniel Fusco, in a sermon on Isaiah 65:17–25, holds out certainty. He says, "Life is full of tremendous amounts of uncertainty. But not everything about the future is uncertain. ... Out of all of the uncertainties of life, there is one thing that isn't a question mark, and that is ... that there is an eternal abode for you."[37] Then he launches into a verse-by-verse exposition of the oracle. The format is effective, because just as Isaiah piles up images and concepts for heaven, so does the sermon. He uses concrete images of children, surgeries, marriages, and movie trailers to draw in listeners. At one point he tells a wonderful story of his 80-year-old grandfather who got both knees replaced. Fusco talks about seeing his grandfather get out on the dance floor and dance with his wife ("And he's got moves!"). But Fusco notices that his grandfather's pants are a little short, the cuffs not coming down to his heels. His grandfather says, "My new knees made me a half inch taller, and I have to get new pants now!" Fusco's story concretely illustrates the comprehensive "newness" of God's

---

37 Daniel Fusco, "Our Forever Home (Isaiah 65:17–25)," August 9, 2017, https://www.youtube.com/watch?v=Y2IzkLP_Qpo.

future: new joy, new legs, even new pants. Everything changes. Images like Isaiah's (and the images we supply ourselves) lend certainty, and certainty encourages.

Apocalyptic oracles are strong medicine. But the prophets did not hesitate to use every nostrum in the box to bring life and healing to their people. If preachers pray, read, and think carefully, they can grasp how the medicine worked, and use it judiciously in their own settings.

Prophetic Epistle and Narrative

Because epistle and narrative appear infrequently in the Prophets but commonly in the pulpit, I have chosen to devote the lion's share of space in this chapter to parable and apocalypse and can only provide the briefest comments here about two other genres.

The prophets at times do write formal letters (e.g., Jer 29). However, those letters do not follow most of what preachers know about epistolary conventions (which are Greco-Roman and were formalized long after the Prophets). Nonetheless, both the few formal letters and most of the oracles are, like epistles, direct corporate address. Thus, what preachers already know about preaching epistles will be helpful, *mutatis mutandis*, for the preacher of the Prophets.

The very few narrative portions of the Prophets (Jonah, portions of Jeremiah and Isaiah) make for wonderful sermons. Because so much of the Bible is narrative, we are on the more familiar ground of plot, character, and setting. Jonah's prejudice is pitted against Yahweh's compassion. The Assyrians are at the gate and Hezekiah is terrified. We can preach these narratives as we preach the other great stories of the Bible.[38]

---

38 On preaching narratives, see the appropriate sections in Long, *Preaching and the Literary Forms*, and Arthurs, *Preaching with Variety*. See also Meir Sternberg, *The Poetics of Biblical Narrative: Ideological Literature and the Drama of Reading* (Indiana University Press, 1987), Steven D. Mathewson, *The Art of Preaching Old Testament Narrative* (Baker Academic, 2002), and Jeffrey D. Arthurs, *How to Preach Narrative*, PBL (Fontes, 2022).

A Final Word on Prophetic Overlap

It bears repeating that when prophets use literary conventions like poetry, parable and apocalyptic, they do so for theological reasons. Prophecy, therefore, is not one kind of literature in the same way that genealogies or acrostics are. The prophets incorporate existing literary forms *in the service of covenant enforcement*. They say what they do to remind people of God's covenant goodness, his demands for covenant faithfulness, and his promises of covenant consequences. Therefore, when they sing lays or spin yarns or whisper secrets, they draw hearers back to their covenant bond to Yahweh. In other words, genre is always a literary means to a theological end.

Remembering this will help preachers to read and to preach well. When they read, they will understand how the prophets are doing covenantal business with their words. And when they preach, they will take a similar stance: the shape of the sermon and its parts must serve the theological ends of the new covenant community.

In the next two chapters we continue our exploration of the features characteristic of prophetic oracles in the OT, examining their use of imagery and emotion.

For Further Reading

See Arthurs, *Preaching with Variety* and Long, *Preaching and the Literary Forms of the Bible*, for helpful guides to preaching parable and apocalyptic.

Collins, John J. *The Apocalyptic Imagination*. 2nd edition. Eerdmans, 1998. 10–42.

Snodgrass, Klyne R. *Stories with Intent: A Comprehensive Guide to the Parables of Jesus*. Eerdmans, 2008. 1-59.

Talk about It

Explore the theology of parables. Read the twin passages about prophetic and parabolic speech in Isa 6:8–13 and Matthew 13:10–17, where Jesus quotes the Isaiah passage to explain why he speaks in parables. Why do you think God would speak in cryptic ways that can leave hearers in the dark? What seems to be the purpose of parabolic speech in God's kingdom?

Dig Deeper

Watch a standup comic to see how their humor works. (Clean ones are hard to find; Brian Regan and Nate Bargatze are both on Netflix.) Why do their jokes work? How do they surprise you?

Watch an apocalyptic or post-apocalyptic movie or show. You will find dozens, covering everything from asteroids to zombies. How does the movie relativize things in our present that we think of as reliable or necessary? What vision of the future does the movie give, and how do the creators want to alter our thinking about our present?

Practice

Think through a prophetic parable for preaching. In Ezek 12:1–16, Ezekiel enacts a parabolic exile for the ruler of Judah and his family. He then explains the parable to his audience. How might you preach this? In other words, how might you preserve the mystery and tension that the prophets' actions evoked, while still helping hearers to understand the text?

Think through an apocalyptic vision for preaching. Ezekiel 47:1–12 is a stunning vision of clean water flowing from God's presence, deepening and increasing as it runs, and bringing life to the land. Is this oracle designed primarily to reveal, to confront, or to encourage? After thinking through the theological and covenantal layers discussed in chapter 2, state how this passage should operate in your own church context. Come up with a summary statement or "big idea" for this sermon.

5

Image

> *The words, too, ought to set the scene before our eyes.*
>
> –Aristotle[1]

ISRAEL STOOD OUT AMONG her Ancient Near Eastern neighbors, in part because her God forbade her from crafting images as objects of worship (Exo 20:4–5).[2] In the innermost chamber of their temple was not a statue of a god but an empty space above the mercy seat. The only adequate picture of Yahweh on offer was humanity itself: men and women fashioned in God's likeness at creation (Gen 1:26–27; Isa 43:7).[3] So central was this prohibition of images that when constructing altars for worship, Israel was not even to cut or shape the stones (Exo 20:25).[4]

---

1 Aristotle, trans. W. Rhys Roberts, *Rhetoric* (Dover, 2004), 1410b, loc 2789 of 3734, Kindle.

2 Scholars debate (here and in the subsequent Golden Calf episode) whether the forbidden idols were images of Yahweh or images of other gods (see Alexander, *From Paradise to Promised Land*, 178–79 and Walter C. Kaiser, *Exodus*, EBC [Zondervan, 1990], 2:422–23 for contrasting opinions on Exod 20). Peter J. Gentry and Stephen J. Wellum, *Kingdom Through Covenant* (Crossway, 2012), 334–336, discuss the grammar of Exod 20:4 and Deut 5:8 and argue for a meaning of "a carved image of any form." This would presumably mean that idols of any god as a form of worship were prohibited.

3 See Gentry and Wellum, *Kingdom Through Covenant*, 181–208, for a discussion of image and likeness in human beings.

4 This does not prohibit the making of pictures *in toto*—merely their manufacture and use as mediators of the deity. Recall the angelic and agricultural carvings in Solomon's temple, or the bronze serpent in the wilderness.

Though images in Israel's worship were sparse, images in the text are plentiful. In spite or perhaps because of God's restrictions on physical representations, verbal imagery flourished in Israelite literature. In particular, the prophetic oracles abound with word-pictures, visions, and evocative descriptions. The "family tree" of David is portrayed as a burned stump with a fragile shoot coming up (Isa 6:13; 11:1–2). Ezekiel sees angels marking people on their foreheads and measuring the dimensions of a new temple (Ezek 9; 40–44). He eats a scroll that is as sweet as honey (Ezek 3). Hosea sings of dew and spring rains (Hos 6:1–6). Malachi says that God's arrival will burn like caustic alkaline soap (Mal 3:1–4). Jeremiah lives among those who have abandoned living waters for cracked cisterns (Jer 2:13). Locusts, snow, worms, offal, potter's wheels, mobile thrones, hammers, lightning, springs, swords and plowshares, lions and lambs, trees clapping hands and mountains riven in two: images saturate the songs of the Prophets.

Images are powerful, taking root in our minds when abstract words blow away like chaff. Modern studies on logos, websites, and branding confirm this phenomenon and explain why images captivate. One study demonstrates that viewers need only about 50 ms (or 1/20th of a second) to form an opinion about a company based on their website's visual design.[5] Long before they read any of the words, customers draw conclusions about a product based on how the site "feels." Even the basic shape of a company's logo matters: "circular- versus angular-logo shapes activate softness and hardness associations, respectively, and these concepts subsequently influence product/company attribute judgments."[6] We are not only drawn to images but make near-instant value judgments based on them.

But what does this have to do with *words* that are pictorial rather than actual pictures? Quite a lot. It turns out that we can recall

---

5 Peep Laja, "First Impressions Matter: Why Great Visual Design Is Essential" (April 2019), CXL (blog), https://cxl.com/blog/first-impressions-matter-the-importance-of-great-visual-design/.

6 Yuwei Jiang, Gerald J. Gorn, Maria Galli, Amitava Chattopadhyay, "Does Your Company Have the Right Logo? How and Why Circular- and Angular-Logo Shapes Influence Brand Attribute Judgments," *Journal of Consumer Research* 42:5 (February 2016), 709–726.

concrete, imagistic words far better than abstract words.[7] Dual Coding Theory, developed by Allan Paivio in the 1970's, postulates "two separate cognitive subsystems. One is specialized for dealing with language, and the other deals with representation and processing of non-verbal objects (imagery)."[8] When concrete words (such as "daisy") enter our awareness, our brains encode them as both a word and an image. This dual coding accounts for why imagistic words stick around, while abstract words (like "concept") tend to fade. In other words, pictorial words act like words *and* pictures in our minds.

In this chapter we will see how the prophets harnessed the power of verbal images for their preaching and how we can do the same.

Prophetic Images

The prophets' images empowered their messages because those images were concrete, vivid, and collaborative.

Prophetic images were concrete. Prophets chose to move down the "ladder of abstraction" from mere ideas to realities that could be touched, smelled, and felt.[9] When Habakkuk wants to communicate his trust in Yahweh even under adverse circumstances, he could have said just that: "I will always trust in God, even when things go poorly. God will strengthen me." But who would be moved by such abstraction? Thankfully, the prophets worked harder than that. Here is what Habakkuk says:

> Though the fig tree should not blossom,
> nor fruit be on the vines,
> the produce of the olive fail

---

[7] Lin Yui, Roslin J. Ng, Hiran Perera, "Concrete vs. Abstract Words – What Do You Recall Better? A Study on Dual Coding Theory," *PeerJ Preprints* (January 2017), https://doi.org/10.7287/peerj.preprints.2719v1.

[8] Yui, Ng, and Perera, "Concrete," 2.

[9] For more on the "ladder of abstraction" see Haddon Robinson, "The Heresy of Application: An Interview with Haddon Robinson," *Leadership* 18 (Fall 1997): 308. Probably the most common advice I give to burgeoning preachers (after "Be clear!") is "Come down the ladder!"

> and the fields yield no food,
> the flock be cut off from the fold
> and there be no herd in the stalls,
> yet I will rejoice in the LORD;
> I will take joy in the God of my salvation.
> God, the Lord, is my strength;
> he makes my feet like the deer's;
> he makes me tread on my high places. (Hab 3:17–19)

Note how concrete his images are: he names the specific products that give life and joy. He pictures fruitless vines, barren trees, decimated flocks, and empty stalls. We can *see* the devastation. Even then Habakkuk will trust. In fact, God transforms his feet into hooves that can climb the mounts and see the horizon of God's purposes! Concrete pictures stick around long after platitudes fade.

Prophets are just as concrete when they threaten as when they promise. Zephaniah portrays the judgment of Jerusalem, predicting that Yahweh "will search Jerusalem with lamps, and [he] will punish the men who are complacent" (Zeph 1:12). Cries of woe and distress will sound from specific places in the city: the Fish Gate, the Second Quarter, and the Mortar district (1:10–11). Zephaniah's audience *knows* these places; they walk in them regularly. They can hear, as it were, the cries of distress rising, the shouts coming closer. The thought of Yahweh going house to house with lamps, searching under every bed, will continue to haunt even when the song ends.

Prophetic images are also vivid. The prophets chose unusual word pictures that arrest hearers' attention and prompt reflection. When Ezekiel eats a scroll (Ezek 3:1–3), this is more than just a way to say that God has put his words in the prophet's mouth. The idea of eating a calfskin scroll makes me pause. Eating is more intimate than reading, touching, or holding. What did it feel like in his mouth? Did he chew it? Why was it sweet when most of Ezekiel's words are sour? Ezekiel's vivid picture packs a square meal's worth of theology into a bite-size phrase.

Or consider another arresting image in Habakkuk:

> Woe to him who gets evil gain for his house,
> to set his nest on high, to be safe from the reach of harm!
> You have devised shame for your house by cutting off many peoples;
> you have forfeited your life.
> For the stone will cry out from the wall,
> and the beam from the woodwork respond. (Hab 2:9–11)

We see in our minds a building project at the top of a hill—an inaccessible nest for a wealthy man who has defrauded his neighbors. Surely, such a man will be out of the reach of vengeance. But the very stones and beams will call out to each other, decrying his sin. It would be easy (and cheap, and utterly forgettable) to toss out a phrase like, "oppressors will not escape justice." It's another thing entirely to put the voice of justice in the mouth of boards and bricks, so that the very gains of sin will harangue the sinner, no matter how high he builds his retreat. Prophetic images arrest by their vividness.

Finally, prophetic images cause listeners to collaborate. Like the parables discussed in the last chapter, images leave the "point" unstated and enlist the hearers as co-creators of meaning who fill in the blanks. Ezekiel's scroll functions this way. We only see a scroll that is eaten and sweet. Its content, nature and function must be inferred. We conclude that he is commissioned by God, that his words are not his own, and that though they sound harsh, there is a sweetness embedded in them somewhere. When we ponder like this, we are already doing Ezekiel's work for him. Images enlist us as (sometimes unwilling) collaborators.

In another example, Jeremiah laments the way that Judah has exchanged her faith in Yahweh for allegiance to foreign gods. "Be appalled, O heavens, at this; be shocked, be utterly desolate" (Jer 2:12). Why would this exchange be so unthinkable? Jeremiah explains with an image: "For my people have committed two evils: they have forsaken me, the fountain of living waters, and hewed out cisterns for themselves, broken cisterns that can hold no water" (v. 13). Jeremiah leaves unsaid what readers must fill in: the priceless and rare discovery in arid Palestine of a "living" well (where water gushes forth instead of being drawn up); the cool refreshment of an underground aquifer; the hot and stagnant taste of old rainwater in a cistern; the rarity and unreliability of rain in that climate; the labor of hewing a container out of solid rock; the heartbreak of finding your cistern cracked and dry. Jeremiah puts a bud in our hearts and allows it to blossom on its own.

I suggest that the combination of concreteness, vividness, and collaboration unite in the prophets' most powerful images. They work together to imprint God's perspective deeply within us. This is what Hosea (whose work is chock full of images) does in Hos 6:3–4. He uses rain as a word-picture to draw a powerful contrast:

> Let us know; let us press on to know the LORD;
> his going out is sure as the dawn;
> he will come to us as the showers,
> as the spring rains that water the earth."
> What shall I do with you, O Ephraim?
> What shall I do with you, O Judah?
> Your love is like a morning cloud,
> like the dew that goes early away.

God's love is faithful like the sunrise, or like the seasonal rains that water crops. Life depends on Yahweh's steadfastness. But Israel and Judah are like a cloud or dew that disappears when the sun comes up. It will be gone in minutes, leaving behind no life-giving moisture. Hosea gives us two species of love, one which reliably gives what it promises and one which fades quickly and proves to be a lie.

Concrete pictures vividly employed that invite collaboration: this is the imagery of the Prophets.

Preaching with Images

Concrete texts demand concrete sermons. As Langley observes, images "make it as difficult as they possibly can for ministers to sally off into vague generalities and call this prosaic speechifying a sermon."[10] The good news is that developing imagery in our

---

10 Kenneth Langley, *How to Preach the Psalms* (Fontes, 2021), 32.

sermons is relatively straightforward and will be successful if we will practice it consistently. We have several ways to employ images effectively in sermons from the Prophets.

Strategy 8.1 Use Images Ancient and Modern

The preacher's first choice is whether to use the prophet's ancient image or to "translate" it for a contemporary audience. Rain and fire (Isa 43:2) are familiar concepts; a cart weighed down by sheaves of grain (Amos 2:13) might need to be updated for an urban congregation.[11] Consider Malachi's depiction of the messenger of the covenant arriving in Judah: "But who can endure the day of coming, and who can stand when he appears? For he is like refiner's fire and like fuller's soap" (Mal 3:2).[12] Preachers can use the images of forges and fuller's soap in their sermons, or they can create equivalent images tailored to their context. We will explore both options.

Some preachers will conclude that Malachi's images work just as well now as they did then: pregnant with emotion and implication, they underscore the pain of the messenger's arrival. His "coming," for which the returned exiles pray, will be surprisingly unpleasant because the messenger's task will be not to restore but to refine, not to comfort but to cleanse. Fire burns away impurities. A little online research can fill out the picture of "refiner's fire" for use in a sermon: iron ore must be smelted in a forge (i.e., combined with charcoal or another agent to temperatures nearing its melting point of 2200° F) where the impurities will leave the iron and combine with the chemical reagents to produce slag (a waste product). The "bloom" of porous iron, interspersed with slag particles, is taken out of the forge, and repeatedly beaten with a hammer to knock off the slag. In other words, ancient iron production was blistering, laborious, and violent, and depicting the Judeans as the ore was an arresting way to warn them of a fiery beating on its way!

---

11 Nonetheless, even universal images like rain connote different ideas and emotions for people living in a desert and others living in a swamp.

12 The specific identity of the messenger, his ties to earlier OT patterns or to Malachi or to later NT figures, and his relation to Yahweh do not affect the present discussion—though they are critical for an effective sermon from Malachi 3.

Sandpaper	Peeling skin after a sunburn
Grinding wheel	Pressure washer
Self-cleaning oven	Roller brushes in an automatic car wash
Paint stripper	Razor burn
Bleach	Scraping the burnt layer off toast
Chemotherapy	Stripping wallpaper
Steel wool	Autoclave
Cheese grater	

Table 5.1: Brainstorming Images for Mal 3

By adding "fuller's soap," Malachi moves the image from a temperature burn to a chemical one. Fullers were the professional dry cleaners of the day. Ancient Near Eastern soap was made from lye (probably potassium hydroxide), an alkaline salt produced by mixing hardwood ashes and water; to form the soap, the lye was then mixed with oil or animal fat. Lye is water-soluble, corrosive, and unpleasant. It decomposes proteins and can cause chemical burns.

Refiner's fire and fuller's soap evoke the caustic nature of the messenger's arrival. Judah's sins will be on display, and the messenger will ignite a cleansing burn to prepare them for God's arrival. Preachers can take Malachi's image as it stands; ancient technology can still singe modern ears.

On the other hand, the local context may benefit from an image closer to home for twenty-first century listeners. Finding modern analogues can be as simple as taking ten minutes to brainstorm. I sat down with Malachi 3 and made a list of modern items that have caustic connotations (see Table 5.1).

Any of the above images can convey Malachi's harsh tone with familiar items. If your context allows it, bringing those items into the pulpit will engage sight as well as hearing. When generating modern counterparts, one must not be satisfied with the first few ideas. In the list above my preference would probably be chemotherapy, both for its frightening implications and for its goal of life and health. But I needed to generate the whole list to push myself to be creative.

Strategy 8.2 Use Images Micro and Macro

Once preachers have settled on a sermonic image, they need to determine how much time and attention to devote to it in the sermon. Will it be a "micro-image," mentioned in passing, or a "macro-image," giving shape and flavor to the entire sermon?

Haggai, for instance, uses a micro-image in pointing out how Israel's hard work results only in poverty. He says that "he who earns wages does so to put them into a bag with holes" (Hag 1:6). In just a few words Haggai captures the futility of fruitless labor. Then he moves on.

Preachers can use brief images like these to great effect. A passing word picture takes effort in the study but virtually no time in the pulpit, and punches above its weight. Sermons on Haggai 1 can talk about finding holes in our pockets or balance sheets where expenses outstrip income. No need to dwell on the image: listeners who have felt the pinch of debt will instantly connect with the words.

On the other hand, preachers can develop "macro-images" that shape and color the whole sermon. For example, Joel uses imagery from a present disaster (locusts) to depict a coming foreign invasion that spells the end for Israel. Locusts are not a major problem in my local economy. However, some contemporary disasters, seen with the eyes of faith, portend the day of the Lord. For example, as I write this chapter in 2021, an overturned cargo ship, the *Golden Ray*, is stranded in a shipping channel off the coast of Georgia where I live. Oil and gas have been leaking from the wreckage and showing up in marshes and beaches. Recently the ship caught fire during efforts to cut it up and remove it, and fuel, oil, and thousands of cars inside the ship caught fire. The conflagration was immense and the toll on our shores has yet to be calculated. On the front page of the paper the following morning was a photo of a man in a red bathing suit, hat, and sandals, fishing off the local pier, a quarter mile from the wreck, while the flames and smoke filled the sky behind him. In Joel 2 the Day of the Lord looks like locusts-turned-invaders; today it might be pictured as an inferno of toxic chemicals whose ashes pour into the waters we eat from.

Life cut off, natural beauty destroyed, seas poisoned, the sun darkened, and on the edge of disaster people blithely pulling fish from the water for supper. The *Golden Ray* foreshadows the coming day.

This "macro-image" is rich and powerful enough to drive the sermon. The sermon introduction can start here and move into Joel, while returning often to the oblivious fisherman and the towering flames.

Most prophetic imagery is flexible enough to allow preachers to decide how extensively the image will feature in the sermon. For instance, Isa 11:6–7 shows readers what the kingdom of Jesse's offspring will be like:

> The wolf shall dwell with the lamb,
> and the leopard shall lie down with the young goat,
> and the calf and the lion and the fattened calf together;
> and a little child shall lead them.
> The cow and the bear shall graze;
> their young shall lie down together;
> and the lion shall eat straw like the ox.

Isaiah predicts a time when even natural forces of aggression inherent in the prey/predator relationships will be altered. The images comprise an implicit *a fortiori* argument: if even natural aggression will be quelled, how much more will sinful violence and unjust predation cease!

A sermon depicting the culmination of Christ's kingdom could use these images in passing or put them on center stage. Some preachers will choose to walk their congregation through the entire oracle in 11:1–9, giving equal time to the restoration of the Davidic monarchy (v. 1), the power of the Spirit resting on the king (v. 2), the actions of the king (vv. 3–5), and the glory of the kingdom (vv. 6–9). The images of animals in harmony would form the first half of the last section and take up just a minute or two of exposition.

However, others will find Isaiah's image so compelling that they will let it drive the sermon. Preachers will use stories of cats and dogs that grow up together or of zoo animals that, left without a need to hunt, find companionship across species lines. The Dream-Works movie *Madagascar* comes to mind, where Alex the Lion and Marty the Zebra are best friends in the zoo, but in the wild as Alex grows hungry his natural instincts kick in and he becomes a predator.[13] In movies and in life, the only reason that predator and prey can get along is because of human interference: a person controls their environment, removing the need for violence. Isaiah's image also applies to other forms of aggression based on scarcity: competition for jobs, vying for the affection of a lover, going to war for land and resources. But a King is coming, a Spirit-filled Son of Man, whose rule will usher in such abundance that aggression and oppression will be a thing of the past. Lions and lambs will recline together, bellies full, drowsing in the sun. The image from Isaiah can function as a gateway into the sermon as well as a controlling metaphor. Preachers can lodge it in listener's minds as a shorthand for all that Christ's reign promises in the world.

A caution about choosing and using images in sermons: do not confuse the prominence of an image with its level of detail. The prophets were masters at "thin" imagery (i.e., very few details) that worked by their thinness, forcing readers to fill in the gaps. Much like Alfred Hitchcock films where what is *not* shown is what truly terrifies—who can forget the shower scene in *Psycho*?—some prophetic images loom large but indistinct, leaving much to the imagination.

For instance, one of Isaiah's favorite word pictures is a flag on a hill.[14] The object itself is simply a piece of cloth on a pole, used to communicate at a distance. But in Isaiah's hands it becomes an icon, appearing in different guises to make profound theological points. Isaiah says that Yahweh can use it to summon nations to attack Jerusalem (5:26) or to bring Israel back from exile (49:22; 62:10). He can signal for the Medes to invade Babylon (13:2) or for the nations to watch the ruin of Cush (18:3). Yahweh is master of all nations, summoning them from and sending them to the ends of the earth.

---

13 Caution: because the movie is an animated comedy, preachers need to ask whether they can make it work with the elevated tone of Isaiah 11.
14 Heb נֵס, a flag, signal, or sail.

Yet Isaiah gives this symbol a surprising twist when he states that *Israel itself* is the signal he will use. In Isa 30:17 the prophet predicts, "A thousand shall flee at the threat of one; at the threat of five you shall flee, till you are left like a flagstaff on the top of a mountain, like a signal on a hill." God will abandon Israel, and her isolation will position her as a signal to the nations to invade. She herself will be the invitation to the predators! Similarly, he says later that the root of Jesse (the coming Davidic monarch) will "stand as a signal for the people—of him shall the nations inquire, and his resting place shall be glorious" (11:10). Now the King stands as Yahweh's signal, the one who summons Israel to return from exile, who draws the nations to Jerusalem in submission.

Isaiah never gives details about the signal; description is not what renders the image so powerful. Rather, the repetition and variation scattered throughout render the signal an evocative device.

Strategy 8.3 Imagistic Language

Imagery in a sermon can be just as effective in the background as the foreground. That is, rather than crafting illustrations or extended metaphors to hold up before the congregation, preachers can instead intentionally choose vivid, pictorial words and phrases that weave images into the fabric of their speech.[15] This is a subtle use of images in sermons, but it can be just as effective as overt illustrations because of the emotional tone that our words set. The following are three methods we can use to render our vocabulary more imagistic.

The simplest method is to develop key phrases and sprinkle them liberally throughout the sermon.[16] Jeremiah, for example, complains that brazen Israel "did not know how to blush" (6:15; 8:12), and speaks again and again of the grievous or incurable wound (10:19; 14:7; 15:18; 30:12) of his people that has been "healed lightly" (6:14; 8:11) by false prophets. Sermons on Jeremiah can repeat

---

15 See also Langley, *How to Preach the Psalms*, 19–21, for what he calls "speaking in pictures."

16 Black preaching has always set a high bar for the church in terms of crafting and repeating powerful phrases. See Henry Mitchell, *Black Preaching: The Recovery of a Powerful Art* (Abingdon Press, 1990), 76–99.

these exact phrases or update them ("band-aids on bullet wounds," for example) and make them a sort of refrain for the sermon. Similarly, R.G. Lee's sermon "Payday Someday" recounts Elijah's oracle against King Ahab and Jezebel over the murder of Naboth and the theft of his vineyard (1 Kgs 21). The haunting phrase sticks in listener's minds, forcing us to contemplate the "payday" that God has in store for those who disregard his will.[17]

Secondly, preachers can craft the general vocabulary and style of the sermon to match the image. In Isa 55:10–11 the prophet compares Yahweh's words to rain. Rather than simply explaining Isaiah's simile or amplifying the image with facts about annual rainfall, a preacher could subtly evoke the image with his or her general vocabulary by using synonyms for "rain." We could talk about God *thundering* from heaven, *showering* us with grace, *drizzling* us with kindness, and *watering* his church. We can describe people who hear from God as *soaked* in his truth, or even *waterlogged*, *glistening* with dew, *saturated* with love and mercy. Contrast the parched, desiccated, dusty lives of those who will not hear. Sermons do not always have to use weighty illustrations that overwhelm or dominate; we can sprinkle in carefully chosen, imagistic speech instead.

Finally, consider using synecdoche: the part for the whole or the whole for the part. When Isaiah tells his people, "You shall be eaten by the sword" (Isa 1:20) the word "sword" stands in for "soldiers wielding swords." But how much more vivid and striking to be eaten by a sword! We can work on developing the same kinds of phrases. Instead of generic phrases about "medical diagnoses or chronic illness," we can talk about "that blue plastic chair in the doctor's waiting room." Instead of "financial distress" we can mention the "bank statement you do not want to open." Wedding photos for marriages, old baby shoes for treasured memories of our kids; pink slips, sprung boots, the bottom of a bottle, that new car smell, tear stains on a pillow, warm hugs, bloodshot eyes, calloused hands. A little forethought in sermon language can evoke powerful feelings in just a few words.

---

17 R. G. Lee, "Payday Someday," https://www.youtube.com/watch?v=0mstq4QTyrQ.

Two Examples: Joel 1 and Isaiah 6

Let us see some imagery in action. The following two sermons show how powerful images can be, whether ancient or modern, large or small.

First, Muboso Zamchiya preached from Joel 1 on God's wrath and our repentance.[18] Although Zamchiya begins in the modern world, his most powerful imagery comes straight off the page of Joel's oracle.

He uses micro-images powerfully by rattling off lists of items. For instance, when canvassing the devastation caused by a locust invasion, he says, "[The market] should be full of grain and wine and oil and wheat and barley and figs and pomegranates and palm and apples and meat and milk and honey and wool. But the market is empty." All Zamchiya does here is compile and list the items that Joel relates. But by pushing them together and quickly rattling them off, we hear the abundance that should be there, contrasted with the emptiness of the market stalls in Israel. This micro-image briefly and powerfully summarizes, letting us see the devastation.

Zamchiya's macro-image in the sermon is a horrifying close-up on locusts. Here is an excerpt, quoted at length to show what a powerful effect a good macro-image can have:

> Locusts are the dark side of grasshoppers.... Unlike other herbivore insects, locusts have an unrestricted diet. Anything that grows out the ground is literally game for them. Rather than bite their food like some other insects, locusts eat by cutting through the vegetation in small chunks with their mandibles and then chewing through it with their jaws.... Serotonin in the brains of these insects triggers astonishing changes.... They develop a strong affinity for each other and converge in very large proximate groups. When together in such close contact, ... higher levels of serotonin will cause the locusts to eat much more, to breed abundantly and even to change color. This

---

18 Muboso Zamchiya, "Repent (Joel 1)," Anacostia River Church, 2020, https://soundcloud.com/archurch/worship-in-preaching-the-message-of-joel-repent.

> phase of their existence is known as swarming. These swarming locusts can number in the billions of insects, spread out over hundreds or thousands of kilometers.... They eat absolutely everything.... As they move together these cutting, swarming, hopping locusts are like a rolling fireball of consumption....
>
> Given their large numbers, many of them actually die along the way. Their millions of carcasses emit a vulgar, horrible stench. Their cadavers attract rats and vultures and flies and other disease-transmitting creatures. In this way, locusts and their corpses can cause the contamination of water sources, the drying up of grasslands, the wilting of both wild and horticultural vegetation, the equivalent of drought conditions across the land. All sorts of airborne, waterborne, food-related and infectious diseases can occur with a viciousness that can bring a human community down to its knees.

His chilling description brings out the terrifying devastation inherent in Joel's oracle and shows the power of imagery deployed in the service of the prophetic word.

Consider another example, this one from Bryan Loritts on Isaiah 6:1–8.[19] Although he gives attention to Yahweh's glorious appearance in the passage, Loritts chooses to lean on mostly updated imagery for the sermon. For instance, instead of trying to get listeners to sympathize with the death of King Uzziah and the resulting social upheaval, he tells a story of traveling on a plane when one of its engines failed. In this macro-image, Loritts conjures fear and panic using a images that allows us to be there with him: a flight on a 747 from Atlanta to L.A., looking forward to renting a car and going down La Cienega Avenue to the Grand Lux restaurant to eat crispy caramel chicken. At 7,000 feet the left engine blows. Smoke, fire, screens on the planes blank, flight attendants with "I've never seen this before" written on their faces. The plane no longer climbing, people grabbing hands and praying. A woman takes a Sharpie marker and writes her social security number on her arm, so her

---

19 Bryan Loritts, "2020: The Year We Must Never Forget," One Community Church, January 4, 2021, The Bryan Loritts Podcast.

body can be identified. We are in the plane with him and can feel the shocking disappearance of certainty and safety. This is what it felt like for King Uzziah to die.

The sermon abounds with micro-images, too, such as his 19-year-old son leaving home, and his barber who also cuts Zion Williamson's hair. Loritts uses both extended and brief imagery to match the fear, pain, and splendor of Isaiah's vision.

Additionally, his language is sown with carefully crafted phrases, giving us brief flashes of insight in just a handful of words. He says, "In life there are no wasted experiences. You can learn just as much from your tragedies as you do your triumphs. You can learn as much from the mountaintop as you do down in the valley.... God speaks to us through pain; God shouts to us through suffering.... How do I know that I can trust God? God says, 'Google me.' Look at my credentials.'" Loritts deploys images—extended, brief, and embedded in his language—that helps listeners feel what Isaiah evoked in his own words.

If we as preachers want to touch hearts and minds the way the prophets did, we can take our cue from the prophets and work hard at crafting and deploying images.

Strategy 8.4 Think Carefully About Technology

Most images in our society live on screens. Finding, creating, or reproducing images of the highest quality is child's play for anyone with a phone or tablet. Preachers can quickly find photos or videos of anything imaginable for use in a sermon. Should we?

For some preachers, the congregation may be so unused to screens in worship that the distraction of the medium would outweigh the benefit of the image. But even in churches where screens are a normal part of Sunday mornings, preachers should run a cost-benefit analysis on using an image. A video can lend vividness to an object or place or concept; showing a film clip can be engaging and entertaining. On the other hand, screen usage costs: it can hijack attention; it moves listeners into an experience (screen watching) that encourages passive consumption; and preachers may find it impossible to follow up a 30-second movie clip that cost $3 million to make, stars an Oscar-winning actress, and uses the latest CGI.[20] After that, we can be nothing but a letdown.

In my own preaching I find that still photos add value without overshadowing the rest of the sermon. Maps of the relevant areas or photos of artifacts like ancient pagan shrines can connect listeners to the text without distraction. Yet, although I use a screen often to display words and pictures, I almost never use video clips.

Instead, low tech visual aids can bring many of the benefits of screens without the costs. Physical objects can underscore ideas without taking church to the movies. For instance, I preached on Isaiah 1 a few years ago, where the prophet asks, "Though your sins are like scarlet, will they be as white as snow? Though they are red like crimson, will they become like wool?"[21] In other words, God asks, do they really think these stains will disappear so easily? I had a large glass bowl of water in the front of the church, and a red piece of cloth. After reading the verse I told the church to watch the cloth closely as I dipped it into the bowl and whisked it around. The moment felt like a magic show as the congregation waited to see what chemical trick I had prepared to turn the red cloth white. The cloth stayed red, of course, and the anticlimax that followed this head-fake helped our people to identify with the wishful thinking of Israelites. Much like we can fool ourselves into believing a magic trick, God's people believed he would wipe out their sins without their becoming "willing and obedient" (Isa 1:19).

One will find opportunities for low tech visual aids in passages like Jeremiah's ruined loincloth (Jer 13:1–11), his broken flask

---

20 For a dated but devastating critique of screens in our society, see Neil Postman, *Amusing Ourselves to Death*, 20th anniv. ed. (Penguin, 2006).

21 Most English versions render this verse as a declaration from God that our sins *will be* white as snow. Along with some OT scholars I find this verse makes more sense in context as an unmarked interrogative (question) in Hebrew, or a sarcastic comment or a conditional offer. The following verse presents Israel with a stark choice: repent or be destroyed. The point of verse 18 is to ask Israel to reason whether they can wipe away their sins and expect no judgment without repentance. They are stained; they must turn and change their ways. For the complexities of this text from those who opt for conclusions as above, see John T. Willis, "On the Interpretation of Isaiah 1:18," *JSOT* 25 (1983), 35–54, and Robert Duncan Culver, "Isaiah 1:18—Declaration, Exclamation, or Interrogation?" *JETS* 12 (1969), 133–141.

(19:1–13), and his burned scroll (36:1–32). Of course, smells and sounds are just as accessible as sights. I have played sounds of a lion's roar when preaching from Amos 1, and fried bacon during a service, updating Jesus' proclamation that "the fields are white for the harvest" (John 4:35). I have known preachers to bake bread, build wooden crosses, and even light campfires. As long as the image doesn't "jump the shark" into the realm of gimmicks or showmanship, low tech objects can powerfully undergird prophetic words.

Conclusion

Images allow the message to transcend words and open another channel in the human mind. They keep our sermons out of the theological stratosphere and anchored to the ground of everyday life. They take work, but by following the lead of the prophets, we can do more than tell them about God and His kingdom. We can show them.

For Further Study

Anderson, Kenton C. "In the Eye of the Hearer: Visuals that Support Rather than Distract from the Word." In Haddon Robinson and Craig Larson, *The Art and Craft of Biblical Preaching*. Zondervan, 2005. 607–609.

Jonker, Peter. *Preaching in Pictures: Using Images for Sermons that Connect*. Abingdon, 2015.

Mitchell, Henry H. *Black Preaching: The Recovery of a Powerful Art*. Abingdon, 1990. Pages 76–99.

Postman, Neil. *Amusing Ourselves to Death*. 20th anniv. ed. Penguin Books, 2005.

Talk about It

What do you think about this chapter's advice for video clips and other electronic images? What would the culture of your local context permit? What is your view on using electronic visuals in preaching?

Dig Deeper

Read Malachi's image of a book of remembrance in Mal 3:16–18. If you were going to preach a sermon on this passage, how extensively would you use that image? Could you build an entire sermon on it?

Practice

Ezekiel 9 contains a vision of a man who has a "writing case," who is instructed to pass through Jerusalem and "put a mark on the foreheads of the men who sigh and groan over all the abominations that are committed in it" (v. 4). How might you update an image like this? List ten contemporary equivalents for putting written marks on people to distinguish them.

6

Emotion

> *Who will deny that true religion consists, in a great measure, in vigorous and lively actings of the inclination and will of the soul, or the fervent exercises of the heart? That religion which God requires, and will accept, does not consist in weak, dull, and lifeless wishes, raising us but a little above a state of indifference. God, in his word, greatly insists upon it, that we be in good earnest, fervent in spirit and our hearts vigorously engaged in religion.*
>
> Jonathan Edwards[1]

DURING THE FIRST GREAT AWAKENING in America there was fierce debate about what role, if any, emotions play in religion. Edwards, quoted above, makes his view clear. I find it hard to disagree, especially when my Bible is open to the OT Prophets. There readers see emotion on full display, as Yahweh burns with anger or grows warm with compassion. Readers also see the prophets overcome with grief, exasperation, or joy. When they delivered the word of God to the people of God, the experience was often intensely emotional.

In this chapter we examine the emotion of prophetic texts and draw conclusions for preaching.

---

1 Jonathan Edwards, *The Works of Jonathan Edwards*, vol. 2, ed. John E. Smith (Yale University Press, 2009), 99.

Emotion in the Prophets

Broadly speaking, prophets deal in the emotional currencies of "woe" and "weal": that is, they either warn the wayward of coming destruction or comfort the downcast with promises of future deliverance. This is in keeping with their function as covenant enforcers, where the covenant consequences have the dual nature of blessings and curses.[2]

Woe and weal, warning and comfort, are emotional concepts. All that a human being would feel in the face of coming disaster, the Prophets exhibit: anxiety, fear, anger, grief, despair. Micah's reaction to coming judgment is typical of the Prophets:

> For this I will lament and wail;
> I will go stripped and naked;
> I will make lamentation like the jackals,
> and mourning like the ostriches.
> For her wound is incurable,
> and it has come to Judah;
> it has reached to the gate of my people,
> to Jerusalem. (Mic 1:8–9)

Jeremiah weeps (Jer 9:1); Isaiah refuses to be comforted (Isa 22:4). The prophets care deeply about Israel and Judah, and when judgment falls, they cannot stand aloof. Their hearts cry out.

Likewise, when God speaks words of grace and restoration, they can hardly contain themselves. Zechariah 9 depicts the coming of a Davidic king and the appearance of God at the restoration of Israel in a passage bursting with triumph and joy. Those who doubt that Prophets are emotional are welcome try to read his words in a flat, calm tone:

> Rejoice greatly, O daughter of Zion! Shout aloud, O daughter of Jerusalem! ... Return to your stronghold, O prisoners of hope; today I declare that I will restore to you double.... I will stir up your sons, O Zion, against your sons, O Greece, and wield you

---
2 See ch. 2.

like a warrior's sword.... The LORD of hosts will protect them, and they shall devour, and tread down the sling stones, and they shall drink and roar as if drunk with wine, and be full like a bowl, drenched like the corners of the altar. On that day the LORD their God will save them, as the flock of his people; for like the jewels of a crown they shall shine on his land. For how great is his goodness, and how great his beauty! (Zech 9:9–17)

Zechariah's words fairly shout: they should be read in a joyful roar.

Of course, sorrow and joy do not exhaust the prophetic emotional repertoire. Readers also find outrage, jealousy, disgust, and relief in their repertoire. The book of Jonah, for instance, ends on a decided note of *schadenfreude* (pleasure at another's trouble), as the narrator shows Jonah in the ridiculous position of being angry over a vine yet apathetic about a great city (Jonah 4). Isaiah 1:2–20 is a litany of exasperation with Judah and Jerusalem. Habakkuk's words in chapter 3 reflect a deep conflict between the horror coming on Judah and his trust in Yahweh's sovereign goodness.

Consider how emotions progress through Zephaniah from low to high (see Figure 6.1). Chapter 1 is all woe, as the prophet predicts the end of Jerusalem in a cataclysmic conflagration. Then Zephaniah shifts gears, after a brief appeal (2:1–3), to oracles against the Philistines, Moabites, Cushites, and Philistines, as well as Judah (2:4–3:8). The tone of the text is still gloom and doom, but judgment now falls on other nations because of their wickedness. (Recall the discussion in chapter 2, where oracles against foreign nations are often intended as comfort for Israel.) Finally,

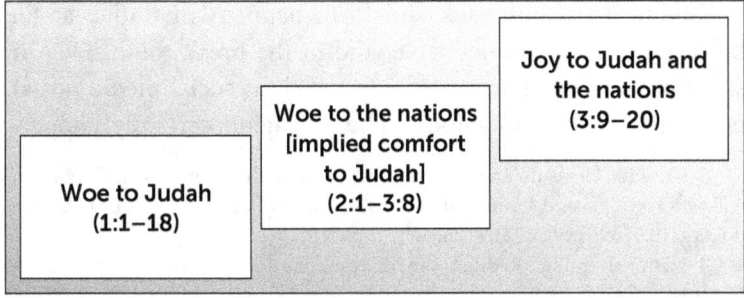

Figure 6.1: The Emotional Progress of Zephaniah

in 3:9–20 the prophet moves into reassurance and even joy: the conversion of the nations, the removal of the proud, the safety and humility of the remnant, and Yahweh's absolute delight in his people. Zephaniah takes readers on an emotional journey from the depths to the heights.

The prophets' ministry was deeply emotional: they experienced emotion, they expressed emotion in their oracles, and in so doing they evoked emotion in their audience.

Preaching with Emotion

When it comes to emotion, preachers do the same as prophets: they experience emotion as they study and preach, they express those emotions (carefully) in the pulpit and by doing so, enable hearers to feel the same things. Yet how do those actions work in concert? How do emotions travel from one person to another?

Emotional Contagion and Preaching

"Emotional contagion" describes the dynamic whereby "humans tend to align with the emotional states they perceive during interactions."[3] When people see someone smile, their own faces will begin to stretch into an involuntary smile in a mirroring gesture. But emotional contagion means more than expression: people also start to *feel* the same happiness that they perceive in others.[4] I live in the deep South, and when a person understands someone so well that he starts to feel what the other feels, he simply says, "I smell what you're stepping in."

Passing emotions back and forth happens in traffic, at the bank, around the dinner table, and in the break room. Even in situations without non-verbal cues (such as social media posts), emotions can be contagious.[5] The contagion certainly happens

---

3 Caroline Herando and Efthymios Constantinides, "Emotional Contagion: A Brief Overview and Future Directions," *Frontiers in Psychology* 2021, https://doi.org/10.3389/fpsyg.2021.712606.

4 National Public Radio, "When Emotions Are Contagious," *Invisibilia* (podcast), July 21, 2019.

5 Herando and Constantinides, "Emotional Contagion."

in preaching. What preachers feel, express, and describe can spill over the pulpit and seep into the pews. The preacher's expression and depiction of emotion helps a congregation to feel the text and the sermon.

Emotional contagion is not just a contemporary phenomenon. Witness the emotional contagion implicit in an oracle from Jeremiah:

> Is there no balm in Gilead?
> Is there no physician there?
> Why then has the health of the daughter of my people
> not been restored?
> Oh that my head were waters,
> and my eyes a fountain of tears,
> that I might weep day and night
> for the slain of the daughter of my people!
> Oh that I had in the desert
> a travelers' lodging place,
> that I might leave my people
> and go away from them!
> For they are all adulterers,
> a company of treacherous men. (Jer 8:22–9:2)

First, we notice the tight link between Jeremiah's emotions and Yahweh's: in this passage, as in many prophetic oracles, the prophet's words and Yahweh's overlap and intermingle. Thus, the grief and repugnance at Judah's corruption and calamity flow back and forth between God and his spokesperson. As Jeremiah gives vent to his feelings, some of his hearers would likely absorb his rage and sadness. Emotions spill from the Lord to the prophet to his hearers (who have ears to hear).

Today, when preachers immerse themselves in this text, they too begin to taste the bitterness of seeing disobedience in God's people. The result is that the church can sense and share the emotions of the text, of the prophet, of the preacher, and of the Lord during the sermon. Preachers thus form a critical link in that emotional circuit, because unless they understand the emotion, experience it, and express it, they interrupt the current between God and his people.

Thus, if "hearing" the word of God in the full, biblical sense includes a deep whole-life engagement with the text, and if emotions are a critical portion of that, then part of a preacher's job is to assist congregations to feel the emotions inherent in or appropriate to the text at hand. They do that, like the prophets did, by first experiencing emotions themselves, and second by expressing them and evoking them in their hearers. To each of these we now turn.

Experiencing Emotion

We cannot give what we do not have. Preachers who try to conjure emotions in others while keeping aloof themselves are flirting with hypocrisy and placing themselves in spiritual danger. Instead, they must feel what the prophets felt.

Strategy 9.1 Practice Emotional Steeping

I use the term "emotional steeping" to describe the way that we can immerse ourselves in a prophetic oracle. Like a tea bag slowly leeches into the hot water around it, the emotion inherent in the biblical text can pass into us. But it does so slowly, and only under the right conditions.

The image of "steeping" helps me because I am an analytical person who would rather study Hebrew syntax or the history of Assyria than experience emotions. I am tempted to jot down observations about the emotional tone of a passage as one more exegetical data point and move on. But emotions do not work that way. I must sit patiently in the text until what the prophet felt begins to soak into me, too.

Emotional steeping is part of sermon preparation, especially in the Prophets. Here I offer three suggestions on how to immerse yourself in their emotional world.

First, understand that your pastoral calling includes emotional awareness and experience, and plan accordingly. Those of us in pastoral ministry know that our "job" calls for lifestyle commitments that go beyond office hours. We pray with people in the produce section; we are a frequent visitor at the hospital; we strive always to live holy lives; in our free time we read and listen to and watch media that deal with Jesus and the spiritual life; we carry the joy and the grief of our people wherever we go. What if we also knew that being a fully human pastoral presence required us to *feel* as much as to learn or pray or act?

We can adopt regular habits that put us in touch with our emotions. We can journal. We can read (good) poetry. We can visit art galleries. We can read books that grieve us.[6] We can watch documentaries that stir us up. We can put lament and joy on our playlists.[7] We can find ways to engage emotionally in worship, whether that means adjusting our role on Sundays to allow us to be fully present or holding mid-week worship when we are not preaching or even attending services at another church. We can also learn and practice the art of spiritual direction (which involves a lot of empathetic listening). What in your regular schedule encourages you to experience emotions? If you cannot come up with much, consider making some changes.[8]

Second, increase your understanding of how your cultural identity shapes your approach to emotions. Your racial and cultural heritage, your nationality, your regional identity, and the groups with which you affiliate all contribute to your own emotional identity. Some cultures embrace emotion and emotive expression. People find it normal to weep or laugh or rage—in healthy or unhealthy ways, but in other spaces such expressions are considered inappropriate or signs of weakness. In my own cultural mix (white American evangelical male in the South, plus smaller contexts like my

---

6 Books of this nature that have grieved me: Ronald J. Sider, *Rich Christians in an Age of Hunger*, new ed. (Thomas Nelson, 2005); Michael O. Emerson and Christian Smith, *Divided by Faith: Evangelical Religion and the Problem of Race in America* (Oxford, 2000); David F. Wells, *No Place for Truth: Or Whatever Happened to Evangelical Theology?* (Eerdmans, 1993).

7 One group that has stirred godly grief in me, and ministered to me in that grief, is Common Hymnal. See their albums *Unproduced* (November 2018) and *Praise and Protest* (January 2021).

8 For additional guidance, see Kenneth Langley, *How to Preach the* Psalms (Fontes, 2021), 111-131.

family and church background) expressions like laughter or hugs are acceptable but showing grief or anger or fear are not. Knowing that helps me not to "trust my gut" when I shy away from those emotions, but instead to lean into them. Understanding your own background and its impact on your emotional life can be a helpful step in finding a way into a godly emotional life.

Third, find ways that work for you to steep in specific prophetic oracles. For example, practice pinpointing the prophet's emotions in an oracle. An emotional wheel can be a great tool because it starts with broad categories like "happy" or "angry" and refines them to specific emotions like "confident" or "jealous."[9] Try emotional readings of the passage (alone or in groups) that express out loud what is inherent in the oracle, or get help in "feed forward" sessions where you share some insight into the oracle and let others express what they feel and why. Their emotions can jumpstart your own.

In my own sermon preparation process, I always take a prayer walk after I finish exegesis and before I start thinking through contemporary application. That unhurried time (without a notebook or a screen) helps me to slow down and wonder, in God's presence, what Isaiah saw and felt, what his people did, what I feel, and what my people will feel when they hear his words.[10]

Whatever practices work for you, devote yourself to them with patience. Steep.

Strategy 9.2 Remember Who Will Drink the Tea

We steep in the emotions of a passage so that we can serve Christ's church. Our emotional experiences and expressions are for them. This simple reminder can prevent two mistakes.

First, we do not serve ancient Israel. Therefore, wise preachers will ask whether every emotion that the prophet felt or wanted his people to feel is theologically appropriate for the church. As chapter 2 argued, historical and theological differences between then and now will affect our interpretation and preaching. When

---

9 See, for instance, https://feelingswheel.com.
10 I started this practice on the advice of Kent Edwards. See his *Deep Preaching: Creating Sermons that Go Beyond the Superficial* (B&H, 2009).

prophets predict disaster that has already come on Israel or Judah, those consequences may have already taken place from our own point of view, and therefore preachers should offer the church the reassuring faithfulness of God rather than an ominous warning of judgment. Likewise, promises of restoration may not directly apply to the church. When Haggai predicts that "the latter glory of this house shall be greater than the former" (2:9), preachers must think through what that oracle says to the church before taking up an emotional stance for the sermon.

Second, we do not serve ourselves. The pulpit is not the place to vent feelings for our own benefit; the pulpit is a place where our words, thoughts, energy, and feelings serve the goal of bringing the word of the gospel to bear in our congregations. Consequently, wise preachers will not only seek to feel appropriate emotions, but to express emotions in ways that serve the church.[11] Paul's emotions were often on display to his churches (Rom 9:1–3; 1 Cor 11:17–22; most of 2 Corinthians; Gal 5:12; Phil 4; 1 Thess 2:7; 2 Tim 1:3–7). Yet those displays served pastoral goals. We must follow suit by placing our emotions in the service of the gospel in the same way we place our intellect, our time, and our treasure.

For instance, consider an oracle where the prophet is angry. Amos castigates the luxurious apathy of the rich with angry words: "Woe to those who are at ease in Zion.... Woe to those who lie on beds of ivory ... who sing idle songs to the sound of the harp ... who drink wine in bowls ... but are not grieved over the ruin of Joseph!" (6:1–7). The oracle is a heated warning from the prophet, depicting luxury and self-indulgence in a time of imminent moral and spiritual disaster. When we steep in this passage, we too will feel anger, not just at the prophet's countrymen but at our own.

Anger in the pulpit can be appropriate and helpful.[12] In fact, to preach this oracle without anger seems unfaithful to the text.

---

11 Preachers do need safe environments to express unvarnished emotion. A spiritual director, a godly therapist, or an elder board may be appropriate; the pulpit is not.

12 If this statement strikes us as dangerous, perhaps a cultural bias operates in you. After all, the Black church has shown that anger can make for powerful preaching in the service of the gospel. See the previous section for cultural self-examination.

But preachers must do more than absorb and regurgitate Amos's emotions. Blasting away at our congregations for their luxurious habits from a lofty moral perch is not a theologically informed use of emotion. Anger, like all pulpit passions, must serve to build up the church.

One way we can do that is to notice not just prophetic emotion but prophetic rhetoric: how does the prophet's emotion impact his hearers? What is its purpose? In this example, Amos's anger humbles his listeners, comforts those oppressed by the wealthy, and summons people to repentance. We can do likewise. As we "preach angry," we can humble our congregations *by placing ourselves first* under the prophet's rebuke, showing them how to feel convicted. In other words, we can be angry with ourselves first. We can also use our anger to comfort the oppressed in our midst, assuring them that God sees and will rectify injustice. Finally, we can set our anger in a gospel context, inviting people to come home to a Father who waits to receive them. "Those whom I love, I reprove and discipline" (Rev 3:19). Neither in the Prophets nor in the pulpit does anger mean flat condemnation.

Emotional steeping is essential for accurate and effective preaching. Only we absorb prophetic emotions carefully, and with our own people in mind, so that those emotions will build them up, not tear them down (2 Cor 13:10).

Strategy 9.3 Learn to Drink Tea

What if you just never drink tea? In attempting to preach from the Prophets, preachers may find that they are unable to experience much genuine emotion at all. The mind is engaged while the heart sits idle. Such situations are deep waters and deserve far more space (and expertise) than is available here. But as a fellow preacher and a brother in the Lord, may I suggest that you pay close attention to that lack of emotion? It indicates more than a need for enhanced homiletical technique. It may be that you are disconnected from your flock and unable to empathize with their pain. Perhaps the Lord is kindly urging you to leave the study and be with your people in their daily ups and downs. Or it may be that you have little emotion left to give at all. Weekly Sabbaths, time off, regular sleep, and private counseling are essential parts of a vital pastorate.[13] The Lord may be inviting you to some significant changes to bring healing into your life, and through you to your congregation. Learn to drink the tea.

Expressing and Evoking Emotion

If preachers burn with zeal, weep with grief, and rejoice in hope, how can they effectively convey those emotions in ways that invite people to feel as they do? Note that this discussion is about emotions, not *emotionalism*. Preachers do not tug on heartstrings disingenuously. "We refuse to practice cunning or to tamper with God's word, but by the open statement of the truth we would commend ourselves to everyone's conscience in the sight of God" (2 Cor 4:2). But given that we want to express and evoke biblically appropriate emotion, the following are ways that we can do so.

Strategy 10.1 Watch What You Say

Preachers' words can express and evoke emotion by choosing their words with care (see Figure 6.2).

For instance, sometimes preachers can simply state their own emotions and invite the congregation to join in. In a sermon on the messianic predictions in Isaiah 9, Eric Mason gives direct expression and invitation a central place throughout the sermon, interrupting his explanation with exclamation:

> This is dope, y'all.... That's God, y'all, you should clap where you're sitting.... I hope y'all are having as much fun as I am.... I don't know about y'all, but I'm getting happy.... I'm trying not to run off the stage when I break this down! ... Y'all don't know when to SHOUT![14]

---

[13] See, among others, Peter Scazzero, *Emotionally Healthy Spirituality*, updated ed. (Zondervan, 2017); Eugene Peterson, *The Contemplative Pastor: Returning to the Art of Spiritual Direction* (Eerdmans, 1993).

[14] This sermon, despite the emotional invitation, is heavily loaded with

> **Watch What You Say:**
> - Direct invitation to emotion
> - Use of the prophet's imagery
> - Updated emotional imagery
> - Emotional vocabulary

Figure 6.2: How to Express and Evoke Emotion

The congregation can see and experience Mason's emotions, and he expects that they too will share in the joy of Christ's advent. While sometimes direct appeal can slip into scolding, judicious use can give the congregation permission and encouragement to feel.

Less direct methods of expression can be even more effective. Preachers can choose specific images and phrases from an oracle to bear the emotional weight of sermon. For instance, Isaiah 16:11 says, "Therefore my inner parts moan like a lyre for Moab, and my inmost self for Kir-hareseth [a city in Moab]." Isaiah literally says his intestines make the mournful sound of a small harp. Preachers can give a thoughtful, mournful exploration of this phrase. What is it like when we hear tragic news? We feel a vibration deep in our gut; we may moan softly, involuntarily. Our pain resonates inside our bodies. When the preachers' innards moan, it can be heard in the pew.

Or consider Amos's warning about the day of Yahweh (5:18–20):

18 Woe to you who desire the day of the LORD!
Why would you have the day of the LORD?
It is darkness, and not light,
19 as if a man fled from a lion,
and a bear met him,

---

systematic theological terms relating to the incarnation. The juxtaposition of intellect and emotion is what drives the sermon. Eric Mason, "Fresh Expectations," December 9, 2020, Epiphany Fellowship, https://www.youtube.com/watch?v=1QE_dtF1R0U.

> or went into the house and leaned his hand against the wall,
> and a serpent bit him.
> 20 Is not the day of the LORD darkness, and not light,
> and gloom with no brightness in it?

This image can be updated in a way that retains the emotional fervor of the oracle: I once asked listeners to picture a man soaked in gasoline, with an unlit cigarette in hand, yelling for someone to please give him a light. The pain and surprise generated by the prophet's images can draw us into the pain and surprise of getting exactly what we have asked for. It was a brief metaphor, but I tried to pack the same emotional content into a more modern image.

To give another example: Isaiah sings of non-Israelites who assume that, because of their ethnicity, "The LORD will surely separate me from his people," and of eunuchs who say, "Behold, I am a dry tree" (Isa 56:3). In Israelite culture, where the outsider status of foreigners and eunuchs was common knowledge, such images were sufficient. Not so for most contemporary churchgoers. Nonetheless, connecting people to feelings of abandonment, loneliness, and isolation from God will take you just a few minutes of thought. Who among us, after all, has not known the feeling of being an outsider in some way: suffering from a chronic illness, lacking financial resources, being an immigrant, being outcast because of one's race, spending time in foster care or caring for those who are, wrestling with mental illness? At one time or another most of us have felt cut off from people and God. We all know what it feels like to be a dry tree, and we can invite listeners into that space with us.

Finally, as chapter 3 noted, sermons can express and evoke emotion by a careful use of words. Just one example to bring this idea back to mind: In Malachi 1 Israel's unrighteous conduct combines with her worship to evoke Yahweh's disgust and outrage. God complains that the priests offer polluted food on the altar, giving God the blind, the lame, the throwaway animals. God's anger is conveyed in the form of an exasperated appeal: "Oh that there were one among you who would shut the doors, that you might not kindle fire on my altar in vain!" (Mal 1:10). Of course, Yahweh doesn't want worship to stop. The appeal to shut the doors reflects the depths of his anger and frustration.

I tried something similar in preaching from Mark 11:15–19/Isaiah 56:7/Jeremiah 7:11 (Jesus' temple cleansing with a focus on the prophetic citations). The exegetical idea of the passage was, "Jesus symbolically halted temple worship because of the inappropriate function it had assumed." Even if that idea is true to Mark's intent, it misses the emotion of what Jesus did and what the disciples experienced, as well as Jeremiah's excoriation of corrupt temple worship. To capture the disgust inherent in Mark and Jeremiah, I wrote a sermon with the big idea, "Just stop!" By making the preaching idea a terse imperative, I tried to imitate the emotional experience of those who were present when Jesus flipped tables and drove people out. We can phrase our words to pass on not only the ideas of the Prophets, but also the emotions.

Strategy 10.2 Watch How You Say It

We express emotion not just with our words but also with our voices. Anyone who has been in a tense conversation with an irate coworker, an offended spouse, or a surly teenager knows that bland words can bite deeply when spoken just so. The questions, "What did you do?" and "Where are you going?" can be neutral requests for information or thinly veiled accusations, depending on how they are said.

The same is true in sermons. The way preachers speak invites listeners into (or shuts them out of) the emotion of the text. Preachers can do all the exegesis and explanation they want on a text like Hosea 2:14–15, where Yahweh woos his faithless bride in the wilderness, but it will not be enough. Word studies on "allure" or an explanation of the Valley of Achor will not astonish hard hearts with the covenant love of Yahweh. They must experience the emotion of the oracle, where tender restoration surprises the guilty bride. Cold explanation not only fails to move God's people, but it also fails the Scriptures and the one who breathed them out. We must watch how we say it.

We can do that by paying attention to how we use our voices.

Most preachers have a default tone of voice and pace when they preach. Unless they take care, they will use that single voice all the time. The voice can be anything from a light conversational tone (entirely inappropriate for Hosea 2) to the well-known "preacher's voice" that some adopt in the pulpit. We also develop verbal tics in the way we speak. A friend of mine—a gifted and careful preacher—tends to state the last three words of every sentence with a slowed ... down ... pace. Each thought ends on the same ... emotional ... tone.[15] To break habits like these, we can pay close attention to our tone, our speed, our cadence, and our volume, and make sure that the sound of our voice matches the emotion of the text.[16]

Your congregation may have a culture that values emotional preaching, or you may minister in a church where such expression is frowned upon. Two bits of advice: First, think less on how loud or extreme your tone is than on how loud or extreme it may be *relative to your average*. In some pulpits a very slight increase in volume or change in pace will go a long way to conveying powerful emotion. Ashley Mathews preached a sermon on Isaiah 61:1-4 on the third Sunday in Advent. Her Anglican church context is not normally given to grand gestures or shouting, but she is still able to evoke emotion in a quiet, heartfelt tone. She says that this oracle is "A reminder to rejoice while we are still in the dark, while we are still waiting.... Tell them, God is still at work. God is still delivering, he is still healing, he is still restoring. His promises are still being worked out."[17] It was quite an emotional moment, though her voice was not raised at all. She turned her volume and speed down slightly, rather than up, and it was wonderfully effective.

---

15 To be fair: this same friend pointed out to me recently that I was developing a similar tic of ending important thoughts with the rhetorical question, "Right!?" He *was* right, and I've had to mend my verbal ways. Preachers must do the painful work of listening to their own recorded sermons (watching on video if possible) and soliciting feedback from honest folks—preferably other preachers—if they want to avoid these traps.

16 Haddon Robinson memorably talks about our "pitch, punch, progress, and pause." *Biblical Preaching: The Development and Delivery of Expository Messages*, 3rd ed, (Baker Academic, 2014) 161-163.

17 Ashley Mathews, "Isaiah 61:1-4," December 13, 2020, Trinity Anglican Church, https://podcast.atltrinity.org/episodes/isaiah-61-1-4-westside.

Second, with patience, you can shape the emotional culture of your congregation. That is, you can teach your congregations over time to accept more emotional expression in sermons. Start small, practice it regularly, and expand their horizons (and yours) over time.

Strategy 10.3 Watch Someone Else Say It

One of the best ways to learn to express emotion is to listen to and watch preachers who do it well. For instance, John Piper's preaching has a distinctive feel, not only because of his theological content but because of his "blood earnestness" about the realities of God and the gospel.[18] In a sermon on Isaiah 12, Piper outlines the dangers of spiritual dryness in the midst of ministry:

> One of the greatest dangers for missionaries, pastors, and Christians is drying up and dying. Losing all interest, losing all hope. Not having any care, any desire, and any joy in God or Christ or salvation or the church or the word anymore. It's just all blank. That's dangerous and scary when that starts to happen in a saint's life.[19]

These are serious words, and Piper delivers them in a serious tone. He almost moans them. His low pitch, his slow pace, and the heavy tread of his voice lend power and depth to his description of barrenness in the faith. I encourage you to listen to the sermon online to understand that *how* Piper speaks underscores *what* he says.

Similarly, Eric Mason's sermon on Isaiah 9 (cited above) offers another glimpse into how preachers use their voice. Mason's cadence builds at critical moments to support the emotion of the text. For instance, when expanding on Isaiah's description of the coming king as a "wonderful counselor," Mason argues that the

---

18 Piper borrows this phrase from John Mason. See John Piper, *The Supremacy of GOD in Preaching* (Baker, 2015), 47-63.

19 John Piper, "Persevering in God-Centered Missions," September 8, 2013, https://www.desiringgod.org/messages/perseverance-in-god-centered-missions.

word "counselor" here means "military strategist." He then says that Christ-followers need a military strategist to bring them through life's challenges:

> If you've got COVID right now, he can bring you through it. If you lost somebody to COVID, he can bring you through it. If you're dealing with spiritual warfare, he can bring you through it. If you're dealing with financial challenges, he can bring you through it. If you're dealing with suicidal thoughts, he can bring you through it. Whatever you're going through the counselor can give you a military strategy.... And if you don't think the devil is in your house trying to press on your mind, trying to press on your heart, trying to make you think crazy thoughts, ... trying to make you think about jumping off bridges, about taking a bunch of pills ... that's the enemy and you need a wonderful counselor to give you some military strategic formats on how to fight the enemy.[20]

Notice how his parallel phrasing builds, and how the escalating energy invites listeners to feel the grandness of God's promised King. Watching preachers like Piper and Mason can calibrate our own emotional expression.

Strategy 10.4 Watch What You Do While You Say It

People express and evoke emotion with their bodies as well as their voices. We smile or grimace; we slump or puff out our chests; we lean in or draw back; we talk with our hands. Often all that is needed to help listeners catch hold of a preacher's emotion is an intentional use of the body. Preachers rarely think about their posture or how closely they stand to the congregants, or whether and how they use a pulpit, a stool, or a table.[21] They should. Deliberate postures and positions (practiced enough that they do not feel

---

20 Mason, "Fresh Expectations."
21 See Jeffrey D. Arthurs, *Devote Yourself to the Public Reading of Scripture: The Transforming Power of the Well-Spoken Word* (Kregel, 2012), 79–87, 111. The book includes a DVD that fills in the written instruction with effective models.

mechanical) convey emotion. Thinking about gestures is also worth a preacher's time. Is there a key gesture that might go along with the sermon's central idea and its associated emotion? Raised arms, a closed fist, hands open in a pleading position? Facial expressions can also be deliberate without being artificial. For instance, remembering to smile during the introduction not only conveys warmth, but also helps the preacher feel the warmth necessary for pastoral engagement.

Preachers who were raised with emotionless or emotionally monotone preaching will have to work hard to catch up. Try watching a reality show where people feel actual stress, anger or surprise, or a well-made drama in which great actors express emotion.[22] Notice what they do, and what that does to you. Go and do likewise.

Strategy 10.5 Watch This

Preachers can also structure the sermon or the service to underscore the emotion of the prophetic oracle. For example, first-person sermons can help congregants to feel the emotion of the text by eliminating the emotional middleman.[23] Instead of emotions passing from the ancient world through a pastor to a church, they can pass directly from the prophet (or a contemporary of the prophet) embodied in the pastor to the church. First-person sermons arise most naturally out of a narrative text like Jonah or autobiographical passages in Jeremiah. But they do not have to be restricted to narrative texts. For instance, preachers could deliver the book of Obadiah as a first-person sermon. Preaching as "Obadiah" could help the audience to feel the grief of what it was like to see Jerusalem attacked, with Edom (a nation related to Israel through Esau, Jacob's twin brother) gleefully gloating on the sidelines. Obadiah's helpless rage could pass directly to hearers.

Second, think about how the entire service can foster appropriate emotions of joy, grief, or anger. Music, Scripture readings,

---

22 A good place to start: *Marriage Story*, directed by Noah Baumbach (Netflix, 2019).

23 See J. Kent Edwards, *Effective First-Person Biblical Preaching: The Steps from Text to Narrative to Sermon* (Zondervan, 2005).

prayers, and moments of reflection can reinforce emotional tone.[24] I once preached a sermon on Isaiah 6 in a church setting where we had a talented band with drums, keys, bass, and guitar. The band and I worked together to try to help the church feel the emotional burden of the passage: the awful weight of Yahweh's holiness. Instead of finishing the music before the sermon, the band continued to play a progression quietly as I narrated Isaiah's encounter with Yahweh in the temple. They increased slowly in volume and energy, and I spoke louder and faster as Yahweh appeared, Isaiah collapsed, and the angel came flying with a burning coal. When we reached the moment where the coal touched Isaiah's lips and his sin was atoned for, the band hit a crescendo and came to a sudden stop, and the church went from overwhelming sound to silence. The music simulated the unbearable pressure of holiness, relieved by God's atoning work. I never could have generated the intensity of that moment without their help, but our people were better off for it. At times the text depicts and demands large emotions; wise preachers use all the tools at their command to deliver it.

For Further Study

Arthurs, Jeffrey D. "The Place of Pathos in Preaching." *JEHS* 1:1 (December 2001): 15-21.

Getting better at preaching with emotion is normally a journey of just getting better at emotions. The following are books that can help.

Manning, Brennan. *Abba's Child: The Cry of the Heart for Intimate Belonging.* NavPress, 2015.

McRoberts, Justin and Scott Erickson. *Prayer: Forty Days of Practice.* Waterbrook, 2019.

Ortlund, Dane. *Gentle and Lowly: The Heart of Christ for Sinners and Sufferers.* Crossway, 2020.

---

24 See David A. Currie, *The Big Idea of Biblical Worship: The Development and Leadership of Expository Services* (Hendrickson, 2017); see also Langley, *How to Preach the Psalms*, 137–142.

Scazzero, Peter. *Emotionally Healthy Spirituality*. Updated edition. Zondervan, 2017.

Vroegop, Mark. *Dark Clouds, Deep Mercy: Discovering the Grace of Lament*. Crossway, 2019.

Talk about It

Have you ever experienced emotional contagion in a sermon? Describe what the preacher did, and how you felt.

Can you think of effective gestures or postures for the following emotions: boredom, rage, joy, fear, frustration, shock, contentment?

Dig Deeper

Record your emotions for 24 hours. It may help to set an hourly reminder on your phone during your waking hours. For each hour, record 1) what was happening, 2) how you felt, and 3) how aware you were of it. What did you notice about yourself?

Practice

Try some emotional contagion. Tell a story to a friend: something funny that happened at the store, an episode of loss in your life, or even the plot of a good book. Tell it with emotion and see if you can bring them into the emotion with you by the way that you tell it.

7

Confusion

It seems that, if you just present the correct information, five things happen. One, [people] think they know it. Two, they don't pay their utmost attention. Three, they don't recognize that what was presented differs from what they were already thinking. Four, they don't learn a thing. And five, perhaps most troublingly, they get more confident in the ideas they were thinking before.

—Derek Muller[1]

In the information age, clarity is currency. The ability to take the torrents of data coming in on all fronts and piece them into a coherent picture is worth billions. The world's largest companies wield power and win profits by their ability to collect, sort, and interpret data, and to predict the preferences and behavior of billions of people.[2] Big data is a meta-industry that operates in fields as disparate as meteorology and the music industry. The one who can understand, explain, and predict, wins.

Of course, the craze for data-driven understanding is simply the latest stage in Western civilization's drive to know, the addition of AI technology to an existing culture hungry for conceptual control. We have known, since the Renaissance cry of *ad fontes*, that knowledge is power.

---

[1] Quoted in Steve Kolowich, "Confuse Students to Help Them Learn," *The Chronicle of Higher Education,* August 14, 2014.

[2] For a rather terrifying documentary about these companies, see *The Social Dilemma*, directed by Jeff Orlowski (Netflix, 2020).

Preachers—especially those who hold a high view of the power and authority of Scripture—generally agree. They view teaching, explaining, and demonstrating as part of their duty. They hold sacred the responsibility to absorb the data streams from Scripture, history, theology, contemporary culture, and the lives of their parishioners, and help the people of God understand the word of God in their time. Consequently, homiletics has traditionally stressed clarity in the pulpit.[3]

Nonetheless, beneath the cultural flood of explanation and clarity, there runs a quiet countercurrent: an approach to learning that values mystery as much as mastery, confusion alongside clarity. It recognizes that when people wrestle with apparent contradictions, they can emerge with a deeper and stronger form of comprehension.[4]

This countercurrent flows most swiftly in the fine arts. Consider a brief example from Shirley Jackson's short story, "The Lottery":

> The morning of June 27th was clear and sunny, with the fresh warmth of a full-summer day; the flowers were blossoming profusely and the grass was richly green. ... The children assembled first, of course. School was recently over for the summer, and the feeling of liberty sat uneasily on most of them; they tended to gather together quietly for a while before they broke into boisterous play, and their talk was still of the classroom and the teacher, of books and reprimands.[5]

---

[3] Haddon Robinson's *Biblical Preaching: The Development and Delivery of Expository Messages*, 3rd ed, (Baker Academic, 2014) is a prime example of a homiletic formulated to produce clarity in the mind of the preacher and in the sermon. See below for a discussion of a contrary trend in twentieth century mainline homiletics.

[4] Here we stand at the edge of deep waters because we are talking about what it means to genuinely understand something. "Hermeneutics" is a branch of philosophy that explores what it means to understand something. Understanding involves far more than in an intellectual grasp of something, involving our emotions, our habits, and our character. For an accessible introduction, see Stanley E. Porter and Jason C. Robinson, *Hermeneutics: An Introduction to Interpretive Theory* (Eerdmans, 2011).

[5] Shirley Jackson, "The Lottery," (*The New Yorker*, June 1948).

This idyllic summer scene from a small town is interspersed with strange clues, like the fact that the children are collecting piles of stones. The town gathers for some sort of traditional lottery, with families standing together, gossiping and making small talk. As the story progresses it becomes apparent that the lottery is the random selection of one person for the town to sacrifice by stoning so that crops will grow. The power of the story—and its ability to move and educate readers—derives from confusion. Hints of violence and fear stand alongside typical conversations, old jokes, and playful children. The juxtaposition confuses, disturbs, and forces readers to reflect on how atrocities can become commonplace given enough time. By the final phrase of the story ("and then they were upon her"), perplexity has given way to horror. "The Lottery" is powered by confusion.

Biblical writers, too, knew the value of confusion. Perhaps the most extended example in the Scriptures is the Gospel of Mark, where the journey of the disciples is marked by different stages and levels of confusion.[6] Their progress in discipleship revolves around a profound misunderstanding of who Jesus is and what he has come to do. They are led slowly to the realization that Jesus is "the Christ" (Mark 8:29), but immediately fall back into bafflement over what his identity entails (8:31–38). They only ever partially grasp the reality that being the Christ requires suffering and death followed by resurrection. Even at the end, when disciples discover the empty tomb, are told that Jesus had risen, and are sent to tell others, "They said nothing to anyone, for they were afraid" (16:8). In their incomprehension we are invited to see our own, and to ask ourselves what it means for Jesus to be the Son of God, and for us to follow him. Mark's use of confusion, rather than illuminating the path of discipleship, takes readers by the hand so that they can walk on it.

The formation of disciples is a multi-layered process, and moments (or long seasons) of confusion, doubt, and mystery are entirely appropriate to that journey. Preachers can do more than

---

6 R. T. France, *The Gospel of Mark,* NIGTC (Eerdmans, 2002), 15–35, offers a helpful introduction to the relation of confusion secrecy, and mystery to discipleship in Mark.

acknowledge this and explain it: they can invite people to experience it.

This is especially true when preaching from the Prophets. In this chapter we will (carefully) examine the presence and use of confusion in the OT Prophets, and (cautiously) offer strategies for preaching these passages in ways appropriate to their original intent.

Confusion in the Prophets

Were the prophets always confusing, or is it just present-day readers that find them so? Robert Carlson argues, "To their original audiences, we can assume that the prophets were very clear."[7] In many cases I agree, but not all. Though our contemporary confusion with prophetic oracles often stems from the cultural and theological distance between their world and ours, the prophets in fact sometimes deliberately confuse their audience. As we will see, confusion is a prophetic tool to render readers more amenable to the message. Confident people lean back with their arms crossed, but uncertain people lean in, brows furrowed in search of answers. Confusion puts people off-balance and shifts them to a posture of curiosity and openness. This is exactly the stance the prophets needed to evoke in people who were in covenant with Yahweh but did not grasp the implications of that covenant bond.

Below I examine four examples of confusion in the Prophets. In each case, the prophets use confusion as a rhetorical tool to accomplish specific pastoral tasks in their audience.

Nahum: Confusion to Empathize

Confusion in the first chapter of Nahum reflects and reinforces the confusion that his people already feel. The prophet confuses his readers throughout his first chapter by interleaving poems of salvation with oracles of judgment, and by using only pronouns and vague descriptors. The chapter is thus unclear on the identity

---

7 Robert Carlson, *Preaching Like the Prophets: The Hebrew Prophets as Examples for the Practice of Pastoral Preaching* (Wipf & Stock, 2017), 93.

of Yahweh's "adversaries" (v. 2) and of "those who take refuge in him" (v. 7). He says "you" to an enemy in v. 9 and "you" to a friend in v. 12. Who is "you"? Who is "they"? As Longman states, "This use of pronouns without apparent antecedents lends an element of suspense to the prophecy."[8] Readers wonder who is getting Yahweh's favor and who is getting his wrath.

This is exactly what his people are confused about in their current context, as Ninevah grows in power and splendor while Israel languishes. Are his readers Yahweh's enemies or friends? Is this a word of comfort or condemnation? Who has God's favor? Not until Nahum finally names Judah in 1:15 and Ninevah in 2:8 does the thrust of the message becomes clear: despite confusing appearances, God will bring Ninevah to justice and rescue his faithful people. Confusion in Nahum 1 offers an empathetic word to confused people, preparing them for the reassurance of the rest of the book.

Joel: Confusion to Instruct

In the first two chapters of Joel, the prophet depicts an invasion of locusts as a sign of Yahweh's judgment (1:2–12), then follows this with a call to repentance (1:13–20). The locusts are likened to a foreign "nation ... powerful and without number" (1:6). So far, so good. But then in chapter 2 Joel appears to repeat himself by speaking about another invasion:

> Like blackness there is spread upon the mountains
>   a great and powerful people. ...
> The land is like the garden of Eden before them,
>   but behind them a desolate wilderness. ...
> Like warriors they charge;
>   like soldiers they scale the wall.
> They march each on his way;
>   they do not swerve from their paths. ...
> They climb up into the houses,
>   they enter through the windows like a thief. (2:2–3, 7, 9)

---

[8] Tremper Longman, III, "Nahum," in *The Minor Prophets*, vol. 2, ed. Thomas Edward McComiskey (Baker, 1993), 795.

In this chapter Joel blends the imagery of a locust horde with that of a military invasion. Are we still talking about bugs? It takes some untangling to discover that the second invasion is a human army, advancing and devouring as inexorably as locusts.

Joel's purpose in blending the two visions is not merely to confuse, but to confuse so that readers will connect a (past) locust invasion with a (future) military invasion. The one foreshadows the other, both as signs of Yahweh's judgment and call to repentance (2:12–17).[9] Confused readers lean in, wondering if these are insect or infantry, and experience an "Aha!" moment that is far more effective than a direct statement from the prophet. Confusion instructs.

Ezekiel: Confusion to Undermine

Sometimes prophets confuse readers to challenge their deeply held assumptions. Ezekiel 1:4–28 recounts a staggering vision of Yahweh's throne appearing out of a storm cloud by the Chebar canal. Amid all the images of gleaming metal, flashing light, living creatures, eyes and wings, perhaps the strangest details involve mobility: the entire throne of Yahweh moves; the four living creatures carrying the throne have four faces looking in four directions so that they can move without turning; wheels are interlocked within wheels so that the throne can move in any direction (including straight up in the air!) without turning; and all are under the direction of the "the spirit/Spirit/wind" (1:4, 12, 20, 21). Confused readers wonder why Yahweh's throne (which is "established from of old," Ps 93:2) is moving and rising. Why a throne with wheels? And why the emphasis on not turning or changing as it moves?

The riddle is not solved until Ezek 10, when Yahweh's throne leaves the temple in Jerusalem. The throne is mobile, it turns out, because its Occupant is not tied to the temple or the city. Yahweh reigns even when his people rebel; he rules even when they fall.

Separating the throne from the temple is a drastic theological move because it undermines some of Judah's deepest convictions.

---

9 John replicates this confusion on an apocalyptic scale in Revelation 9:1–11.

Didn't Yahweh say he would put his name there forever (1Ki 9:3)? The exiles in Babylon continued to put their hope in the temple establishment, believing that Yahweh would bring them home quickly because he would not allow the temple to be ruined. Ezekiel's confusing vision undermines that confidence by implying three radical ideas: 1) Yahweh is able and willing to abandon temple and city if they continue in unfaithfulness; 2) Yahweh can rule anywhere, even over a community of exiles in Babylon; 3) Yahweh's relocation does not "turn" or change his character at all. He can leave the temple and move to Babylon and be the same God he always has been.

At the end of the book, Yahweh's throne returns to the new temple in Jerusalem. The final phrase in Ezekiel rings out with finality: "The LORD is there" (48:35). But note that his return is not because he changed (which he never does). Rather, Israel has changed and now has a new Spirit to obey his laws (36:25–27). The confusion of a wheeled throne spans the arc of the entire book. It serves to undermine deeply held assumptions about Yahweh's ties to a particular city and a particular building. Confusion serves spiritual formation.

Confusion that Remains

Sometimes the formation of readers calls for more than temporary confusion. It requires unrelieved confusion. This is often the case in eschatological scenes, where the images, though striking, are never clearly explained. Malachi depicts a sunrise that is also a burning oven (Mal 4:1–3), and the reader is left to figure out the comparison. Ezekiel sees dead bones revived by the Spirit of Yahweh into an army (Ezek 37), but never says whether that is literal or symbolic for national revival. Joel predicts that the heavenly bodies will become dark and bloody (Joel 2:10, 30–31; 3:15), and the reader senses drastic upheaval but cannot describe it literally. It seems evident that such confusion puts readers in a state of expectant hope, knowing that they await something momentous, but not knowing when it will happen or even what exactly will take place. All we know is that God will do it and that we will see it. But the confusion remains with us, prompting us to place our hope in God himself rather than in specific events and timelines.

Confusing Preaching?

In a book on genre-sensitive preaching, readers might think that this section of the chapter will make a case for confusing preaching. After all, preachers want to recreate the effects of the prophetic oracle.

Not so fast: here the preacher is on treacherous ground, because confusion is almost always the *enemy* of effective sermons. How often have listeners lost the thread of a talk, wondered what the point might be, and eventually given up six minutes into a sermon?

Therefore, three strong caveats are in order. First, most confusion during a sermon is unintended, a result of the preacher's own lack of clarity, preparation, and skill. This is not the type of confusion advocated here! As Robinson notes, "A mist in the pulpit can easily become a fog in the pew."[10] Preachers should never be misty; in fact, sermons that use confusion effectively come only from exceptionally clear and well-prepared preachers.

Second, we must remember the theological distinction between a prophet like Isaiah who was called to preach in such a way that would result in a refusal to listen and an acceleration of judgment (Isa 6:9–13), and a preacher whose job is to proclaim the gospel clearly, making it plain to meanest understanding (2 Tim 4:1–2). Confusion that will result in hardening and judgment is not within the scope of our vocation.

Third, confusion works in moderation; too much leaves listeners hopelessly lost. As Kolowich, argues, "Confusing [people] on purpose is more like loading the elastic of a slingshot: It creates tension that can propel them into higher altitudes of understanding; pull too far, though, and the elastic will snap."[11] It takes great care to know how far to stretch listener's minds.

Having said that, confusion has its uses. When done well it can enhance listeners' interest, participation, and eventually their

---

10 *Biblical Preaching*, 101.
11 Kolowich, "Confuse Students."

understanding. The Prophets demonstrate that for the sake of the spiritual formation of God's people, preachers can and should (occasionally) employ confusion.

Literary scholars have long understood the benefits of taking readers on a journey that involves frustrating and confusing stages embedded in the "form" of a text. As Kenneth Burke argues,

> Form is the creation of an appetite in the mind of the auditor, and the adequate satisfying of that appetite. This satisfaction ... at times involves a temporary set of frustrations, but in the end these frustrations ... serve to make the satisfaction of fulfillment more intense.[12]

When form is used skillfully, it generates frustration and then brings satisfaction. Confusion is one species of frustration, and if done well, it creates and satisfies listeners' appetites. Moreover, Paul Ricoeur postulates that true understanding of a text moves in an arc from a first and simple reading through a second stage of critical reflection—confusion, where initial understandings are undermined—to a final full inhabitation of the world generated by the text.[13] Again, confusion and doubt ultimately serve understanding.

What is true about confusion in literature holds true in homiletics. Fred Craddock was a strong advocate of the inductive form in sermons: that is, rather than stating a proposition at the beginning and reasoning deductively from it, the sermon takes pieces of evidence and builds to an idea that comes at the end of the sermon. He argues that all of us tend to live and think inductively, and that sermons in this form are more powerful and engaging than blunt and pedestrian deduction.[14] The experience of an inductive sermon is

---

12 Kenneth Burke, *Counter-Statement* (University of California Press, 1968), 31.

13 This is a bald statement of a complex theory. For an accessible summary, see Paul Ricoeur, *Interpretation Theory: Discourse and the Surplus of Meaning* (The Texas Christian University Press, 1976). For an alternate perspective on how readers navigate confusion, see Wolfgang Iser, *The Act of Reading: A Theory of Aesthetic Response* (Johns Hopkins University Press, 1978).

14 Fred B. Craddock, *As One Without Authority*, rev. ed. (Chalice Press,

often one of initial confusion: we have observations or experiences and driving questions, but no answers. In one sermon, Craddock wonders, "Why is Jesus asleep in the middle of a storm?" He intensifies the listener's confusion for most of the sermon. That confusion prepares them for his idea about exhaustion and rest.[15] Confusion draws listeners in and helps them participate in the sermon.

Similarly, Eugene Lowry's homiletical plot sketches a formal outline for sermon that thrives on confusion and dissatisfaction. Problems get worse and worse until, at the climax of sermon, the gospel is unveiled: an indicator of what the good news is and how it might lead to resolution.[16] David Buttrick's homiletic emphasizes the formation of a gospel consciousness in listeners. This happens not by clear explanation but by sermonic moves that imitate the flow of the text, so that listeners can experience its dynamics.[17] If the text confuses, so should the sermon.[18]

Thus, while preachers must employ confusion with care—and never because of poor comprehension or preparation on their part—there remain pastoral uses for confusion, and preachers can wield it, not as the primary tool in the homiletical kit, but as a specialized instrument to be used in imitation of the prophet.

Preaching with Confusion

How can preachers carefully allow and even encourage a beneficial, gospel-saturated confusion that will turn out to be good news

---

2001), 43–62.

15 Ibid., 137–143.

16 Eugene Lowry, *The Homiletical Plot: The Sermon as Narrative Art Form*, exp. ed. (Westminster John Knox, 2001), 22-26.

17 David Buttrick, *Homiletic: Moves and Structures* (Fortress, 1987), 321–323.

18 The astute reader will note that Craddock, Lowry and Buttrick are all mainline homileticians deeply involved with the New Homiletic, an approach to preaching that favors induction over propositional content, focuses on the experience of the listener, and sees the sermon as an event. The New Homiletic has come in for its fair share of criticism, and its aversion to propositional truth (so apparent, for instance, in Buttrick) is not only too radical for effective ministry, but also at times unbiblical and impossible to practice consistently. Nonetheless, the New Homiletic was onto something: biblical writers were not always deductive and didactic, and neither should we be.

for hearers and for the church? This chapter suggests three strategies, each of which require preparation and practice to perfect.[19]

Strategy 11.1 Wander with Them

Fred Craddock suggests that the movement of the inductive sermon can mimic the preacher's own struggle to grasp the text.[20] In other words, we recreate in the pulpit the confusion we experienced in the study, finally arriving at a homiletical idea. This can be particularly effective because preachers can take congregants by the hand, as it were, and wander with them along the path laid out by the prophet.

For instance, recently I preached on Isaiah 46:1–4, an oracle where the prophet uses limited perspective, gradually revealing more and more, to bring listeners from confusion to clarity (see Figure 7.1). The passage proceeds in four stages, and so did the sermon. The first stage (46:1a) begins, "Bel bows down; Nebo stoops." Bel and Nebo are foreign idols of the powerful Babylonians. The vision of the inanimate idols bowing down is not only fantastic but counter to the current power dynamics of Isaiah's hearers, where Babylon bows to no one. So, the vision makes no sense. In the second stage (46:1b–2a) it becomes apparent that the idols are bowing down because they are being carried by weary livestock, who stumble in the way and cause the statues to dip in apparent submission. Isaiah zooms out further (46:2b) and reveals that the livestock are weary because they walk into exile with defeated Babylonians. The mightiest people on earth depend on weary animals to carry their idols—the very idols that seemed to give them such prosperity. In each stage, Isaiah's masterful passage

---

19 The reader should note that the sermon examples in this chapter and the next generally follow a covenant context model of interpretation. The preachers move from corporate Israel to the corporate church, with awareness of the New Covenant in Christ. Creative homiletics is consistent with solid theological interpretation.

20 Craddock, *Without Authority*, 98–100. His appendices (131–16) offer four sample sermons—unfortunately for our purposes, all are from the NT—showing how sermons can be a series of questions seeking answers. They all thus use confusion in one form or another.

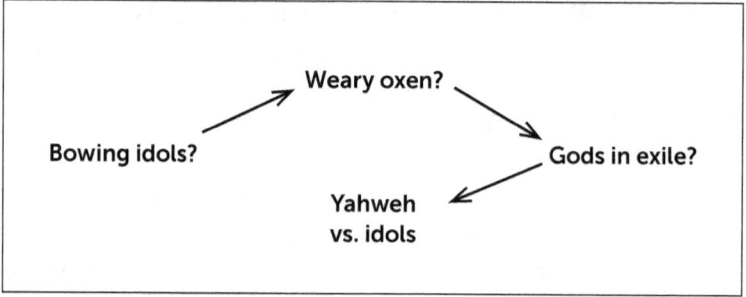

Figure 7.1: Confusion in Isaiah 46:1–4

solves one apparent mystery by introducing another: Why do the idols bow? Why are the oxen weary? Why are they going into exile?

The fourth stage of the oracle offers a crushing contrast between idols, who never deliver on their promises and become a burden that must be carried, and Yahweh, the one who carries his people: "Listen to me, O house of Jacob, all the remnant of the house of Israel, who have been borne by me from before your birth, carried from the womb; even to your old age I am he, and to gray hairs I will carry you. I have made, and I will bear; I will carry and will save" (46:3–4).

Just as the oracle proceeds in four stages, my sermon walked through four movements of confusion, asking question after question, not just about Babylonian idols but about our contemporary objects of devotion. We pretend that our careers or kids or health or talent or government will save us. But they all turn into burdens that we must carry, that force us to pretend that they have more power than they do. The final question, and the big idea of the sermon, was "Do you carry your savior, or does your Savior carry you?" I wandered with my congregation in the confusion of the passage, because solving the riddles too early would have robbed the oracle of its suspense and power. Who, after all, would be interested in an introductory statement that set the scene with flat clarity, then immediately solved the puzzle, and then laid out the fine points of application for the next 20 minutes? Far better to wander with them.

Because this type of sermon is tricky, I offer a second example.

Pauli Murray preached a sermon on Isaiah 53:3-6, a section of the final Suffering Servant song that describes the Servant's quiet submission to violence and injustice.[21] Murray's sermon begins as a straightforward exegesis of the passage, noting that while Israel expected social restoration from the Servant, what God had in mind was redemptive suffering. Murray concludes that the oracle's "most perfect expression" came in the life and ministry of Jesus Christ.[22]

So far, so good. Israel may be confused, but we are crystal clear. But then Murray says these verses are difficult because they also form "the standard [God] has set for us to attempt to meet." We, too, must be "self-giving, pouring out love upon others even when they are unlovely and unlovable."[23] And then she gets to the crux of her dilemma, which applies specifically to minority Christians:

> For those of us who have been born into a group which has been the object of contempt, injustice, and oppression, the figure of the Suffering Servant, the example of Jesus Christ, presents us with a most difficult dilemma. On the one hand we strive for self-respect and pride in ourselves and our achievements against those who would deny our humanity and our personhood. On the other hand we are told that self-pride is a stumbling-block to salvation. Are we expected to endure injustice submissively? To give our backs to the smiters? Not to be rebellious when all around us we see evil and injustice?[24]

Note Murray's subtle rhetorical strategy: she outlines Israel's confusion over the choice between restorative conquest and redemptive suffering, and then her (minority) listeners find themselves in the same trap! Shall they seek social equality and human dignity, or like God called Israel to do, trust in redemptive suffering?

---

21 Pauli Murray, "The Dilemma of the Minority Christian," May 19, 1974, in Bettye Collier-Thomas, ed., *Daughters of Thunder: Black Women Preachers and Their Sermons, 1850-1979* (Jossey-Bass Publishers, 1998), 257-62.

22 Ibid., 259.

23 Ibid., 259-260.

24 Ibid., 261.

Murray wanders with her listeners, and by the end of the sermon, they resonate with Israel's own struggle to find hope in God's plan for his servant(s) to suffer.[25]

To use confusion in your own sermons, keep on the lookout for when prophets *intend* confusion (as opposed to when we contemporary readers are confused by temporal and cultural gaps between Israel and us). Also, observe how that intended confusion operates in you as you read and study. Be mindful of your own process; take notes in real time, jotting down your questions and objections. And then plan—oh so carefully!—how you can generate a gentle confusion in congregational minds, leading them to a moment of clarity and discovery along with you. Your aim is to share not only the puzzling feeling of being lost in the dark forest, but also the delight of finding your way back to the sunlit path.

Strategy 11.2 Drop It on Them

Sometimes confusion in the Prophets is a feint with the right hand that sets up a surprise left hook. Patterns are violated, expectations dashed, roles reversed. The Prophets use confusion to set up repentance because off-balance fighters are susceptible to a knockout blow. Like Jesus declaring that the tax collector rather than the Pharisee went home justified, prophets and preachers can use confusion to slip past hearers' defenses.

I once preached from a passage in Amos that delivered a prophetic one-two. The passage is a series of oracles against foreign nations in Amos 1:3–2:16, where the prophet excoriates the surrounding people—Syria, Philistia, Tyre, Edom, Ammon, and Moab. Six nations come under the harrow of Amos's tongue, and the Israelites cheer because God sees and will hold the nations accountable. Over and over Amos sings, "For three transgressions… and for four, I will not revoke the punishment." In other words, these people are right on the edge of disaster: three strikes and

---

25 Space limitations prevent a fuller explanation of the way Murray preserves the tension and provides an answer that gives ample space to justice concerns while fixing our gaze on the eternal kingdom of God.

they are out! Then the seventh oracle increases their delight by targeting Judah, those self-righteous know-it-alls down south, who think that because they have the temple and a Son of David on the throne that Yahweh will give them a free pass. Not so: only three strikes left for them, too! Seven wonderful oracles, seven songs of judgment on our enemies. It's a good day at church!

Good, that is, until Amos pronounces an eighth oracle. Eight, of course, is one too many. Seven rounds things out to perfection; no one is looking for an eighth. Even worse, the eighth is against Israel, and issues the same warning: "For three transgressions of Israel, and for four, I will not revoke the punishment" (2:6). Amos causes confusion and surprise with his eighth oracle. The 7+1 pattern sets up an expectation and reverses it: judgment is *not* complete until it comes home.

In my sermon, I drew the parallel that we, too, must reckon with our sins. Our proximity to God and our prior relationship with him do not allow us to ignore our own rebellious ways. Amos's oracle was meant to land hard on Israel. The sermon followed suit, giving comfort for six and even seven passages, and then changing tone for the eighth. Though we as believers would like to stand behind our covenant relationship with God to excuse our failings, he is unfailingly righteous. The cross is no place to continue in sin with impunity.[26] As Paul says, we must not continue in sin so that grace will abound.

As always, pastoral wisdom is called for here. These types of passages and sermons can hit so hard that they do damage rather than heal. If our role, along with Paul, is "for building up and not for tearing down" (2 Cor 13:10), then we must look for ways to soften the blow. One option is to use appropriate self-disclosure, so that we sit together with them in the ring and show them how to take a punch. Another would be to end the sermon with the gospel message, not as an invalidation of the oracle, but as a hand raised in surrender by the boxer lying on the mat, and a reminder that "He has torn us, that he may heal us; he has struck us down, and he will bind us up" (Hos 6:1).

---

26 See Lee Beach, and Joel Barker, "Springing the Trap: The Rhetoric of Amos as a Strategy for Preaching Justice and Judgment," *JEHS* 12 (2012): 4–10.

Strategy 11.3 Leave It with Them

As we saw above, sometimes prophets apparently felt that confusion should abide. It should linger and continue to haunt the audience. We can consider whether the same strategy would be appropriate for our people. Of course, it may not: the mysterious prophecy about the Spirit being poured out in Joel 2 finds its fulfillment at Pentecost (Acts 2:1–41). Christian churches who hear Joel should delight in a question answered rather than leave wondering how God will keep his promise. In some cases, however, leaving the congregation with a bit of confusion can be helpful.[27]

Tony Fernandez provides a fine example in his sermon, "Hope When It's Hard," on Habakkuk 1:1–11.[28] Habakkuk questions God about why he seems indifferent to injustice and pain (Hab 1:2–4). Yahweh's reply to Habakkuk seems only to worsen things: he will use the Chaldeans to come and terrorize Israelite sinners (1:5–11).

Fernandez gives the prophet's questions full vent in the sermon. He takes his time exploring the situations where God's apparent indifference to our pain makes no sense. Over halfway through, Fernandez is still asking, "How can God be good when life is not?" When he reads God's counterintuitive answer to Habakkuk, his counsel to the church is, "Embrace and wrestle": embrace God amid pain and continue to wrestle with your faith and your circumstances. Fernandez resists the temptation to pull in the rest of Habakkuk—or the New Testament, for that matter—to undermine the mystery. He leaves listeners with the uncomfortable truth that God does not always operate the way we expect him to and tells them to grab on while also asking why.

---

27 Here I gently remind preachers to consider educational levels in their congregation. Some minds, by constant training, are accustomed to solving abstract problems or working things out for themselves. Others have very little such experience. It would be not only unfair but also counter to the nature of the gospel to throw out riddles and questions that only some (usually those on the higher end of the socioeconomic scale) could untangle.

28 Tony Fernandez, "Hope When It's Hard: Habakkuk 1," Broward Church, July 8, 2019, https://www.youtube.com/watch?v=8Imn1sJjNdg.

Fernandez allows the confusion inherent in Habakkuk to shape the church. He does so by taking measures to frame listeners' experience. He warns early on that "this is not going to be a sitcom sermon.... What we're talking about today cannot be resolved in 30 minutes." In other words, he prepares his people for perplexity, so that when it comes, they will know that they are not just misunderstanding the preacher. Confusion is intended. He also suggests some things that, while not relieving the confusion, offer direction: "The way to true intimacy with God is not on the mountaintops but to get to know his faithfulness when you're in the valley." And again: "What if it takes real pain to experience deep and abiding hope?" Fernandez offers pointers to confused parishioners. They *should* feel confused; perhaps this is the way to a deeper faith.

Throughout, Fernandez walks a fine balance between explaining too much and leaving his people in the lurch. He not only strikes this balance with skill, but also demonstrates how well he knows his people and what will be beneficial for them.

This strategy requires even more care than the prior two because we deliberately allow some knots to stay tied when the service ends. We want to leave them with enough of a puzzle to nag them, but with enough direction (like Fernandez's "embrace and wrestle") to help them know which strings to tug after they leave.

Conclusion

The prophets knew that when used skillfully, confusion can be a powerful tool for discipleship. The prophets confused, not simply to befuddle their people, but to shake their listeners' firm and faulty convictions about themselves, their God, and his ways, and to open them up to the word of the LORD.

Preachers today must be careful that the confusion they generate results from intention and skill (not from their own lack of understanding), and helps people grow in their faith. But given that caveat, they can use confusion as a pastoral prybar to open closed ears and shut eyes, jarring loose false assumptions to replace them with God's word.

For Further Study

Craddock, Fred B. *As One Without Authority*. Revised edition. Chalice Press, 2001.
Lowry, Eugene L. *The Homiletical Plot: The Sermon as Narrative Art Form*. Expanded edition. Westminster John Knox, 2001.

Read through The Gospel of Mark in one sitting, noticing the disciples' journey into and through confusion.

Talk about It

Think about a book you have read or a movie you have watched that confused you along the way. How did your own confusion shape your experience of the work? Do you think it was intended by the writer? Was it helpful? Why or why not?

Dig Deeper

Confusion can be helpful or harmful. Where is the dividing line? What makes it a path sometimes and an obstacle at others?
 Read Paul's remarks about prophecy and tongues in 1 Cor 14. How does his explanation inform the answer you gave above?
 Can you think of situations in a disciple's life where confusion would spur her on to love and good deeds?

Practice

Three traveling salesmen arrive at the same time at a roadside motel one evening. The motel has only one room left for the night, and the men agree to split the room and the cost. The bill comes to $25, and each salesman hands the manager a ten-dollar bill. She says that she has no change now but will send it up to them later.
 A few hours after, she sends the bellhop up with five one-dollar bills. Knowing that five bills will not split evenly between three customers, the bellhop gives each salesman $1 in change and pockets the remaining two bills for his trouble. Thus, the three salesmen

have each now paid $10 − $1 = $9 for the room, for a total of $27. The bellhop kept two, which makes $27 + $2 = $29. But the original amount was $30. So where did the extra dollar go?

After you have found the extra dollar, reflect on your experience trying to solve a puzzle. Did the confusion motivate you? Discourage you? If you cheated and googled it, what do you think you might have missed by not staying with it?

Shock

> *But, on the other hand, those whom not even scourges restrain from iniquities are to be smitten with sharper rebuke in proportion as they have grown hard with greater insensibility.*
> —Gregory the Great[1]

TAKE YOUR TIME READING "in Just" by e. e. cummings:

in Just-
spring   when the world is mud-
luscious the little
lame balloonman

whistles   far   and wee

and eddieandbill come
running from marbles and
piracies and it's
spring

when the world is puddle-wonderful

---

1 Gregory the Great, *The Book of the Pastoral Rule* (Fig books, 2013), book III, chap. 13, loc. 1355 of 2709, kindle.

> the queer
> old balloonman whistles
> far   and   wee
> and bettyandisbel come dancing
>
> from hop-scotch and jump-rope and
>
> it's
> spring
> and
>
>   the
>
>   goat-footed
>
> balloonMan   whistles
> far
> and
> wee[2]

At first, we revel in an innocent spring day of puddles and games; a balloon man whistles to summon children. The balloon man is first "lame," and then "queer," and finally "goat-footed." By the end of the poem, we see an old satyr whistling for innocent children, hinting at darker sexual themes.[3] By shocking its readers, "in Just" evokes surprise, anger, and disgust.

When preachers must conjure these kinds of emotions, shock may be the right homiletical tool. By "shock" I mean more than the confusion or emotion of prior chapters. I use the term here to indicate an intense reaction. Shock is sharp and sudden fear, anger,

---

    2 e. e. cummings, "in-Just," Poetry Foundation, accessed January 23, 2022, https://www.poetryfoundation.org/poems/47247/in-just.

    3 See, for instance, an analysis at "in Just- Summary and Analysis," LitCharts, accessed June 5, 2022, https://www.litcharts.com/poetry/e-e-cummings/in-just.

disgust, or delight. It reflects a reversal of the expectations of what a story or sermon or text will do and produces a visceral reaction.

If the previous chapter on confusion was cautious, the present one will be more so. Shock lies in the bottom tray of the preacher's toolbox, covered in sawdust and hidden beneath anecdote, poetry, alliteration, and even props. Perhaps that is appropriate: shock is somewhat of a last resort, meant to jar hard hearts and unplug clogged ears. But for this reason, shock appears often in the Prophets, and wise preachers who want to say what the text says and do what the text does will know where to find it and how to wield it.

Shock in the Prophets

Bible readers are in for some surprises after Psalms and Proverbs: bizarre behavior, dire warnings, outrageous promises, and profane scenes await those who open to the Prophets.

For instance, Isaiah knows the value of shock. He mocks the upper-class women of Jerusalem (Isa 3:16–4:1). He strolls around naked to give people a stark visual of what captivity will be like (Isa 20:1–4). And at the end of his work, he presents a vision of the new heavens and the new earth, glorious and full of the redeemed, enduring forever. His final words predict that those who worship God will travel outside of the city to gaze upon the bodies of rebels, burning forever and eternally eaten by worms (Isa 66:24). This whiplash from salvation to judgment closes the book.

Or take Amos: in the first two visions of chapter 7, he sees a locust swarm descending on Israel and a judgment of fire on the whole land. The prophet's intercession leads to relenting: "'It shall not be,' said the LORD" (7:3). But in the third and final vision Amos sees the LORD standing by a wall with a plumb line in his hand (a weight on a string that indicates up and down precisely, thereby measuring whether a wall is straight or crooked). In other words, the crooked wall will be torn down: "The high places of Isaac shall be made desolate, / and the sanctuaries of Israel shall be laid waste, / and I will rise against the house of Jeroboam with the sword" (7:9). The days of relenting and mercy are past; judgment has arrived.

Delight, not just outrage and distaste, can also shock. Yahweh, after describing in detail the adulterous behavior of his "wife" Israel, says that he will take away her riches, strip her naked, shame her publicly, end her festivals, destroy her crops, and punish her sins (Hos 2:9–13). He continues:

> Therefore, behold, I will allure her,
> and bring her back into the wilderness,
> and speak tenderly to her.
> And there I will give her her vineyards
> and make the Valley of Achor a door of hope.
> And there she shall answer as in the days of her youth,
> as at the time when she came out of the land of Egypt.
> (Hos 2:14–15)

What a tremendous reversal of expectations! Deliverance and delight spring up in the unlikeliest of circumstances. Hallelujah!

Living as he does amid disaster, Ezekiel utilizes shock more frequently than any other prophet.[4] After all, he speaks to exiles in Babylon who cling to the false hope that Yahweh will quickly bring them home. He overwhelms with a vision of Yahweh's holy throne (ch. 1), depicts idolatrous abominations in back rooms of the temple complex (ch. 8), pantomimes a prolonged and painful defeat (ch. 12), enacts the squalor of exile by burning food over dung while lying on his side (ch. 4), and declares that when Yahweh restores Israel it will not even be for her sake (36:22–32). He uses salacious imagery to depict his countrymen's unfaithfulness (chs. 16, 23). With these kick-down-the-door, take-no-prisoner oracles, Ezekiel makes one final push to break the proud hearts and bend the stiff necks of his people.

The prophets sang, questioned, called, offered, invited, and rebuked. But they were not afraid to jolt or to astound when necessary.

Nonetheless, prophets did not shock for thrill of it. As always, they said what they did in service to the covenant between Yahweh

---

4 See Daniel I. Block, "Introduction," *The Book of Ezekiel Chapters 1–24*, NICOT (Eerdmans, 1997), 1–74, on the urgency and crisis that drove Ezekiel to such extremes.

and Israel, to call God's people back to him and to give hope to the despairing. In the most extreme cases of rebellion or depression, shock was the appropriate tool for covenant enforcement.

Preaching with Shock

Is shock ever called for in a sermon? Lest preachers toss it on the trash heap as inappropriate for new covenant believers, they may recall that Jesus himself used shock in similar situations.[5] He responded to the disciples' awe at the temple buildings with stark predictions of its destruction (Mark 13) and pronounced harsh woes against those who rejected him (Matt 23:1–36). Likewise, Paul was not above saying shocking things to the church (e.g., Gal 5:12). Even a cursory glance at Revelation should put to rest the idea that shock is inappropriate for NT believers: plagues (6:8), conquest (6:4), demonic locusts flying out of smoke (9:1–11), mutant beasts (13:1–18), blood pooled up to a horse's bridle (14:20), swords protruding from mouths (19:15), slain animals living again (5:6), thunder speaking (10:1–4), cities falling (11:13), and skies rolled up as a scroll (6:14) fill the pages of John's vision. The advent of Christ does not remove the need for strong and surprising words.

Shock is thus (occasionally) appropriate to the church and the pulpit. Tony Campolo provides a helpful example. He often began sermons by telling congregations that he had a few things to say: "First, while you were sleeping last night, 30,000 kids died of starvation or diseases related to malnutrition. Second, most of you don't give a s***. What's worse is that you're more upset with the fact that I said s*** than the fact that 30,000 kids died last night."[6] Shock—for a purpose. Campolo allows congregations to feel outrage over his profanity, but immediately the outrage turns to conviction. Listeners who fixated on the four-letter word must reckon with the fact that they skipped over a massive amount of suffering to do so. Campolo is driven to wake up listeners to misaligned priorities; shock helps him to do that.

---

5 On the prophetic nature of Jesus' ministry, see N.T. Wright, *Jesus and the Victory of God* (Fortress, 1996), 147–197.
6 Quoted in Ted Olsen, "The Positive Prophet," *CT,* January 1, 2003.

Nevertheless, preachers should think twice before they start slinging profanity from the pulpit. Some preachers are contrarian, or frustrated in their ministry, or simply enjoy pushing the envelope. For them, shock can be attractive for its own sake. This is an unbiblical perspective, devoid of that pastoral care enjoined upon those who are told, "The Lord's servant must not be quarrelsome but kind to everyone, able to teach, patiently enduring evil, correcting his opponents with gentleness" (2 Tim 2:24–25).[7]

Preachers should prayerfully consider whether shock is the right tool for the job. The following four guidelines may help. First, consider the culture. Different churches have different tolerance levels for strong words or odd behaviors. Say it too softly and no one will notice; push too hard and the offense will eclipse the point. My own church culture is loose and casual, and our people are used to strong words on hard topics. I must push volume or language or emotion to a high degree to shock them. Yet just down the street from me are churches where coming out from behind the pulpit to emphasize a point would raise some eyebrows. If preachers don't gauge the culture well, the shock will be either ineffective or distracting.[8]

Second, consider the moment. Shock is for when things are at a sad standstill, when normal persuasion or rebuke or encouragement is not enough. Shock can be appropriate when evil is the norm and people have forgotten how to blush, or when despair is in the air and people think the Lord has forgotten them. It should be used with discretion and restraint. Although the prophetic literature is full of shock, they are anthologies of the prophets' teachings over time. Years of faithful ministry are often compressed into a few pages. The extreme moments will garner a disproportionate share of attention.[9] Our proportions should be suited to the ordinary

---

7 See also the NT injunctions to pure speech, e.g., 1 Tim 4:12; Eph 4:29.

8 Under this warning can go a catalogue of "overkill" moments where one wonders whether the shock factor was planned around the sermon or vice versa. I recently watched a sermon about what God calls us to do where the preacher spit in his hand and rubbed the saliva on someone's face. Apart from any concerns about whether this is a biblical point, the shock of the illustration eclipsed the point of the message.

9 Note the concentration in Isaiah 1–39 on the Assyrian invasion and its

rhythms of our peoples' lives. While we can and should use shock at appropriate moments, we should guard against overuse.

Third, consider the sermon, which must be more than a single moment of shock. In particular, the sermon must go on appropriately after the moment of surprise.[10] Wise preachers know that astonishment must lead somewhere. For example, if the point is to convict the congregation of sin, what then? How will the sermon take that conviction and walk people through appropriate response? What will the tone be in the moments following? A strong shock will affect everything that follows: it will, for instance, be almost impossible to follow shock with dispassionate exegesis of a passage. The sermon must take the result of the shocking moment and use it.

Finally, consider yourself. Be aware of how much trust you have earned in your congregation and ask whether this is the right time to expend some of that precious resource. Shocking your people is a form of aggression, and it will tax the relationship with your church.

I once preached an Advent sermon on the shepherds and the angels in Luke 2. I wanted to help my people understand the audacity of entrusting the announcement of Christ's birth to agricultural workers far down the socioeconomic ladder in Israel. So, without introducing the text or topic, I started the sermon by talking about how my family raises cattle on land in the next state and telling a story of going down there and finding our workers gone, the gates open and the cattle wandering loose. When the workers came home in the middle of the night, they seemed drunk and delirious and told me an outlandish story of a giant glowing man saying something about a baby. Then I had someone get up and read the story from Luke 2.

Not a great idea, as it turns out. The sermon generated a lot of confusion among those who didn't get it, and anger among those

---

result, or the focus on single moments and issues in Obadiah, Nahum, Habakkuk, and Haggai.

10 Unless, of course, the very end of the sermon forms a terrific surprise. See, for instance, Don Sunukjian's first person narrative sermon on Esther ("My Name is Harbona," *PT,* September 2006).

who did when they realized I was making it all up. The format eclipsed the point; the church was not used to these homiletical games, and I had not earned the trust to play them anyway. It was a sharp lesson in choosing my moments.

If, after all of this, it seems like the right moment for shock, then the following strategies can help preachers deliver it with power and with care. Note that some will seem mild while others may be entirely beyond your congregation's tolerance level. Choose wisely.

Strategy 12.1 Shock from the Start

At the beginning of a sermon, our listeners are rearranging their bulletins, smoothing their skirts, shushing their children, and settling in for some gentle words of encouragement or, failing that, a power nap. This is a great place for shock. Opening words or music that is bizarre, counterintuitive, offensive, or just plain unbelievable will have more impact here than almost anywhere else in the sermon.

I began a series through Amos in this way: "We are going to walk through the book of Amos for the next few weeks. Has anyone ever read Amos? Reading through Amos is like this." I had an audio clip cued of a lion roaring and asked the sound technician to make sure the volume was turned all the way up. I then read Amos 1:2, "The LORD roars from Zion." On another occasion I began a sermon on Isaiah's warning to the women of Zion (Isa 3:16–4:1) with Beyonce's "All the Single Ladies." In both cases the sound gained attention and directed us to the harsh oracles that followed.

A video introducing a sermon series can also provide a note of shock. Russell Howard preached a series through Amos where each week an introductory video played. The video had dramatic music and a voiceover that summarized the message of Amos, who foretold "the onrushing fire of [God's] judgment."[11] In churches used to sermons about God's patience and forgiveness, even this sentence can shock hearers into paying attention.

---

11 Russell Howard, "Unboxing Amos," October 7, 2020, https://www.youtube.com/watch?v=0gI_HcS4bZI.

Whether through video, music, or the spoken word, we can provide an initial shock to garner attention and signal that something important is about to be said.[12]

Strategy 12.2 Shock Yourself

One way to help people feel a shock while maintaining a pastoral connection is to feel it with them. Rather than standing over a congregation hurling thunderbolts, preachers can let the prophet sit on high while they seek shelter from the storm alongside their people. First, we will look at how an OT prophet did just this, and then suggest some ways we can follow suit.

Habakkuk takes the shock along with his readers. The prophet delivers very bad news to his people: God will punish the evil of Judah by send the Chaldeans (Babylonians) to invade, and then in turn bring judgment on the invaders. This plan gives little comfort for those sitting in the Babylonian crosshairs. Habakkuk's approach is to be shocked along with his people, delivering his oracles in the form of a painful series of prayers to and answers from Yahweh. As the catastrophic divine plan is unveiled, Habakkuk shows himself to his people complaining (1:2–4), objecting (1:12–17), eagerly awaiting (2:1), and professing trust (ch. 3). At the height of the pain, he shows his own pivot from panic to confidence:

> I hear, and my body trembles;
> my lips quiver at the sound;
> rottenness enters into my bones;
> my legs tremble beneath me.
> Yet I will quietly wait for the day of trouble
> to come up on the people who invade us. (Hab 3:16)

Habakkuk's own dismay allows his listeners to be shocked along with him.

---

12 Of course, this means that there had better be something important coming! Shock simply to get attention will not only disappoint listeners but will also condition them to expect over-promising and under-delivering.

In a sermon on Habakkuk's final oracle, Jeffrey Arthurs takes a seat beside the prophet as Habakkuk prays, waits, and groans.[13] When the sermon comes to 3:16, Arthurs has surveyed the injustice within Judah, the horrifying invasion to come, and the scorched earth that the Babylonians will leave behind them. He asks, "How is this possible? How can one dwell in scorched earth and still rejoice? How can we rest in quietness and rejoice in confidence even while lamenting?" Rather than delivering shocking news to the church, Arthurs receives shocking news along with the church. He postures himself as a fellow wanderer and a guide.

Strategy 12.3 Shock with Anachronism

Biblical passages—especially Old Testament pericopes—can strike contemporary ears with all the urgency of a weather report from last year. Preachers can be hard put to make Israel's terror or joy resonate today. One way to do this is through deliberate anachronism, where ancient words take on a jarring modern format or tone.[14] Once again, we will look first at how prophets used this strategy, then suggest ways we can do the same.

Ezekiel, when predicting Jerusalem's coming devastation, asserts, "Even if these three men, Noah, Daniel, and Job, were in [Jerusalem], they would deliver but their own lives by their righteousness, declares the Lord GOD" (Ezek 14:14).[15] Heroes from the past are conjured for comparison. Even these men would not stop the judgment to come! Similarly, the entire thrust of Isaiah's new exodus motif—a divinely provided return from exile that the prophet describes beginning in chapter 40—is one large anachronism, using the memory of the exodus from Egypt to give hope to Babylonian exiles. Anachronism, by bringing the past forward in surprising ways, can shock listeners and force them to reevaluate their present circumstances.

---

13 Jeffrey D. Arthurs, "What to Do When Your Fig Tree Doesn't Blossom," *PT*, November 2011.

14 I owe this insight to Casey Barton, *Preaching Through Time: Anachronism as a Way Forward in Preaching* (Cascade: 2017), 111-162.

15 The identity of "Daniel" in this passage is uncertain. See Block, *Ezekiel*, 447-449.

Preachers today can also fuse the past and present in unexpected ways to reinforce the shock of a prophetic oracle. They do so in two ways. First-person narrative sermons are a particularly effective method for anachronism, when preachers assume the role of someone from the time of the oracle.[16] The presence of someone who feels the weight and urgency of an oracle can transport the distant past to the vivid present. Preachers can of course play the role of the prophet, but perhaps more effective (and easier to pull off) might be to play the role of an ancillary character like Baruch to Jeremiah or King Hezekiah to Isaiah. Easier still (particularly for female preachers), they can be an unknown bystander: a merchant's wife in Jerusalem, a farmer outside of Samaria, an Assyrian soldier.

If the point is to deliver a shocking anachronism, consider delivering the entire sermon in character, with no introduction. The character can either be aware that he or she has been transported to our present, or else be entirely in his or her own era. The merchant's wife, for instance, could just be coming home from the temple on a Sabbath. She walks to the front of the church, sits down, and delivers the "sermon" as if she is talking to her husband. She has just heard Jeremiah outside the temple gates haranguing the crowds and tells her husband how the prophet's words frightened or angered or inspired her. The entire sermon can be a recollection of her experience a few blocks away. First-person anachronism can help the shock of the past be felt with immediacy.

Secondly (and more simply), preachers can "translate" oracles into contemporary language. For instance, Amos's final oracle is one of staggering abundance and favor. He paints a picture of ludicrous agricultural bounty where the one who plows new ground overtakes the one who harvests, because the harvests are so plentiful and the weather so propitious that no fallow period arises between crops (Amos 9:13). Such agricultural bounty indicates the fulness of Yahweh's favor on his people in the future. In preaching a sermon on this oracle I tried to capture the heart of this passage

---

16 This paragraph and the next are dependent upon Kent Edwards, *Effective First-Person Biblical Preaching: The Steps from Text to Narrative to Sermon* (Zondervan, 2005), 13-29, 98-99.

for people in my southern town. I told them that Amos was predicting a time when

> there will be jobs for everyone with full medical and dental, they're going to start giving away groceries and fixing cars for free, the fish are guaranteed to bite every day, and if you don't have time to wait, they will jump into your boat and clean themselves. The temperature will drop by ten degrees, it won't rain on weekends, and all the sand gnats are going to hell.[17]

No matter how you choose to do it, consider anachronism. It can help people feel the shock of a prophetic oracle.

Strategy 12.4 Shock with Delight and Disgust

Whether rapture or repugnance, when prophets resort to extremes, preachers can do the same. We start with delight, and then move to disgust—in the Prophets and then in the pulpit.

The prophets generally deliver more bad news than good. But when the news is good, it is amazingly good! Let us focus on the passage quoted earlier from Hosea (2:14–15). Here the prophet shocks his readers with delight: after an unanswerable indictment of Yahweh's unfaithful wife Israel, rather than passing judgment Hosea promises a stunning reconciliation between Yahweh and Israel. Hosea 2 is set up to shock readers. The "therefore" in verse 14, which normally indicates punishment to come, leads instead to reunion and restoration.

But this delightful surprise can fall flat if not handled with care. A traditional deductive path will undermine the shock inherent in Hosea. I watched a sermon where, after reading the passage in full (!), the preacher introduced the sermon by discussing the anticipation that normally precedes a wedding. But this wedding, he said, could never have been anticipated. It was a wedding between God and his people. After the introduction he launched into exegesis of

---

17 Care must be taken in this kind of "translation" to avoid generating a new, unbiblical contemporary prediction. Use general language, as in the above example.

the passage. Only the shock was already gone; we now knew that an unlikely wedding would take place between God and Israel. He later stated, "This is a bad breakup with no hope of reconciliation." Which then makes the 'therefore' in verse 14 shocking to say the least." But telling the church that something is shocking is not the same as letting them feel it.

Instead, preachers can structure what they say to preserve the surprise. Another sermon on the same passage handles the shock more effectively.[18] The preacher begins by playing an Adele song about being betrayed, and asks, "What would you do if the person you loved betrayed you? This is the pain Hosea felt." He then talks about how we (God's people) have broken his heart and have forgotten him. Then just before he reads verse 14, he declares,

> God steps in with grace and mercy. God acts in a totally counterintuitive countercultural way. And God calls out to his children.... You might have rejected me, but I'm not going to reject you. You might say you don't love me, but there's nothing you can do for me not to love you.... As long as you're drawing breath, God says, it is not too late.

Here the emotional flow of the sermon follows Hosea's lead and preserves the delightful surprise of God's mercy to sinners who deserve none of it. Preachers can shock with delight.

As with delight, so with disgust: when prophets use revolting words and themes, so can we. To name but a few: Ezekiel relates a vision where throughout the temple complex, Israelites gather in pagan worship of carved images, animals, pagan deities, and even the sun (Ezek 8). Prophets say that Yahweh will spread offal on the faces of disobedient priests (Mal 2:3), while Moab will swim in the mire of a dung heap (Isa 25:10–11). Bodies lie in the streets; adulterous women are stripped naked; the winepress of Yahweh's wrath stains his garments red with blood.

The prophets use disgust just like they wield all the rhetorical tools at their disposal—in the service of God's covenant. When

---

18 "God's Love Never Gives Up," Vanguard Church, February 7, 2016, https://vimeo.com/154492339.

hearts are hard, disgust makes its entrance: prophets use offensive images to describe situations that would otherwise seem commonplace, and the repugnance felt for the image is transferred to the situation. Political machinations really are adultery; disobedient priests really are defiled. The disgust becomes a kindness that leads to repentance. Preachers can imitate the prophets' tactics if they do so with similar motives.

Disgust need not be prolonged or accompanied by vivid photographs; a brief description may work admirably. In planning a sermon on Isaiah 1, I came to verse 15, where Yahweh says, "When you spread out your hands, I will hide my eyes from you; even though you make many prayers, I will not listen; your hands are full of blood." God does more in this verse than express his displeasure; he intimates that the blood on the hands of the worshippers from their animal sacrifice is (in Yahweh's eyes) the blood of the fatherless and widow (v. 17). It did not take much homiletical maneuvering to get Isaiah's image to hit home. A simple gesture of hands raised in worship and prayer (which was a part of our church's worship culture), and the quiet statement, "Your hands are filled with blood." Keeping hands lifted as I explained that worshippers' hands in the OT could often be bloody, but that Isaiah meant something far darker. The shock (in Isaiah's time and now) urged us to ask what God sees in our hands as we lift them in prayer.

Delight and disgust can serve covenant purposes in a sermon.

Strategy 12.5 Shock with Satire

Fans of late-night TV know that satire is endlessly entertaining because it shocks. Ridicule gets attention, and the storehouse of prophetic technique contains an entire shelf devoted to it. People and gods, foreigners and natives—all are candidates for the prophets' satire. Isaiah mimics drunken Ephraimites (Isa 28) and helpless pagan idols (Isa 44:9–20); Amos mocks the decadent rich (Amos 6:1–7); the book of Jonah in its entirety is incredibly unflattering to the prophet who is so consumed by ethnic hatred that he entirely misses the point of his mission.

As with most of the tools in this chapter, one must take care.

Biblical satire is not just an ancient political cartoon: it does more than elevate one faction against another or reduce someone else's viewpoint to lunacy. The point of the prophets' satire is to show by exaggeration the folly of those who will not listen to the Lord, hoping that those whom they mock (and others who observe them) would change their ways and come home.

Therefore, I find that the best practice is normally to mock myself or a group of which I am a member. It preserves the humor but removes some of the sting that can prevent people from listening. For instance, Micah 6 taunts the Israelites for their hypocritically extravagant worship, when they have always known that what Yahweh desires is to do justice, love kindness, and walk humbly with their God (Mic 6:8). In a sermon on this oracle, I talked about similarly misguided attempts in our own church culture. The evangelical subculture presents a large target, and I had a lot of bullets. I made fun of how we display our faith with T-shirts, bumper stickers, and "Test-a-mints" breath mints (with a Bible verse in the wrapper) that I found at a Christian bookstore. I teased us about our compulsion to make a Christian version of everything from YouTube to Facebook to professional wrestling. Micah tells us, instead, that we have no need to invent things to do for God. We already know that God wants justice, mercy, and humility from us. The point of the (self-directed) satire was to expose these silly substitutes and call for repentance.

If you do choose to mock another person or group (for edifying purposes), be sure to qualify it in some way: noting that you often have behaved similarly, or that while this behavior may be objectionable, we affirm the worth and value of all people and hope for better for them. Unadulterated satire that has a superior tone will turn away those in your congregation who are filled with the fruit of kindness and reinforce cruelty in those who are not.

Strategy 12.6 Shock with the Liturgy

Service elements can add a punch to pulpit speech. The culture of your congregation will determine which of the options below will provide a shock appropriate to the message.

Use the sounds available to you in your church. Pastors have long used an organist or a full band behind them to "pad" sermon moments and evoke emotion—particularly during the conclusion.[19] In many churches such practices are standard procedure. Consider silence instead, or a sudden stop in the music. Or go further and use the sharp percussive sound of a cymbal crash, a sharp discord on the keys or a loud crash of some sort. Shocking noise proclaims that this is not business as usual.

Scripture readings or other performances are normal parts of Sunday morning. But what if that reading came from people who stand up without warning from the pews, or walk down the aisle and yell their verses, or interrupt the announcements? A talented speaker who has memorized the passage and can deliver it with passion could render Obadiah's words in unforgettable fashion. Readings like this provide a shock, so that the preacher can focus on expositing and applying the text.[20]

Any element of the service can function as a shock or interruption. What if congregants came in and all the chairs were gone? Or, as in a Tenebrae service, all the lights go out?[21] Or the bulletins were blank, or the service ended in the middle of a song? The only limitations here are what the congregation will tolerate, and what you will dare.

And Yet

This chapter has offered some possibilities that are perhaps over the line for some congregations; the shock would be so intense that it would overwhelm whatever homiletical point was on offer. But are there *passages* that are similarly beyond the pale?

---

19 A side note: a friend of mine once called this practice "instant Holy Spirit." The comment irked me, but I had to admit he had a point. Perhaps you should take time to have a prayerful discussion with musicians, preachers, and liturgists in your church about how we can cooperate with the Spirit without trying to assume his role in persuading others.

20 For more ideas on creative ways to do Scripture reading well in church, see Jeffrey D. Arthurs, *Devote Yourself to the Public Reading of Scripture: The Transforming Power of the Well-Spoken Word*, (Kregel, 2012), 105–122.

21 Be careful here that you provide enough light for those in transit in and out of the sanctuary. A slip-and-fall is not the kind of shock we're looking for.

Theologically I am committed to a negative answer. I trust that "all Scripture is breathed out by God and profitable for teaching, for reproof, for correction, and for training in righteousness" (2 Tim 3:16). I have tried to live by that assertion in preaching and other forms of ministry of the word.

But some passages put that conviction to the test. In Ezekiel 23 the prophet offers an allegory of two debased sisters (representing Israel and Judah) who commit adultery in the lewdest fashion. The oracle goes well beyond a celebration of physical love as one finds in the Song of Solomon; it descends into debauchery. Some verses I would blush to explain on a Sunday morning.

The reason for Ezekiel's breach of etiquette, of course, is the present crisis of hardheartedness in Jerusalem and Babylon, where the faith of God's people is in a sorrier state than ever before, and catastrophe is right around the corner (Ezek 24). In other words, Ezekiel is screaming. Perhaps it may be best to reserve this passage for the most extreme situation when we also must scream to a church, "You have the reputation of being alive, but you are dead. Wake up, and strengthen what remains and is about to die" (Rev 3:2).

Conclusion

Shock jocks on the radio make a living from being offensive, opinionated, and perverse. If you delight in shock for its own sake, then consider a change in career. Preachers, like the prophets who preceded them, use shock only for kingdom purposes.

But when hearts harden and ears close, preachers can reach for the bottom drawer of the tool chest. They can, in empathetic mercy, craft sermon moments that will shock dull senses awake, and open stopped ears.

For Further Study

Block, Daniel I. "Introduction." In *The Book of Ezekiel, Chapters 1–24*. NICOT, 1997. 1–74.

Barton, Casey C. *Preaching Through Time: Anachronism as a Way Forward in Preaching*. Cascade, 2017.

Heath, Chip and Dan Heath. *The Power of Moments*. Bantam Press, 2017. 69-92.

Talk about It

What is the most shocking sermon you've ever heard? How did the shock affect you as a listener? Was it effective or distracting, and why?

What would count as an effective level of shock in your own church context? What would go too far?

Dig Deeper

The prophets generally reserved shock for the direst situations. What contemporary situations facing the church today merit a shock treatment in the pulpit? What makes those issues so urgent?

Practice

Appropriate shock is impossible to practice in the absence of an urgent reason to disturb someone. However, you might choose (gently, legally) to violate a social norm to see how it affects others. For instance: have a very loud conversation in a restaurant; sit in the seat right next to someone on an otherwise empty bus or subway; under- or overdress for a social event; organize a flash mob. Who pays attention and how do they react? What are possible ways you could bring appropriate shock to the pulpit?

Part III

Make Straight in the Desert a Highway: Obstacles to Preaching the Prophets

This book began by introducing the Prophets and giving some guidance for interpreting their oracles. Part II surveyed the Prophets' literary methods and offered strategies to adapt their techniques for the pulpit. Part III turns to those tricky features of the prophetic corpus that can send preachers scurrying in fear back to the New Testament and provides some homiletical paths through the wilderness.

Three obstacles will occupy our attention: an ethical one (justice), a hermeneutical one (the distance between their world and ours), and a literary one (prophetic monotony). To the first of these we now turn.

9

Justice

Justice is in fact perfect virtue.

—Aristotle[1]

Justice is a habit of the mind which attributes its proper dignity to everything.

—Cicero[2]

Justice is revenge.

—Saad Hariri[3]

WHEN PROPHETS CALL FOR justice, some preachers start to sweat. As I write this, the current cultural and political climate in America makes justice a particularly thorny issue in the church, and for this reason preachers may decide to dodge passages about justice.

Yet justice talk is difficult to dodge without avoiding the Prophets altogether. Alongside idolatry, justice is one of the most frequent topics in the prophetic literature. A word study on *mishpat* (the most common Hebrew word for justice) reveals that although the Prophets comprise 25% of the Old Testament, they contain 34% of the word's occurrences. When ranked by the relative frequency of

---

1 Aristotle, *Nichomachean Ethics* Book V, trans. D. P. Chase, in *Aristotle Collection*, ed. Jefferson Cabell Douglas, Kindle edition.

2 Cicero, *De Inventione* Book II, trans. C. D. Yonge, *Cicero Complete Works*, Delphi Classics (2014), Kindle edition.

3 Quoted in Daniel Schorn, "The New Beirut," *60 Minutes*, December 22, 2005, https://www.cbsnews.com/news/the-new-beirut/.

the use of *mishpat*, the top four books are prophetic books.[4] Several of the most famous passages in the Prophets deal with justice: Isaiah's chapter on fasting (Isa 58) is all about justice; Micah tells the people to do justice, love kindness, and walk humbly with their God (Mic 6:8); Amos prays that justice would roll down like waters, and righteousness like an ever-flowing stream; prophetic visions of restoration predict that every Israelite will be able to sit under his own vine and fig tree (Zech 3:10); and the year of God's favor would be characterized by justice to those who suffer (Isa 61).[5]

The Prophets are deeply concerned for justice. Our challenge is bringing their words into our current context.

Justice as a Problem

As Nicholas Wolterstorff observes, "Justice and rights are the most contested parts of our moral vocabulary."[6] The first two decades of the twenty-first century have seen sharp conflict over the meaning and practice of justice.

To take an example current at the time I write: I live in Brunswick, Georgia, where a young Black man named Ahmaud Arbery, jogging on a public street, was shot and killed after being pursued

---

4 In fact, 9 of the top 15 are prophetic books. Five prophetic books contain no mention of justice: one discusses justice without using the term (Joel 3:3), two are addressed strictly to foreign nations (Obadiah and Nahum), and two address special topics (Jonah and Haggai).

5 Note that Jesus quoted this last passage in Luke 4:18–19 to explain his own mission. Justice is not absent in the NT; it is simply easier to avoid, for two reasons. First, the relative powerlessness of the Christian community in the Roman empire meant that justice concerns were not primarily about structural and social change, which were mostly out of the reach of the NT church. Thus, NT justice is often about treating people in the church community well, whereas in the OT, where Israel at times did have significant political power, justice more often included broader social and economic factors. Second, the vocabulary used to talk about justice in the NT normally centers on *dikaios* and related Greek terms (usually translated as "righteousness"). Justice/righteousness talk then gets absorbed into theologically loaded discussions of righteousness-as-forgiveness and substitutionary atonement. On this latter point, see Nicholas Wolterstorff, *Justice: Rights and Wrongs* (Princeton University Press, 2008), 96–108.

6 Ibid., 1.

in trucks by three white men in February 2020. The murder trial took place just a few blocks from my office, and I (along with members of our local clergy) spent many hours outside of the courthouse listening, speaking, and praying with residents and with those who came from all over the country. Cries for "justice" were ubiquitous, but it was apparent that the word meant different things to different people. By "justice," some meant a fair and impartial trial; some meant a conviction on some or all counts; one memorable speaker meant by justice a conviction, a death penalty, and a short trip to eternal judgment. Likewise, some felt that the presence of protesters outside the courthouse would help ensure justice, while others believed that protesters would intimidate the jury and obstruct justice.[7]

Justice in the Church

Talk outside a Georgia courthouse reflects a broader cultural disagreement over the meaning of the term. That disagreement is especially sharp in the American church.[8] I write from a broadly evangelical perspective, where the tension has been acute and prolonged.[9] The debate over justice in evangelical circles has increased in volume and divisiveness in recent years. In fact, a search for articles on justice in *Christianity Today*, a leading evangelical magazine, returned 8 results for 2017, 5 for 2018, 2 for 2019—and then 19 for 2020 and 21 for 2021. Moreover, while recent evangelical works on justice discuss the topic and affirm both its presence in

---

7 In December of 2021 all three men were convicted on multiple charges, including murder. They were sentenced to life in prison, two without the possibility of parole.

8 See, for instance, the polemical declaration, "The Statement on Social Justice and the Gospel," https://statementonsocialjustice.com. For one article among many on justice controversy in the church, see Rebekah Thompson, "Social Justice and Biblical Justice are Actually the Same," *CT*, October 6, 2021.

9 Even the term "evangelical" has become extraordinarily problematic, for many of the same reasons that complicate the term "justice." I use the term here in a purely theological way, devoid of any political overtones. See the "Statement of Faith of the National Association of Evangelicals," accessed June 12, 2022, https://www.nae.org/statement-of-faith/.

Scripture and its importance for the church, they sharply disagree on the meaning of justice.[10]

The conversation is intensifying.

Preachers to whom I have spoken (particularly white preachers) tell a similar tale. "Justice," for one preacher, is hard to distinguish from "politics." Even his sermons that to him have not seemed "too controversial" have resulted in people leaving the church. Another pastor told me that people nowadays are more often staking their ground in their preferences. In other words, disagreement about justice can quickly become a fundamental disagreement about worldview, or politics, or basic theology. The anticipation of hard conversations and the loss of members makes preachers uneasy when they encounter biblical texts on justice.

It has in fact become sadly commonplace to hear stories of families leaving churches over sermons that "got too political" when a preacher tackled the topic of justice. The result of this reshuffling of flocks is a landscape of politically monolithic churches that belie the beautiful variety inherent to the body of Christ.[11]

It should be noted that justice conversations go differently in the Black church. Eric Price observes, "While [B]lack Christians hold many beliefs that are theologically evangelical, the [B]lack experience of oppression and suffering in the United States leads to divergence from majority culture Christians in how those theological beliefs are applied to the public square."[12] That application (in

---

10 To name just two: Thaddeus J. Williams, *Confronting Injustice Without Compromising Truth* (Zondervan Academic, 2020) and Timothy Keller, *Generous Justice: How God's Grace Makes Us Just* (Viking, 2010). When the subject of justice overlaps with issues of race, economics, gender or politics, things get even more complex. For contrary views on justice, race, and the gospel, see Jemar Tisby, *How to Fight Racism: Courageous Christianity and the Journey Toward Racial Justice* (Zondervan, 2021); Voddie T. Baucham, Jr., *Fault Lines: The Social Justice Movement and Evangelicalism's Looming Catastrophe* (Salem Books, 2021).

11 For a recent example of church division along political lines, see John Burnett, "Christian Nationalism is Still Thriving—and Is a Force for Returning Trump to Power," *National Public Radio*, January 23, 2022, https://www.npr.org/2022/01/14/1073215412/christian-nationalism-donald-trump.

12 Eric Price, "Situating Black Evangelical Preaching Within Scholarship on Black Homiletics: William E. Pannell as a Case Study" (paper presented at the annual meeting of the Evangelical Homiletics Society, October 15, 2020).

part through preaching) includes a readiness to address issues of justice. A young Black pastor I know told me that he gets excited at the prospect of preaching on justice. "It's not hard for me," he said, "but it may be for other people." By "other people" he means preachers in white evangelical churches.

In addition to the divisions within evangelicalism, one also finds a pronounced difference between the mainline and evangelical churches regarding justice.[13] Very broadly speaking, the former tends to view justice/righteousness in public and structural terms (including topics like social welfare programs, affirmative action, and broad economic inequality), while the latter uses the same words to describe personal moral issues (like abortion, the importance of a strong work ethic, and the rights of individuals against government overreach).[14] This is one reason that many Black churches and pastors, even when espousing a strong commitment to the authority of Scripture, tend to associate with mainline groups rather than evangelical ones.[15]

Despite all this disagreement, the Scriptures continue to direct our attention to justice. As Proverbs 28:5 states, "Evil men do not understand justice, but those who seek the LORD understand it completely." And the Prophets are especially loud in their insistence on justice. What is a preacher to do?

I believe that rather than glossing over those differences, the

---

13 This history can be traced all the way back to the fundamentalist controversies of the early twentieth century, the emergence of the Social Gospel, and the growing split between theological liberals who embraced social justice as central to the gospel and theological conservatives who worked hard to distance themselves from liberal theology and practice. See Walter Rauschenbusch, *Christianity and the Social Crisis,* (1907; rev. ed. Harper and Row, 1964); David O. Moberg, *The Great Reversal: Evangelism and Social Concern*, rev. ed. (J.B. Lippincott Company, 1977).

14 See the section below on different definitions of "justice," especially the sections on libertarianism and equity.

15 See the discussion of this scenario from a homiletical and theological perspective in Jesse L. Nelson, "Barriers: The Challenge for Evangelical Homiletics in the African American Church and Community," (paper presented at the Annual Conference of the Evangelical Homiletics Society, October 19–21, 2019). Nelson names, among other causes, a theological shift in evangelical beliefs away from social activism.

way forward requires taking a closer look at them. The controversy over the practice and preaching of justice rests on divided conceptions of what the word "justice" even means. We first look at the different ways that philosophers have defined justice, and then ask how those differences have surfaced in the pulpit.

Justice among the Philosophers

Philosophical conceptions of justice are myriad. The following is a rough categorization of contemporary versions of justice.[16] I intend this list less as a comprehensive survey of thought on justice and more as a heuristic tool to underscore the complexity of the subject.[17]

Justice as right order. On this view, justice is when peoples' behavior conforms to a common standard or order (often understood as given by God). In other words, people do not have rights; they have obligations to act in certain ways. Justice exists when people meet those obligations and thus society is well-ordered.[18] For example, in asking whether my speech practices are just, the question is not, "Have I enjoyed the right of free speech?" but rather, "Have I used my powers of speech to promote God's order in the world?" The focus is on duty rather than entitlement.

Justice as general welfare (utilitarianism). Utilitarian theories of justice say that one can determine the right action by looking at its

---

16 This list is adapted from that offered by Michael J. Sandel in *Justice: What's the Right Thing to Do?* (Farrar, Straus and Giroux, 2009). His basic categories are justice as welfare, freedom, and virtue. I have added "right order" theorists to reflect a strain of thinking that emphasizes obligations over rights, and what Timothy Keller calls "postmodern" justice, which is about power differentials between groups. Keller offers his own version of Sandel's list in "A Biblical Critique of Secular Justice and Critical Theory," *GL*, August 2020. Keller's own preference is what he calls "biblical justice." But see the critique of Keller's article in David Fitch, "Tim Keller, David Fitch, and Justice," *CT*, August 4, 2020.

17 This survey does not address some older versions of justice. For an illuminating discussion of the historical development of views of justice, see Alasdair MacIntyre, *Whose Justice? Which Rationality?* (University of Notre Dame Press, 1988). For simplicity's sake, I have also passed over the differences between primary (distributive) and secondary (rectifying) justice. For more on this distinction, see Wolterstorff, *Justice*, ix–x.

18 See Wolterstorff's explanation (and critique) in *Justice*, 21–64.

consequences: actions are just if they produce the greatest good possible.[19] This means, however, that denying people freedom or choice may in some cases be preferable, if the results increase the welfare of society generally. For instance, if taxing a wealthy person $10,000 does not significantly reduce his standard of living while giving ten people in poverty $1,000 each would make a huge difference for them, then those results make the action just because they increase the general welfare.

Justice as individual rights (libertarianism). Advocates of libertarian justice say that justice is served when everyone in society enjoys the same rights, which are normally construed as freedom from interference by others (e.g., the right to own property, the right not to be over-taxed, the right to self determination). So, justice will mean a society of free individuals who do whatever they like, so long as they do not infringe on those same rights for others.[20] For instance, if the government does not interfere with my right to purchase a firearm, and I do not use that right to shoot others without cause, that is a just state of affairs.

Justice as individual rights (equity). Here, too, justice is expressed in terms of people enjoying their rights. But on this view, rights are more extensive than the ability to act freely. They may include rights to "life-goods" such as education, healthcare, and economic opportunity. Justice exists when those rights apply equally to all.[21] This view emphasizes equity (similar outcomes for all) over equality (similar starting points or opportunities for all).[22] For

---

19 See Sandel, *Justice*, 31–57.

20 Ibid., 58–74. He cites Robert Nozick as espousing this view, which derives from John Locke.

21 Ibid., 140–166. The argument for equity is a little more complex than stated above: the reason why a person has a right to an equitable share in life-goods is that if, hypothetically, people had to choose how to organize society without knowing what assets, talents, or social position they would enjoy in that society, they would freely choose an arrangement organized around the principle of equity. For more, see John Rawls, *A Theory of Justice*, rev. ed. (Belknap Press, 1999). Wolterstorff's view in *Justice* could fall under this category: he thinks of rights as positive life-goods, but his list of those rights is so meager that in practice he would look much more like a libertarian than a Rawlsian theorist.

22 For a quick primer on equity versus equality (a contrast which carries its own controversies), see Susan K. Gardner, "Equity vs. Equality," https://www.

instance, if a college education is increasingly necessary to make a living wage, the government would be acting justly if it imposed taxes to provide me with a free college education rather than merely granting the *opportunity* to go to college to anyone who can afford it.

Justice as rectification of power differentials. Here justice is understood in terms of the respective power of different groups. Historically, groups in power tend to stay in power by oppressing other groups in unjust ways and incorporating those injustices into social systems that perpetuate that inequality. Justice, then, is conceived of as something that reverses those power inequities.[23] For instance, if the local schools in a community show a disparity in racial composition, average household income, and test scores, then it may be just to redirect funding and personnel from better-performing schools to those schools. Although such action is technically unequal and deprives some students of resources, the power differential between groups is being reversed.

Justice as virtue. This final view, first propounded by Aristotle, says that justice exists when people get the resources that they deserve. What they deserve, in turn, is determined both by the purpose of that resource, and by a person's ability to use that resource to promote goodness or virtue in specific ways. Thus, if a flute's purpose is to make beautiful music, then justice does not give everyone a flute; it gives flutes to the most talented players. It will be just for those people to receive flutes because they will use them for the right purpose and thus promote the virtue of beauty. Likewise, if a society's purpose is to cultivate certain virtues in its citizens, then justice will give the most power and influence (e.g., political offices, commercial resources, speech opportunities) in that society to those who can best direct it to developing those virtues in citizens.[24]

---

youtube.com/watch?v=nCS7Rus4_-Y.

23 This school of thought, called "postmodern" by Keller ("A Biblical Critique"), is often tied to Critical Race Theory and the legal writings of Derrick Bell. The path between Critical Race Theory and philosophical postmodernism is tortuous and need not be detailed here. For an accessible work that operates with this view of justice, see Ibram X. Kendi, *How to Be an Antiracist* (One World, 2019).

24 Sandel, 184–207. If this view feels like the odd one out, that is a reasonable

Of course, two or more of the above could be combined, while some approaches to justice fit none of these categories precisely. The point of this list is not to map out all the views of justice but to survey how rough the terrain is. Below I will discuss a biblical definition of justice and how it compares to the models above.

What keeps these differences from being dry academic debates is what hangs in the balance. Individuals, families, businesses, and entire economies can shift fundamentally if the definition of justice moves from one category to another. The stakes are extraordinarily high.

Different and highly charged versions of justice help to explain why the conversation about justice in the West has become polarized and politicized. If one feels as if one is on the side of "justice," then what side are the opponents on? We are no longer exploring ideas together; we are fighting for what is right against unjust enemies. People develop strategies not for dialogue or persuasion but for political dominance. As I write this, Congress continues their investigation into the attacks on the U.S. Capitol building on January 6, 2021. The labels ("insurrectionists" or "patriots") and narratives of conservatives and liberals are diametrically opposed. It appears unlikely that all parties will come to a compromise on what happened and what consequences should follow. Nonetheless, both sides are still talking about justice. In this instance and more generally in our society, the rhetoric of discussion and persuasion is giving way to the rhetoric of warfare and survival.

Justice in the Pulpit

Now add a layer of biblical morality and authority to the conversation, and we see why any politically loaded discussion inside the church is at least as heated as the debate outside. In fact, James Davison Hunter has shown that the American church, far from

---

conclusion. Neither rights nor freedoms nor equity are paramount here—virtue is. Additionally, while most of the other views take no stance on what people should aspire to, this view requires a common conception of what the goal of humanity or society is. For more, see Alasdair MacIntyre, *After Virtue*, 3rd ed. (University of Notre Dame Press, 2007).

toning down divisive rhetoric within its walls, has leapt headlong into the political fray.[25] Whether the Christian Right or the Christian Left, church subcultures have generally aligned with one of the major political parties and adopted a narrative of entitlement and victimization around issues like justice. Both sides tell a story of loss and resentment, with a fierce determination to regain the upper hand.[26]

Thus, a quick Google search for "sermons" and "justice" will return a result like Lee Steiner's "Justice Demands the Truth" (a 50-minute exposé on Black Lives Matter, Critical Race Theory, Marxism, and how the social justice movement today wants to eliminate capitalism, redistribute wealth, and unravel the nuclear family).[27] Just a few results down sits Teresa Fry Brown's "Surviving Justice Fatigue" (a call to perseverance to those who suffer from "microaggressions, ... the conspiracy of silence, ... political inaction, ... re-traumatization, ... having spent their entire life watching others run and soar and fly and move around at will without anyone asking why they were there").[28]

Both sermons are from Isaiah.

As a result of this ecclesiastical polarization, there remains little space for discussion and disagreement. Any mention of justice can quickly spark resentment and anger. The sad irony is that for brothers and sisters in Christ, one person's "justice" will be *precisely* another's "injustice," with each side believing that they hold the moral high ground.

Hence the preacher's perspiration at the prophet's proclamation. When justice comes up in the Prophets, preachers can feel like they stand in a minefield. Not only will a sermon on justice address an explosive topic, but *because the sermon is based on*

---

25 James Davison Hunter, *To Change the World: The Irony, Tragedy, and Possibility of Christianity in the Late Modern World* (Oxford University Press, 2010), part II. Kindle.

26 Ibid., part II.

27 Lee Steiner, "Isaiah 59:14–15, Justice Demands the Truth," Trinity Baptist Church, Shreveport, LA, October 4, 2020, https://www.youtube.com/watch?v=oH_kUrCNoQo.

28 Teresa Fry Brown, "Surviving Justice Fatigue," Candler School of Theology Fall Convocation, Atlanta, GA, August 25, 2016, https://vimeo.com/180328468.

Scripture, it will claim an implicit authority. Preachers do not just tiptoe through the minefield; they march across it in hobnailed boots.

The homiletical options are few and unattractive: step on the mine to the left, step on the mine to the right, or slink off the battlefield and look for greener pastures. No wonder we run to the New Testament.

Do Not Step Here

If you find yourself in a church context where sermons on justice could blow up in your face, how do you lead your people through safely? Below I list three places to avoid stepping.

Strategy 13.1 Do Not Shy Away

Some preachers feel so unprepared or afraid of these topics that they avoid them altogether, either out of a sense of inadequacy or a desire for peace. I advise against it, for two reasons. The first is for our own sake. We are to proclaim the whole counsel of God, and God included these passages in the canon for a reason. If we trust him to deliver his word to us, then we must trust him to proclaim it, or we ultimately surrender our integrity and fail in our pastoral responsibility. Remember that Ezekiel was commissioned to be a watchman for the house of Israel, and that his sacred responsibility was to deliver God's words of warning. If he fails in that task, Yahweh tells him, "[Israel's] blood I will require at your hand" (Ezek 3:18).

The second reason is for your people's sake. They need to hear it as much as you need to say it. If the church concludes that she can connect to God without caring about something so near to his heart, then in short time or long, they are in for a rude awakening. They need to be exposed to biblical teaching about justice.

Justice, in fact, is like any other difficult issue in Scripture: genocide, polygamy, sexual immorality, apocalyptic imagery, or the sovereignty of God. Wise preachers do not run from these issues, lest they have nothing left to talk about but what they already think they know. Avoiding sections of Scripture holds danger for shepherds who are commanded to feed his sheep, and danger for the people under their care.

Strategy 13.2 Do Not Split the Difference

In speaking of opposing views on justice, preachers today sometimes try to play the neutral mediator between factions. But mild critiques of both the Left and the Right followed by a generic appeal to love God and neighbor can do more harm than good, and that in three ways. First, it minimizes the complexities of justice in the modern world by commending abstract, simple solutions. If it were simple, we would have already figured it out. Second, it implies a general symmetry between viewpoints. Both sides are sort of right and sort of wrong, so let us all be humble and try to get along. But each side is not wrong in the same way and suggesting that this is the case obscures the real differences at play and makes it more difficult to expose and discuss them.

Third, splitting the difference allows preachers to excuse themselves by pretending to neutrality. This last point is especially important: as a white middle class American, I occupy a particular social space in our culture. Donning vestments does not remove me from that space or erase my own actions or those of my forbearers. I must come to the table aware of and vocal about the place where I stand. The word of God judges; I sit with my people beneath it.

Although it may seem wise to play the dispassionate sage, this practice ultimately undermines the discussion it seeks to foster. Far better to admit publicly how difficult, complex, and emotional this issue is, and how much you have yet to learn.

Strategy 13.3 Do Not Do It Alone

Finally, some preachers prepare and deliver their messages without consulting other people. They closet themselves with a book or some podcasts to beef up on terms and statistics, and then step to the pulpit, ready to deal out justice, with weapons in the right hand and the left. Carnage often ensues.

Instead, why not begin with discussion? Gather people who have different perspectives and take time to listen before you speak. Hold low-stakes meetings where the only goal is to learn with and from others. Read books (note the plural). Read them *together*. In the past few years, as justice in the Prophets and in our world have become more important and visible to me, I have had conversations with other pastors and priests, elected officials, law enforcement officers, non-profit leaders, retired businessmen, students, and others. Without exception they have sharpened me and helped me to avoid homiletical blunders that could have hurt my people.

Step Here

The following are four practices that can help you grow more skilled and comfortable when preaching from passages in the Prophets that call God's people to justice.

Strategy 14.1 Learn About Justice

Before you preach, think and pray. Consider putting off that sermon series on Micah until next year and give yourself time to learn about what Micah meant when he wrote.

Begin to define justice by searching the Scriptures. I suggest that none of the models of justice described above fully capture the rich texture of biblical justice. Like everything else the Prophets say, justice lives within the framework of the covenant people of God. It goes beyond minimal principles and is aimed at reflecting the full character of Yahweh in the laws and conduct of Israel.

It may help to ask some questions: How is the term "justice" used in the Old Testament? Why does it so often (84 times) occur alongside "righteousness"? When does *justice* address issues like private property, individual liberty, poverty, public health, racial inequality, the power of various groups, or the correct order of a society? And how does that relate to the character and deeds of Yahweh and his covenant with Israel? Spend some *unhurried* time in the Scriptures, asking good questions and prayerfully seeking answers without a Sunday deadline.

After that (and not before), seek out a trusted guide to the biblical material. No book is perfect, but Tim Keller's *Generous Justice* is a good place to start.[29] Spoiler alert: Keller shows that although some passages in the Prophets deal with property rights and justice as personal liberty, more often they address the poor, the sojourner, the widow, and the orphan. His description of biblical justice does not perfectly align with any of the models above. Additionally, passages about justice are deeply tied not to humanistic goals of social progress but to the glory and holiness of Yahweh and the appearing of his kingdom. Biblical justice involves caring for the most vulnerable in society and doing so within a strong covenantal framework.

Strategy 14.2 Learn About Injustice

As the biblical material about justice becomes more familiar, it will also be necessary to learn about injustice in the contemporary world. It will not help to preach from Joel, "[You] have cast lost for my people, and have traded a boy for a prostitute, and have sold a girl for wine and have drunk it" (Joel 3:3) without explaining how those dynamics endure today. If you do, listeners will just congratulate themselves on not being slave traders, rather than taking a hard look at the economics of modern human trafficking and how they may be unwittingly supporting that industry. Your people need guidance.

You can learn to guide them by studying modern justice issues that affect the most vulnerable of our society. Gary Haugen's *Good News About Injustice* is a great introduction.[30] Helpful works on specific topics like racial or economic justice are also available.[31] You can find a list of books to get started at the end of the chapter.

---

29 Keller, *Generous Justice*. See also Mark Labberton, *The Dangerous Act of Worship: Living God's Call to Justice* (IVP Books, 2007).

30 Gary Haugen, *Good News About Injustice*, 10th anniversary edition (IVP Books, 2009). See also Richard Stearns, *The Hole in our Gospel* (Thomas Nelson, 2010).

31 For the former, see, among others, Douglas Blackmon, *Slavery by Another Name: The Re-Enslavement of Black Americans from the Civil War to World War II*, reprint ed. (Anchor, 2008); Richard Rothstein, *The Color of Law: A Forgotten*

Do not limit yourself to national or global perspectives. Learn about your own town. I live in a small enough community that it was easy to get to know our Mayor and City Commissioners; I sought out activists, attorneys, clergy, educators, and business owners. I discovered the local history section at the library. I made friends with people whose lives have been very different from my own. The resources are there for the finding.[32]

In my experience, learning about injustice in my own society (and my own life) has allowed me to feel a measure of the prophets' passion and urgency when they call for righteousness and justice. It has nurtured in me a love for justice and set me at the feet of the men who sang of it long ago. I am more committed now than ever to be a student of their words and of my world.

Strategy 14.3 Let Them See You Learn

Paul writes to his protegee Timothy, "Practice these things, immerse yourself in them, that all may see your progress" (1 Tim 4:15). In other words, Paul thinks it important not only for Timothy to grow in his ministry skills but also for the church to see him grow. Preachers can have a hard time with this advice. We sometimes dream of stepping out of the study to astound the church with profound wisdom and powerful speech. Moreover, we may fear being exposed as people who have a lot left to learn. Paul gently reminds us that we need not be afraid—that, in fact, our people benefit when they see us making progress.

Be honest, then, about your own journey as you learn about justice. Be open about what you know, what you suspect, and what

---

History of How Our Government Segregated America (Liveright, 2018); George Yancey, *Beyond Racial Gridlock Embracing Mutual Responsibility* (IVP Books 2006); for the latter see Ronald J. Sider, *Rich Christians in an Age of Hunger,* new ed. (Thomas Nelson, 2005).

32 Note: learning about global, national, or local injustices does not force us to equate Israel with our modern nation-state. As ch. 2 explained, these oracles apply to God's covenant people, the Church. Nonetheless, as God's people we live within a broader society and are entangled (wittingly or unwittingly) in such injustices. We do not preach *to* the nation, but your people live *in* a nation as representatives of Jesus' kingdom.

still confuses you. It can encourage your people to see you stepping into unfamiliar territory because the Word of God requires it, and you are devoted to the God of the Word. If you can have honest conversations about hard things—especially when you are not yet an expert—then maybe they can, too.

Strategy 14.4 One Step at a Time

When you begin preaching from the Prophets on justice, resist the temptation to develop a biblical theology of justice in the first sermon. Stay close to the text, showing your people that the reason you say what you do is that the Prophets said it first. Trying to accomplish too much will likely backfire, especially with people of a different political view that your own.

Instead, begin slowly and carefully. When Jeremiah complains that Judeans "judge not with justice the cause of the fatherless, to make it prosper" (5:28), then stay close to that concern in your sermon. Those without caring parents are a vulnerable class in our society; the foster care system in America is woefully overloaded; many older children and sibling sets wait for adoptive parents. The sermon can stay tightly focused on children without parents and how the church can make their cause prosper.

As you handle passages like these more frequently, you will gain more competence with the text and more confidence from your people. You can begin to reason from this one text to broader justice concerns, sharing what you are learning about injustice locally, nationally, and globally. If you have worked to earn their trust, walked them carefully though confusing topics, and been vulnerable enough to let them see you learn, your people will be more likely to listen with open ears.

Example: "Worship in Justice"

Navigating the minefield is possible. Bret Johnson preached "Worship in Justice" on various passages from Isaiah 56–59.[33] This

---

33 Bret Johnson, "Worship in Justice," Valley Bible Church, March 21, 2021, https://vimeo.com/526178997.

sermon represents a genuine effort to wade into issues of justice in a congregation that is mostly unused to such topics. In a mostly white congregation in rural Virginia, Johnson knows the minefield is loaded. So, he is careful but bold.

First, he acknowledges the complexity: there are different definitions of justice, he says, and sometimes "justice has been coopted" by political factions. At the same time, "Sometimes there is overlap [between biblical justice and secular justice]: Praise God! ... So, we should be people who join in sometimes with the justice that is happening around us. But there will be times where we can't join in with the justice around us, because that justice has been coopted and made into something else." He urges caution and discernment.

Second, he does not stay safe in abstractions, or play the neutral middle. He gets (for his church) uncomfortably specific: "We should be a people who are grieved when people of color ... are not treated the way they should be treated.... There are definitions of white supremacy that I can get on board with. There are definitions of white privilege that I can get on board with." For some churches, these statements do not go nearly far enough. In Johnson's context, they are quite provocative. Isaiah's passage addresses Israelite ethnic prejudice, and Johnson, staying close to the text, does so as well.

Finally, he models and commends humility. He speaks about his friendship with a Black pastor in an urban context a few towns over and what he (Johnson) is learning. In several places near the end of the sermon he counsels his people to a similar humility and growth:

> Don't assume that you know what your neighbor needs.... Have you talked to them? ... Can you let them define what they need? Are you willing to listen? ... Maybe we misunderstand more than we understand as far as the work of justice ... and that's ok, what you have to say is, I need to learn and grow and change. ... Go do justice. Do justice. Do it. But you can't know what you're doing if you're not having a lowly listening posture.

In the end, Johnson says, the job of the church is not to have all the answers (and not to wait until they do), but in their practice of justice, "Your job is to repent your way forward." Minefields can be navigated with courage and care.

Note how this sermon neither adopts a strident, one-sided posture like the sermons from Fry Brown and Steiner, nor pretends to neutrality by avoiding real-life justice issues. Johnson takes steps, based in the text, guarded with humility, toward building a theology of justice for his people. This sermon cannot be the last word in his church on justice, but it can serve as a significant step on a longer journey.

Conclusion

Tyshawn Gardner writes that when preaching about justice, preachers must declare "God's alternative vision, pronouncing the redemptive themes of the Bible to the disenfranchised and powerful alike, ... call[ing] the congregation to speak and act on the behalf of the victims of injustice and unfairness."[34] The prophets did so with passion and perseverance. We can do the same.

So let us neither shy away, nor feign neutrality, nor rush in with guns blazing. Let us listen and learn in the company of the saints, inviting our people to journey with us to a place where "justice will dwell in the wilderness, and righteousness abide in the fruitful field" (Isa 32:16).

For Further Study

Sandel, Michael J. *Justice: What's the Right Thing to Do?* Farrar, Straus and Giroux, 2009.
Keller, Timothy. *Generous Justice: How God's Grace Makes Us Just.* Viking, 2010.
Labberton, Mark. *The Dangerous Act of Worship: Living God's Call to Justice.* IVP Books, 2007.

---

34 Tyshawn Gardner, "Beginning with the End in Mind: Redeeming Social Crisis Preaching from Social Justice Idolatry," paper presented at the annual meeting of the Evangelical Homiletics Society, October 15, 2020.

Haugen, Gary. *Good News About Injustice*, 10th anniversary edition. IVP Books, 2009.

MacIntyre, Alasdair. *After Virtue*, 3rd edition. University of Notre Dame Press, 2007.

Rothstein, Richard. *The Color of Law: A Forgotten History of How Our Government Segregated America*. Liveright, 2018.

Sider, Ronald J. *Rich Christians in an Age of Hunger*, new edition. Thomas Nelson, 2005.

Talk about It

Which of the views of justice presented above is closest to your own? How did you come to that view? Has it changed over time?

Find someone in your congregation whom you suspect holds different views than you do and talk to them about a justice-oriented topic in the news.[35] What do they think, and why? How, if at all, does that relate to their faith or to the Scriptures? What can you learn from them?

Dig Deeper

Do a word study on *mishpat* (justice) in the Old Testament.[36] What stands out to you?

Practice

Read Isaiah 5:8–25. What is going on in ancient Judah? How might that apply in our context?

If you were to preach this passage to your congregation, how would you handle vv. 8–10?

---

35 If you don't know someone like this—or your congregation does not have anyone like this—I encourage you to ask why not.

36 If you do not have access to theological dictionaries or Bible software, you can find free tools at https://www.blueletterbible.org.

10

Distance

> *It is a wonderful and beneficial thing that the Holy Spirit organized the holy Scripture so as to satisfy hunger by means of its plainer passages and remove boredom by means of its obscurer ones.*
>
> —Augustine[1]

THE PROPHETIC CORPUS is not the oldest part of the Bible, but it can feel like the most archaic. It can be easier to relate to tales of Abraham's wanderings or to the sharpness of Job's agony than to the complex, politically charged, poetic oracles given by the prophets (often with no explanatory comments).

The formidable distance between the Prophets' time and our own is a major hermeneutical obstacle to preaching from them. And the distance comes in several flavors. In an article on the difficulties of preaching from Isaiah, Carl Bosma lists no less than *nine different types of distance* internal to the text—before he moves on to external factors![2] Preachers who tackle the Prophets will confront strange customs, opaque phrases, disturbing talk about God and people, and unexplained references to current events. Thus, a sermon series on the Minor Prophets can seem like a great idea

---

[1] Augustine, *On Christian Teaching*, trans. R. P. H. Green, (Oxford, 1997), 2.15.

[2] Carl J. Bosma, "The Challenges of Reading the 'Gospel' of Isaiah for Preaching," *CTJ* 39 (2004), 11–53. These include its length, its composite nature, lack of perceived order, textual difficulties, and mixture of genres.

when preachers are putting rough notes on a white board. But when the time draws near and they begin to read Nahum, regret sets in. How can preachers even explain these poems, much less have enough time left to talk about God in the here and now?

In a word, how do we deal with distance?

Deal with it we must. In ministry (and in preaching) we help people see that what God did and said back then operates now, in the concrete structures of our present lives and institutions. "Prophetic imagination" is the ability to fix one's eye on the distant world of Samaria and Jerusalem, Nineveh and Babylon, while pointing to the concrete realities of our own world and saying, "This is that."[3] Such imagination requires that we address the (sometimes daunting) distance between the Prophets' time and our own.

This chapter discusses the various forms of distance one encounters in the OT Prophets. It first categorizes the common types of distance, and then offers methods for handling them in the pulpit.

Distance in the Prophets

Sometimes the distance between the biblical world and our own can be crossed with a small imaginative jump. Ezekiel's stirring vision of the Valley of Dry Bones (Ezek 37), though strange, speaks intimately to us. Who has not longed for life from death: for God's Spirit to animate lives with power and vitality? Yet read on to Ezekiel 38, where God tells Ezekiel, "Set your face toward Gog, of the land of Magog, the chief prince of Meshech and Tubal, and prophesy against him" (v. 2). Now the canyon is so wide we need heavy equipment and a team of civil engineers.

Distance, great and small, crops up everywhere in the Prophets.

---

3 Brueggemann offers some rich examples of this practice in his *Hopeful Imagination: Prophetic Voices in Exile* (Fortress, 1986). His discussion is helpful and should stir your own imagination. However, in my view he is sometimes too free in his associations. For example, he suggests that the exile from Jerusalem in 587 can be "a way of speaking about the end of any known world, about the dismantling of any system of meaning and power" (4). My own view is that such connections should be constrained by covenant similarities between then and now. See ch. 2 for more.

To help preachers make sense of it, we can categorize distance into three types.

Cultural Distance

Ancient Israel is unlike the church in the way she looks, sounds, and smells. She speaks a different language, wears different clothing, tells different stories, and sings different songs. Consequently, when the Prophets draw on cultural artifacts to make a connection to Israel's heart, those same artifacts become an obstacle between God and the contemporary church.

The prophets, being resourceful and imaginative, constantly used cultural material in this way. Isaiah gives a satirical description (3:16–23) of the fashion accoutrements of upper-class Israelite women, to contrast their current high living with the stench and baldness of exile (vv. 24–26). Haggai creates a metaphor from cleanliness regulations (Hag 2:10–14) that would resonate with post-exilic priests and worshippers. Zechariah's series of visions (Zech 2–6) moves from one cultural object to another: horseman on patrol, craftsmen and iron horns, a measuring line, priestly vestments, a golden lampstand, olive trees, a scroll, a basket, chariots, and a crown. In each case, the prophets connected to their people on a frequency beyond the range of our cultural receivers. Thus, rather than an intuitive connection forged almost instantly, their words now must first be explained, then the meaning explicated, then perhaps a different, contemporary cultural connection forged. The immediacy and power of the Prophets' words can be lost along the way.

Historical Distance

Some of the distance in the prophetic oracles is due to the geopolitical setting and national histories of Israel, Judah, and the Ancient Near East. Of course, every pericope in Scripture carries this kind of distance, but in the Prophets the problem is particularly severe. In some parts of the Bible, the political environment is minimal (e.g., Job, Genesis, the wilderness wanderings), while in others the context is quite simple (slavery in Egypt, judges, monarchy, or Roman oppression in the Hellenistic world). The most complicated political scenario exists in the divided monarchy, with two royal dynasties, a host of surrounding nations, and almost always an empire or two in the offing. Within the country, kings and nobles, priestly classes, merchants, and prophets of different stripes all play their own power games. During the exile we find all these groups, but now in two locations: the exiles scattered abroad and the holdouts at home. After the return to Jerusalem *three* groups coexist: the poor of the Promised Land who stayed and assimilated, those still in exile, and those who have returned to rebuild Jerusalem. The only parts of Scripture that cover the same complicated period (Kings, Chronicles, Ezra–Nehemiah) narrate the events clearly; the Prophets simply assume them.

Isaiah's oracles are a case in point. When the prophet preaches against Tyre and Sidon (Isa 23), a world of background undergirds the passage, from the location and relative power of the two coastal cities, to their economic strength through trade, to their complex relationship with Jerusalem and its rulers, to the immediate reasons for the oracle. Later in chapter 30, when Isaiah dubs Egypt "Rahab who sits still" (30:7), that name rests not only on a long history of the waning power of Egyptian dynasties, but also on the name "Rahab" and what it meant to Isaiah.[4] Even a simple phrase like, "in the year King Uzziah died" (Isa 6:1) reaches the reader on a flood tide of information that Isaiah and his people instinctively know, but we do not.

Historical distance is ubiquitous in the Prophets. The prayer of Habakkuk about the Chaldeans, the tirade of Nahum against Assyria, the bitterness of Obadiah at Edom, the precarious position of Jeremiah in the court of Judah, the economic depression in Haggai: every prophetic situation assumes a vast amount of historical background. Without that background, the words of the Prophets

---

4 The understandable reaction—to equate seventh-century Egypt with the Exodus Pharaoh and Rahab with the prostitute of Jericho—will lead the reader wrong in two directions at once. By this time Egypt was far behind other world empires in power and prestige, though still a potential ally for Judah. "Rahab" is a symbolic name for Egypt (Psa 87:4) and apparently refers to a mythical sea monster (Isa 51:9).

are more like the babbling of foreigners than the clear speech of the gospel.

Theological Distance

Yet a third way that Israel is distant from the church has to do with theology—the ways each relates to God, objectively and subjectively.

Objectively, as chapter 2 discussed, the church and Israel live on different sides of the climactic ministry of Jesus. But on an individual scale, there are also significant differences between a prophet and a preacher.[5] Obviously, preachers are not OT prophets, speaking the words of God that they hear directly from him. They instead rely on the foundational words of the prophets and apostles (Eph 2:20) and bring those words to bear on their contexts. Additionally, prophets and preachers have different tasks. Prophets, as Jeremiah says, were "to pluck up and break down, / to destroy and to overthrow, / to build and to plant" (Jer 1:10). Prophets have a destructive function (proclaiming judgment and exile) alongside a restorative one (the coming return and restoration). Yet when the Apostle Paul references this passage, he surprisingly speaks of "the authority that the Lord has given me for building up and *not for tearing down*" (2 Cor 13:10, emphasis added). Paul apparently perceives a new covenant distinction in his role. Even when church dysfunction reached Corinthian depths, Paul's task is to build it up and not to destroy it. Only Jesus has the authority to remove a lampstand from its place (Rev 2:5).

Thus, when we preach from the prophetic corpus passages that seek to uproot—that point toward judgment and exile and punishment and death—we handle these texts as new covenant shepherds who believe that the words that served the *destruction* of Israel should serve the *preservation* of the Church. This does not mean that we never warn or rebuke; it means that we do so in alignment with the command, "Let all things be done for building up" (1 Cor 14:26).[6]

---

5 John Stott (*The Preacher's Portrait* [Eerdmans, 1961], 11–13) is clear and concise in his argument that preachers are not prophets.

6 This new covenant distinction is probably the reason that parabolic speech

For instance, Jeremiah loudly and repeatedly proclaims that Jerusalem will be destroyed and orders the people of Jerusalem to surrender to the invading Babylonians (chapters 21, 24, and 27). He predicts (correctly) that resistance will only lead to more carnage.

However, it would be folly of the highest order to copy and paste this message directly to the Church. Our enemy is not flesh and blood but spiritual (Eph 6:12), who wants to steal, kill, and destroy (John 10:10). How could we ever counsel surrender? Rather, we understand that what God permits evil to do is for our discipline and for Gods' glory (Heb 12:3-11; 2 Cor 12:1-10). Congregants who feel as if their sufferings are punishment, as if God is done with them, must be counseled in the strongest terms to understand their sufferings redemptively, trusting that God is working for their good. Prophets sometimes tear down, but preachers always build up (even when they rebuke).

Subjective theological differences also exist. How Israel and the prophets experienced their connection to God can seem to us strange, obscure, or even disturbing. Therefore, it will take homiletical labor to connect the prophets' words to our ears.

Ezekiel 18 offers a helpful example of subjective theological distance. Here, the prophet delivers an extended argument in favor of the principle, "The soul who sins shall die. The son shall not suffer for the iniquity of the father, nor the father suffer for the iniquity of the son" (Ezek 18:20). In other words, Ezekiel tries to convince his listeners that each person is responsible for his own sin and not the sins of others.

To contemporary Western Christians, what could be more

---

largely ends with the Gospels. The prophetic call to speak in confusing parables is tied to Isaiah's commission to harden hearts and prevent understanding, and so bring about judgment (Isa 6:8-13). Jesus quotes this commission to explain his own use of parables (Mark 4:10-12). He was, in a sense, permitting people to shut themselves off from his words and message, which large-scale rejection would lead to the destruction of Jerusalem (see Mark 13). Jesus here acts in prophetic ways. Nonetheless, after Pentecost we find a strong emphasis on explanation, clarity and understanding as the gospel is preached. The authors of the epistles are at pains to help their readers understand (see Paul's repeated "I do not want you to be ignorant," Rom 1:13; 11:25; 1 Cor 10:1; 2 Cor 1:8). Even the Gospel writers, looking back on Jesus' words, give the readers access to the explanation of the parables (Mark 4:13-20).

obvious? Of course people should not suffer for the sins of others! Subjectively, though, the experiences and beliefs of Ezekiel's audience are such that the prophet takes an entire chapter to argue for this principle. Israel so strongly believes that sins and righteousness pass from generation to generation that they have a proverb to that effect: "The fathers have eaten sour grapes, and the children's teeth are set on edge" (v. 2). When they hear Ezekiel's declaration of individual responsibility, they reply with unbelief and even indignation: "Why should not the son suffer for the iniquity of the father? ... The way of the Lord is not just" (vv. 19, 25). In other words, they not only believe in generational punishment and rewards, but interpret individual accountability as *injustice*.

That stubborn belief drives the progress of the chapter and provides the twist at the end. There, Yahweh says through Ezekiel, "O house of Israel, are my ways not just? Is it not your ways that are not just?" (v. 29). He takes their accusation and turns it around: isn't it the case, he says, that you hold to this conception of inherited sin and righteousness precisely because your own ways are unjust, and you are carelessly relying on the righteousness of your ancestors to outweigh your sins?

Ezekiel's original audience can follow his lead easily. But for today's readers who don't subscribe to a generational conception of sin and righteousness in the first place, the chapter will fall flat without a lot of homiletical help. We will only be trying to explain an argument for a conception that they already hold. The subjective distance between what Israel believed and what we believe makes this passage difficult to preach.

The culture, the history, and the theology of ancient Israel were all ways that the prophets connected to their people. But precisely those things now stand in the way of our hearing the words of the prophets. Bridges have become barricades.

We now move on from recognizing distance to preaching through it.

Distance in the Pulpit

To some extent, of course, preachers are always overcoming

distance when they preach. Every time they look down at the lectern, they see thousands of years into the past; every time they look up, they see faces in the present. Even texts like John 3:16 that have planted themselves firmly in our cultural consciousness present challenges of distance for the preacher. (We encounter cultural distance involving Nicodemus' and Jesus' social status, as well as wordplay on *pneuma* [wind/Spirit] and *anōthen* [from above/again], and we find historical distance when we read Jesus' reference to the bronze serpent in the wilderness.) How much more is this true in the Prophets! The difficulty is not distance *per se* but rather the sheer size of the gap between then and now.

Preachers must develop the skills to cross that chasm. The following strategies and examples can help.

Strategy 15.1 Gauge the Distance

Not all distance needs to be crossed. Preachers do not have to bridge every gap, explain every exegetical detail, map out every theological concept, and address every potential objection. We have neither the time nor the need to do so. Rather, we should be selective based on the needs of our own people.

Therefore, the first step is for preachers to learn how a text worked for its ancient audience, and then to label and categorize the types of distance (cultural, historical, theological) that exist between that audience and their people. Only then will they be able to choose which types of distance need to be crossed for the sermon to work the same way.

For instance, consider Jeremiah 7:30–8:3. The oracle is profoundly disturbing, both in its accusation and its prediction. The prophet speaks of the Valley of the Son of Hinnom, a site near Jerusalem where locals worship idols, even sacrificing their children in rituals to foreign gods. Yahweh through Jeremiah predicts three tragic punishments: that the valley itself will be the site of the unburied victims of warfare (7:32–34), that in the conquest of Jerusalem the bones of kings, priests and prophets would be exhumed and exposed to the sun, moon, and stars that they had worshipped (8:1–2), and that the exiles who survived would prefer death to life (8:3).

The oracle works by the way the punishments fit the crime. Idol worship involved the death of innocent children; thus, the punishment includes the death of the people, the death of the rulers, and the death-wish of the exiles. A just death comes home to roost for those who handed out unjust death.

Yet what a canyon of distance to cross to get from then to now! We want the oracle to work the same way for our people: for them to sense the horror of idolatry, consider the justice of God whose punishment will fit the crime, and turn in fear and hope to the Lord. The question then becomes, what gaps must we bridge for our people to hear Jeremiah clearly? We must gauge the distance and make decisions.

Much of the gap here is cultural: ancient burial practices, the specific religions that called for child sacrifice, the location and history of the valley, the customs of the worship of the heavenly bodies in the Ancient Near East, the role of political and religious leaders in Jerusalem, and common practices during military invasion and conquest. Because the oracle works on the symmetry of crime and punishment, whatever illuminates that dynamic needs to be explained. That means that child sacrifice practices (and their prohibition in the Law), plus practices of conquest and exile are probably the most essential features to explain. The history of the Valley, the worship of heavenly bodies, and the role of leaders are less essential for understanding the oracle.

As for historical distance: this oracle takes place in the run-up to the siege and conquest of Jerusalem in 586 BC. Preachers who try to take listeners all the way from Genesis 12 through Abraham, the Exodus, Sinai, the conquest, judges, Saul, David, Solomon, the divided kingdom, Elijah and the prophets, the fall of Samaria, and the rise of the Neo-Babylonian Empire will find little time left to talk about Jeremiah's oracle (and fewer people in the pews the following Sunday). Relevant history may simply include the Babylonian threat and eventual conquest of Judah.

Finally, one will find less theological distance here than one might suppose. Though the setting seems bizarre, the underlying principles at work find strong NT expression: exclusive devotion to God (Matt 10:37), proscription of idolatrous practices (1 Thess

1:9), severe threats to those who abuse the innocent (Luke 17:2), and symmetrical retribution for sin (Luke 16:7).

By thinking about how the oracle works and categorizing the types of distance, preachers can focus in on the most relevant pieces of information—in this case, the cultural practices surrounding idolatry and conquest at the time and the impending exile. Though thousands of years of history and culture separate us from the prophets, sometimes only a few salient details are required to enable our people to hear their words afresh. Gauge the distance before you preach.

The description above was cumbersome; gauging the distance requires hard work. But when done well, the result can feel effortless for your congregation. Consider an Advent sermon on Isaiah 9:1–7 given by Ashley Mathews.[7] The distance in this oracle is daunting, mostly being historical (the precarious situation of King Hezekiah and the Assyrian threat) and theological (as this prophecy filters through NT quotations about Jesus' birth from a virgin mother). Mathews does a masterful job of boiling the distance down to what is essential for the hearers. After reading the passage, in just a few sentences she highlights important historical factors, makes key theological connections, and gets to the heart of the matter. Her introduction is worth quoting at length:

> It's very likely impossible that we don't all immediately think of Jesus when we read these verses. And well we should. The connection that we make to Jesus we make because Matthew makes it for us. He makes it explicitly in chapter 4, when he quotes from this passage in reference to the life and birth of Jesus. And yet of course we know that Isaiah was prophesying and would have given these words centuries before Jesus was ever born—and most likely in reference to the birth and reign of king Hezekiah and not Jesus. King Hezekiah would be the king whose reign would help to push back the oppressive plague that was Assyria. Hezekiah is the one that would

---

[7] Ashley Mathews, "Isaiah 9:1–7," December 20, 2020, Trinity Anglican Church, Atlanta, GA, https://podcast.atltrinity.org/episodes/isaiah-9-1-7-westside.

institute reforms that would be a light in darkness and help to restore Judah and Israel in the aftermath of king Ahaz. And so, there was good reason for people to hope in Hezekiah's reign. Hezekiah's reign would ultimately pave the way for the life of Jesus who would of course ultimately be the one who would deliver his people from the tyranny of sin and death.... In both instances these verses are referring to the hope that a besieged people feel whenever a new king is born.

Why on earth would an oppressed people ... have any hope at all or care for the birth of a baby? What is a baby in the face of the Assyrian empire or the Roman empire?

This section takes less than two minutes.[8] But at the end, we understand key facts about Isaiah's context, connect the oracle appropriately to Jesus, and get to the heart of God's mysterious promise of a baby as a counter to the threat of all the powers of the world. Massive distance can be crossed deftly, directing the hearer to important truth rather than burdening them with unnecessary detail.

When we take the time to gauge the distance, we can choose wisely which gaps need to be crossed with the limited time we have.

Strategy 15.2 Cross the Distance

Once we understand and prioritize the types of distance to be crossed, the most direct method for overcoming it will also be the most common: just cross it. Relay the necessary information so that your people can hear the words of the Prophets, understand their import, and feel their power.

Because there will usually be a *lot* of explaining to do, even when covering just the essential matters, it can help to spread out the explanation. This may be done in one of two ways. First, rather than try to give all the relevant background in the sermon's

---

8 In fact, the entire sermon (including Scripture reading and prayer) is less than 20 minutes long: a lesson to those like me who struggle to make a point in less than half an hour.

introduction, it can be portioned out in small helpings as the sermon works its way through the passage.

Richard Phillips preached a sermon on Jeremiah 16 that utilized this approach.[9] In this strange and gloomy oracle, Yahweh prohibits Jeremiah from marrying and starting a family and from participating in social activities like feasting and mourning. When people ask him why, he is to tell them that Yahweh will "hurl you out of this land" (v. 13). There then follows an oracle (vv. 14–18) that seems to be about a return from the "north country," although the tone remains glum. The chapter ends with a prayer praising God and predicting that he will be worshipped and known (vv. 19–20). Yahweh says it will be done (v. 21). The passage presents quite a challenge for preaching because of the various types of distance that occur throughout.

Phillips tackles the distance a little bit at a time. In the introduction he briefly outlines the general historical situation. Then he explains different portions as the sermon progresses: marriage and family customs (vv. 1–2); mourning customs (v. 5a); the Hebrew words for peace, steadfast love, and mercy (v. 5b); idolatrous practices of Israel in the time of Jeremiah (v. 11); and the importance of the Exodus for Israelite identity (v. 14). Phillips has a lot of distance to cross and it requires quite a bit of information. Trying to front load all that content in the introduction would overburden people, but he distributes the weight throughout the sermon.[10] Phillips offers a fine example of dealing with distance one typically encounters in the Prophets.

Second, consider preaching from the Prophets in a series. In so doing preachers can stack on information week-by-week instead of having to unload all of it at once. One week can be about God's covenant faithfulness; the next about idolatry; the next about corrupt leadership; the next about exile and restoration. Brief reviews

---

9 Richard D. Phillips, "My Strength and My Stronghold," February 6, 2022, Second Presbyterian Church, Greenville, SC, https://sermons.spcgreenville.org/sermons/27221556164843/.

10 A structural note on Phillips's sermon: he also parceled out the application, once at the end of each section. The same pattern (text, background, meaning, application) repeated for each section, and gave the sermon a rhythm that retained my interest throughout its 44-minute duration.

of prior weeks can help solidify the context so that listeners feel increasingly at home in the Prophets.

Crossing the distance by explaining relevant information will probably be the most common way to deal with it. However, at times the passage at hand may be susceptible to alternative tactics. I suggest two.

Strategy 15.3 Ignore the Distance

Sometimes prophets speak in such general, symbolic, or exalted fashion that preachers may ignore the distance entirely between then and now. Their words connect so powerfully that digression into historical minutiae would only get in the way. Listen to Micah's oracle near the end of his book:

> Rejoice not over me, O my enemy;
>   when I fall, I shall rise;
> when I sit in darkness,
>   the LORD will be a light to me.
> I will bear the indignation of the LORD
>   because I have sinned against him,
> until he pleads my cause
>   and executes judgment for me.
> He will bring me out to the light;
>   I shall look upon his vindication. (Mic 7:8–9)

Micah sings from the pit of defeat, yet trusts in God's mercy, knowing that his pain is discipline from God. God alone has cast down, and God alone will plead the prophet's cause and bring redemption.

Of course, Micah prophesies from within a particular historical situation. But his lyrics are generalized. The foe is just "my enemy," not "Assyria"; his failings are simply called "sins," not "sacrificing your children"; his hope is "judgment," "light" and "vindication," not "retaining your ancestral homeland." Micah sings in universal terms; why not invite the church to sing along? Tedious explanations might detract from the power of a song that we can take up today. When we are defeated and disciplined for our sin, we rely on the one who will vindicate even the sinner who trusts in him.

John Piper's sermon on this passage functions this way.[11] He does include a small section on the wider context of Micah, but when teaching on chapter 7, Piper does almost no historical or cultural or theological puddle jumping. For the most part, he simply ignores the distance, and encourages us to put Israel's song on our lips. His points of application are:

> Experience unshakeable solidarity with God.
> Accept indignation when you sin.
> Take bold confidence in the grace of God.
> Look to God for deliverance.

These could just as well be spoken today as they could 2,700 years ago.

Other oracles may also lend themselves toward ignoring the distance: Isaiah predicts that we will hear the voice of our Teacher guiding us (Isa 30:19–21); Zephaniah declares that Yahweh rejoices over us with singing (Zeph 3:17); Amos asks incredulously why we would long for God to show up (Amos 5:18–20). Sometimes a careful delineation of the differences between then and now would unnecessarily water down words ready made for the church. Ignore the distance and start singing.

Two brief cautions here: First, ignoring distance in the sermon does not permit the preacher to ignore it in the study. Preachers must work hard to understand what the oracle meant and what that implies for the church. Sometimes, after hard study one finds the application to be straightforward and immediate, but one has no way of knowing without first performing the normal labor of exegesis.

Second, ignoring distance should be practiced sparingly. If it becomes the staple diet of a church, the implicit message will be that biblical words are all simplistically applicable in the same manner. For example, immediately following the words cited above, Micah

---

11 John Piper, "When I Fall, I Will Rise," July 24, 1988, https://www.desiringgod.org/messages/when-i-fall-i-will-rise#brokenness-contrition-and-remorse.

declares, "A day for the building of your walls! / In that day the boundary shall be far extended" (Mic 7:11). Ignoring the distance when reading this passage would be foolish, as it could lead to a triumphant over-realized eschatology. Preachers who make a hermeneutical habit of immediacy unwittingly lead their people into dangerous places.

Strategy 15.4 Use the Distance

Occasionally the peculiarity of prophetic oracles can set up a powerful preaching surprise. A sermon might begin by examining the odd words and habits of an ancient people from a safe distance. Images and practices that seem far removed from our lives and times can be studied like strange artifacts unearthed in an archeological site. We clean, weigh, measure, and sketch—until we find our name and address written on the underside! These strange old words have been speaking to us all along. The preacher begins as a tour guide of the site, then suddenly takes on the role of police detective, asking, "Does this object belong to you, sir?"

For instance, in Jeremiah 7 Yahweh tells the prophet to stand in the temple gates and declare, "Do not trust in these deceptive words: 'This is the temple of the LORD, the temple of the LORD, the temple of the LORD'" (Jer 7:4). Apparently, this is a popular piece of doggerel sung by the inhabitants of Jerusalem about the temple. If this is the temple of the LORD, where Yahweh would put his name (2 Kgs 21:7), then how could there ever be a successful foreign invasion? They are safe—no matter their sinful rebellion—if they have "the temple of the LORD." Jeremiah's job is to undeceive them of these notions.

In a sermon on this passage, we can stand with our people at a distance and critique. How foolish those Israelites are! We put our arm around Jeremiah's shoulders, shaking our heads at what a difficult job he has, working with such hypocrites.

But then comes the hinge, when the preacher finds a way to change his role, showing listeners that we may not be as different from them as we thought. For example, our church sings a worship song called "Build Your Church":

Upon this rock, You build Your Church
And the gates of hell will not prevail.
When we bind and loose, we proclaim Your truth
And in Jesus' name, we will not fail.[12]

At one point the song moves into an extended repetition of the phrase "We will never fail," in a call-and-response between the vocalist and the church. The song is a powerful anthem, offered in a spirit of trust in Jesus' indefatigable commitment to the church (Matt 16:18–19). In preaching from Jeremiah 7, one could ask, do we sing our own songs as a screen to conceal the things in our lives that must change? We might hide behind God's promise to be with the church, using the inspiring words to give ourselves false security. If so, then we have some self-examination to do. Beware of superficial and facile trust that downplays sin.

We can use distance, delaying the point until the right moment, and transform a homiletical obstacle into an instrument.

Conclusion

Like any passage of Scripture, prophetic oracles are only effective in the pulpit when they are brought to bear on the here and now. But the cultural, historical, and theological distance between the prophets' scenario and our own can put a heavy strain on our prophetic imagination. We must size up the distance with care and ask how we can overcome it, so that our people can hear the prophetic words in all their intended power and immediacy.

For Further Study

Bosma, Carl J. "The Challenges of Reading the 'Gospel' of Isaiah for Preaching." *CTJ* 39 (2004). 11–53.
Brueggemann, Walter. *Hopeful Imagination: Prophetic Voices in Exile.* Fortress Press, 1986.

---

12 Naomi Raine and Chris Brown, vocalists, "Build Your Church," *Elevation Worship and Maverick City Music* (Heritage Worship Music Publishing, 2021).

Walton, John H., Victor H. Mathews, and Mark W. Chavalas. *The IVP Bible Background Commentary: Old Testament.* IVP, 2000. 581–811.

Seitz, Christopher R. *Word Without End: The Old Testament as Abiding Theological Witness.* Eerdmans, 1998.

Talk about It

What seems to you the hardest kind of distance to overcome: cultural, historical, or theological? Why is that difficult for you in particular? If you could bridge that distance, how might your people benefit? How might God work in your life also?

Dig Deeper

Read Isaiah 19:16–25. What concepts (phrases, nations, names) present a challenge of distance to modern ears?

What can you say about the tone of the oracle, and how it seems to change from the beginning to the end of the oracle? Why is this significant for Isaiah's contemporaries—and how could it be significant for your congregation now?

In a sermon on this oracle, which strategy from this chapter might you use to bridge the distance between then and now?

Practice

Brevity counts! How can you quickly bring your people up to speed on a prophetic oracle? Write an introductory paragraph (less than 300 words) that sets the historical and theological stage for Jeremiah 23:1–8.[13] You should include explanations of the political situation (the immanent Babylonian invasion), the behavior of Judah's recent kings (addressed in prior oracles), and Jeremiah's task.

---

13 It may help to read general introduction to Jeremiah, an accessible example of which can be found in Michael L. Brown, "Jeremiah," in *Jeremiah–Ezekiel*, ed. Tremper Longman III and David E. Garland, EBC vol. 7 (Zondervan Academic, 2010), 23–66.

Monotony

> *Because children have abounding vitality, because they are in spirit fierce and free, therefore they want things repeated and unchanged. They always say, "Do it again"; and the grown-up person does it again until he is nearly dead. For grown-up people are not strong enough to exult in monotony. But perhaps God is strong enough to exult in monotony. It is possible that God says every morning, "Do it again" to the sun; and every evening, "Do it again" to the moon. It may not be automatic necessity that makes all daisies alike; it may be that God makes every daisy separately, but has never got tired of making them. It may be that He has the eternal appetite of infancy; for we have sinned and grown old, and our Father is younger than we.*
>
> —G. K. Chesterton[1]

A chapter titled "Monotony" sounds about as appealing as a cereal called "Stale Flakes." But we cannot get around it: the prophets say the same things over and over. In this chapter we take a hard look at why the prophets repeat themselves day after day, era after era. Then we will see how preachers can take the same old ingredients and serve up a hot homiletical breakfast on Sunday.

---

1 Gilbert K. Chesterton, *Orthodoxy* (Doubleday, 1959), 58.

Monotony vs. Boredom

Before jumping into the Scriptures, it will help us first to distinguish monotony from boredom. Monotony is about content; boredom is about the experience of that content. We must note that the former does not make the latter inevitable.[2]

In high school my older brother joined the wrestling team, and I spent hours in the bleachers watching his matches. To my eyes, each match was the same: sweaty boys pushing each other and falling down, then either staying down or getting back up and repeating the process. Monotony and boredom perfectly overlapped. But the next year I joined the team, and I began to learn about the strategies and tactics of the sport. It was still monotonous, but the boredom dissipated, even when I was a spectator, because I understood the dynamics of a match, and why one hold was slightly different from another. I saw what the wrestlers were trying to do, and how a competitor used his brain as much as his body to position himself and score points. Today I enjoy watching an entire wrestling meet, which consists of 20 or so consecutive matches.

The same dynamics are at play with other sports (such as baseball and stock car racing), games like chess and bridge, and music. Composer Philip Glass writes minimalist works where the same musical phrase repeats time and again. As he says, his music is "like taking a microscope and looking at something very close up and you'll see things that you never would have seen before. ... The music isn't slow but the rate of change is slow."[3] In other words, look closely and monotony becomes a vehicle for creativity, even brilliance. For those who understand, boredom fades while monotony remains.

The same dynamic operates in the Prophets. Once readers understand the what, the why, and the how of prophetic monotony, their oracles no longer bore; they fascinate by their endless variation on just a few themes. To that task we now turn.

---

2 For that matter, the converse also fails: dictionaries are low on monotony and high on boredom.

3 Philip Glass, "Philip Glass: Complex Minimalist," interview by Renee Montagne, *Morning Edition*, October 3, 2008.

Monotony in the Prophets: What, Why and How

What is Isaiah so worked up about for 66 chapters? It turns out that for 39 chapters in a row he has the coming exile to Babylon on his mind, and then in the latter parts he mixes in songs about a future return to the land. Like all the prophets, Isaiah is always exercised about the same two things: judgment and salvation. As we will see, these twin themes explain almost every oracle in the OT Prophets. When the prophets only walk in two tracks, they are bound to wear ruts in the ground.

In a classic study on the form and content of prophetic material in the OT, Claus Westermann suggests why they make ruts.[4] Though some narrative accounts (such as Jonah) and prayers (such as in Habakkuk) appear, Westermann shows that almost all prophetic material is comprised of "announcements" of judgment or salvation. The announcements are made to individuals, to Israel and Judah, and to the surrounding nations, but the content is predictably binary: Yahweh is bringing disaster, or Yahweh is bringing redemption. Let us look at each.

Judgment is by far the more common announcement. It comes in several forms. Sometimes the prophet leaves the nature and timing of the disaster uncertain. Joel, for instance, lacks historical context almost entirely. He proclaims judgment using the image of a recent (undated) locust invasion, with the attackers swarming like insects over walls and mountains. But they are never identified explicitly.[5] At other times the judgment is quite specific. Jeremiah leaves no doubt, for instance, that the invading Babylonians are the instrument of God's wrath (Jer 25:9), and that the current royal dynasty of Judah are Yahweh's target (Jer 21–23). The announcement of judgment varies also in time and addressees: "judgment"

---

4 Claus Westermann, *Basic forms of Prophetic Speech*, trans. by Hugh Clayton White (Westminster John Knox, 1991), 90–98.

5 On the difficulty of dating Joel or describing its historical context with any certainty, see John Barton, *Joel and Obadiah*, OTL (Westminster John Knox, 2001), 3, 13–18. For the possibility that Joel's rather general predictions of woe and weal "is made a type for God's work with the nations and with creation itself," see Christopher R. Seitz, *The Goodly Fellowship of the Prophets: The Achievement of Association in Canon Formation* (Baker Academic, 2009), 87.

can indicate the fall of Samaria or Jerusalem (in Isaiah, Jeremiah, Ezekiel, Hosea, Amos, Micah, Habakkuk, Zephaniah), or punishment during and after exile (in Isaiah, Jeremiah, Haggai, Zechariah, Malachi). And all prophetic books include oracles of judgment addressed to foreign nations. In these varieties, then, judgment plays a lead role in prophetic discourse.

Salvation, though occupying less space, also appears regularly and in various guises. The prophets speak of it concretely in time and space as a return to the Promised Land (as when Jeremiah 29:10 gives a timeline of 70 years). That return signals a renewed covenant and a radical change of heart in God's people (Jer 31).

In many cases the prophets announce salvation in terms that can only be called "apocalyptic": the heavenly bodies will fall (Joel 2:30–32); the desert will bloom (Isa 35:1); the mountains will be leveled (Isa 40:3–5); the fire of Yahweh will burn away enemies and give light to the faithful (Mal 4:1–3); the Mount of Olives will be split in two (Zech 14:1–5); dry bones will be given life by the Spirit of Yahweh (Ezek 37); the land will yield miraculously rich produce (Amos 9:13–15).[6]

The prophets beat out a steady cadence of judgment and salvation. *Why* so monotonous? Why tread the same paths repeatedly for hundreds of years? Recall that OT prophets are the covenant enforcers between Israel and Yahweh.[7] They declare the character of the covenant Lord; they recite the covenant history; they remind Israel of covenant demands; and they proclaim the covenant consequences (judgment and salvation). The prophets' role means that they were not there to deliver new content; they were called to remind and reinforce existing covenant regulations.

Even the specific forms the consequences would take—military victory or defeat, health or plague, abundance or famine, peace or strife, security or exile—were lifted straight from the pages of Leviticus 26–27 and Deuteronomy 28–30. For the prophets, nothing is new under the sun.[8]

---

6 See ch. 4 for a discussion of the interplay between prophetic and apocalyptic literature.

7 See ch. 2.

8 See the list of prophetic predictions and their precedents in Leviticus and

But just as God's demands and consequences did not change, neither did Israel's response. As steadfast as Yahweh's love, so consistently was the people's rebellion. As Hosea complains, "The more they were called, the more they went away" (Hos 11:2). The constancy of both Yahweh's character and Israel's conduct were like two mirrors facing one another, creating an endless series of repeating images and oracles.

In fact, the prophets themselves grew tired of the monotony. How long will God have to demand obedience before he gets it? How long will must we stand on street corners and in the temple gates and among the hopeless exiles, crying out yet again the holiness of Yahweh, his covenant faithfulness, and his commandment to love him in return? Jeremiah asks in frustration, "How long will the land mourn and the grass of every field wither? / For the evil of those who dwell in it the beasts and the birds are swept away, because they said, 'He will not see our latter end'" (Jer 12:4). The people's stubborn refusal to trust and obey made monotony necessary.

In the final analysis, the prophets' consistency reflects the consistent goodness of Yahweh, the stubborn refusal of his people, and the chronic need for a future where their hearts would be circumcised, and they would finally love him in return (Deut 30:6).

So much for *what* and *why*. *How* did the prophets handle their monotonous assignment? Their oracles show that they did it by combining grit and creativity.

The prophets had grit. They did not shirk their responsibility, no matter how monotonous the work.[9] The sheer volume of the prophetic corpus (which was probably only a selection from a larger body of oracles) testifies to their perseverance. Moreover, their words were just as difficult to deliver as they were to devise. They proclaim judgment when salvation is on everyone's mind,

---

Deuteronomy in Douglas Stuart, *Hosea–Jonah*, WBC (Word Books), xxxii–xlii.

9 Fascinating partial exceptions to prophetic obedience include Jonah and Ezekiel. Yet Jonah's unwillingness, which functions as the central plot point of the book, comes not for reasons of monotony but because of his ethnocentrism. Ezekiel, however, perhaps needed powerful pressure from Yahweh before he agreed to prophesy. See Daniel I. Block, *The Book of Ezekiel Chapters 1–24*, NICOT (Eerdmans, 1997), 11–12.

Yahweh brings life in the desert	40:3–8; 41:17–20; 42:14–17; 44:1–5; 45:8; 49:8–12; 51:3
Yahweh's judgment and redemption compared to water (rain, floods, pools, etc.)	43:16–21; 44:27–28; 48:20–21; 50:2; 51:10; 51:15; 55:12–13
Yahweh's cosmic greatness	40:12–17, 21–27; 44:23–26; 45:11–13; 48:12–13; 50:3; 51:4–6
Yahweh's control of the nations and the future	41:1–7; 41:25–29; 43:8–15; 44:6–8; 45:14–25; 48:1–8; 49:22–26
Yahweh's tender care for Israel	40:11, 28–31; 41:11–13; 43:1–7
Yahweh blots out sins	43:25–28
Yahweh kills the sea monster	51:9
Yahweh a potter who shapes clay	45:9–10
Yahweh's words like rain	55:6–11
Yahweh's humble servant	42:1–9, 18–25; 44:21–22; 49:1–7; 50:4–9; 52:13–53:12
Israel Yahweh's treasure	49:13–18
Israel tried in a furnace	48:9–11
Israel an unfaithful wife	50:1–2
Israel a weapon in Yahweh's hand	41:14–16
Israel in the dark	50:10–11
Israel a barren woman who gives birth	49:19–21; 54:1–3
Israel a widow redeemed from shame	54:4–8
Israel sold and redeemed for free	52:3–6
Mockery of idols	40:18–20; 41:21–24; 44:9–20; 46:1–13
Enemies consumed	51:7–8
Cyrus as Yahweh's instrument	45:1–7
Humiliation of the sorceress Babylon	47:1–15
Watchmen calling	40:3–5; 52:7–10
Flee as in the Exodus!	52:11–12
Wake up, drunk Israel!	51:17–23
Dress for a festival!	52:1–2
Eat and drink for nothing!	55:1–5
Faithfulness like the days of Noah	54:9–10
Beauty and stability in the new city	54:11–17

Table 11.1: Variety in Isaiah 40–55

and vice versa. They never seem in step with the culture. Consequently, the prophets are often ridiculed for their words. Ezekiel's bizarre actions appear to be strange and fictional parables (Ezek 20:49); Isaiah is mocked by drunk leaders who thought he talked in an infantile way (Isa 28:7–13); Amos is threatened by a priest (Amos 7:10–13); Micah is told flat out to stop (Mic 2:6); Jeremiah faces imprisonment and kidnapping (Jer 38, 43). Yet they persevere, speaking the same message time and again.

But they also showed tremendous creativity. Their method for serving theological leftovers to picky eaters was to spice up the dish in unexpected ways. In other words, the literary form was as diverse as the message was constant. The prophets were masters at saying the same thing in different ways.

Consider an extended series of oracles like Isaiah 40–55. The section's theme is simple: an exhortation to trust Yahweh to bring salvation in the form of a return from exile. But this scant description is nothing at all like reading Isaiah. These 16 chapters are among the most beautiful and brilliant passages in all of Scripture. The prophet finds ever-new ways to make the same simple point (see Table 11.1). Isaiah 40–55 is a parade example of how the OT Prophets use variety of form to deliver monotony of content.

The dilemma for prophets is inescapable: repeat the message of Yahweh to hard hearts that are not interested. They do so with impressive perseverance and astonishing variety.

Monotony in the Pulpit

In many ways, the preacher's dilemma mirrors the prophet's. When we preach—especially when we preach from the Prophets—we deliver the same message repeatedly. In fact, if one reduces sermons to propositions, the range of ideas delivered by a sermon series on, say, Ezekiel will be quite narrow: judgment is coming to Judah (Ezek 1–24); judgment is coming on the nations (Ezek 25–32); restoration will follow (Ezek 33–48).

That puts us in a preaching pickle. In one sense we know that our task is to tell the old, old story, over and over again. At the same time, as Robinson asks, "How can you shun the sin of boring people?"[10] We can shun that sin and remain faithful to the prophetic message by using the strategies below.

Strategy 16.1 Develop Variations on a Theme

At the beginning of this chapter, we noted that monotony does not always lead to boredom. One way to prevent the former from triggering the latter is to work hard at developing variations on simple ideas. This can be done on a small or a large scale.

On a small scale, we can turn repetition into restatement. Repetition is simply saying the same phrase again and again. A few years ago, I was at a local clergy gathering for my denomination. These sessions took place on Sunday afternoons, after most of us had done the hard labor of preaching in the morning and eaten a hearty meal afterward. The phrase "carb coma" would not have been inappropriate for most of us. The purpose of the meeting was ostensibly to worship together, though we all knew that denominational administrative tasks were the true reason our attendance was required. As we slogged through Scripture readings, prayers, and songs, waiting for the "business" portion to commence, we sang a chorus which repeated the phrase, "This is a holy moment." Perhaps sensing the lethargy in the room, the music leader had us go back over and over to sing that line. A friend leaned over and whispered to me, "It doesn't matter how many times we sing it, just saying that it's a holy moment doesn't make it one." Repetition takes monotony and produces boredom.

But restatement is finding new ways to say the same thing. It takes one topic and turns it over like a jewel, letting each facet catch the light. Cleophus LaRue provides a brief example of restatement in his message on Hab 2:1–4. At one point he describes the frustration of being in a season of uncertainty and disappointment:

> What do you do when you are no longer sure how God is going to work out God's purpose in your life? What do you do when you're not even sure that God is at work in your life? You are

---

10 Haddon Robinson, *Biblical Preaching: The Development and Delivery of Expository Messages*, 3rd ed. (Baker Academic, 2014), 147.

Passage	Variation on "judgment"
1:1–2 (and several other passages in Amos)	God's character means that he judges
1:3–2:16	God's judgment falls on His people just as it does on everyone else
3:1–8	God's judgment always happens for a reason
5:4–15, 21–24	God brings judgment on injustice
6:1–7	God brings judgment on those who hoard their wealth
8:4–14	God's judgment will reach its climax at the return of Christ

Table 11.2: Variations on Judgment in Amos

unhappy where you are, and yet unsure about where God is leading. What do you do when you find yourself in a difficult season of waiting where heaven is silent, or the trumpet of heaven is sounding forth an uncertain sound?[11]

Note that as LaRue restates listeners' situation, the picture develops from uncertainty about the *how* of God's purpose, to uncertainty as to *whether* God has a purpose at all. Then dissatisfaction is added, and finally a metaphor of heavenly silence and confusion. Restatement uses small changes in a simple idea to expose hearers to unseen facets. The sermon is filled with such restatement, plumbing the depths of simple concepts. Restatement, by taking a single idea and unfolding it, can turn monotony into fascination.

We can also develop variations on simple themes using whole sermons. For example, a few years ago I preached a 7-week series through the book of Amos. Amos is a tough book, with every oracle warning of judgment to come until the final section (9:11–15). So, the church heard warnings of judgment from the same prophet in the same context for six weeks in a row. I needed to vary the theme each week, adding a twist to the warning of judgment each

---

11 Cleophus J. LaRue, "It Will Surely Come," February 2002, https://www.youtube.com/watch?v=thUNubGmO4E.

week until a full picture emerged of Amos's theology of judgment (see Table 11.2).

By spending unhurried time listening to Amos, his words provided us with all the variety we needed to spend extended time in the book. This series is like restatement on a large scale. Rather than each sentence, though, it was each sermon that revealed a new aspect of the idea of judgment. With hard work, preachers can vary their content and style in large and small ways to preach monotony without setting off boredom.

Strategy 16.2 Cultivate Grit

Monotony is necessary. In Israel, as in the church, part of the *point* of preaching is delivering the same messages time and again, in season and out of season. Prone to wander, we need repeated summons back to the fold. Monotony is not a random byproduct of the prophetic corpus or of the church's life, but the necessary medicine for a forgetful people. In a sermon in 1855 Charles Spurgeon said,

> The whole Bible tells us, from beginning to end, that salvation is not by the works of the law, but by the deeds of grace. Martin Luther declared that he constantly preached justification by faith alone, "because," said he, "the people would forget it; so that I was obliged almost to knock my Bible against their heads, to send it into their hearts." So it is true; we constantly forget that salvation is by grace alone.[12]

In other words, whether preaching about grace or another topic, one of the major functions of preaching is reminding.[13] This fact places preachers in proximity to prophets, in that we both have

---

12 Charles Haddon Spurgeon, "The Carnal Mind Enmity Against God," April 2, 1855, https://www.spurgeon.org/resource-library/sermons/the-carnal-mind-enmity-against-god/#flipbook/. This seems to be a loose paraphrase from Luther's *Commentary on Galatians*. For more, see James Swan, "Luther: Every Week I Preach Justification by Faith to My People, Because Every Week They Forget It," August 3, 2020, https://beggarsallreformation.blogspot.com/2020/08/luther-every-week-i-preach.html.

13 Jeffrey Arthurs has written helpfully on the role of reminding in preaching: *Preaching as Reminding: Stirring Memory in an Age of Forgetfulness* (IVP, 2017).

a duty to accept monotony as part of the "priestly service of the gospel of God" (Rom 15:16). Nowhere is that task more central than in preaching from the (monotonous) Prophets.

If this is the case, then our task calls for the same grit that the prophets demonstrated. We must not flinch in the face of monotony. Some preachers lean so heavily on surprise and novelty in their preaching that monotony feels like failure. I am one of them. I love sermons that present new concepts, that astonish and delight, or that correct misunderstandings in moments of fresh insight. Of course, there is nothing wrong with Sunday surprises. But preaching habits calcify over the years, and we can develop a tendency to pursue novelty for novelty's sake, to stay away from themes we have already "covered."[14] When that happens, we are in danger of rating originality too high. The question is not, "What will be new and interesting?" but rather, "What do my people need to hear (perhaps again)?"

One way we can cultivate grit is to listen to preachers who have it. In 1934, Ida B. Robinson gave a sermon on Malachi 3:2 entitled, "Who Shall Be Able to Stand?" Witness the grit on display from an African American woman in the Jim Crow era:

> Jesus is coming back for a church without spot or blemish.... Tell me who, then, shall be able to stand? Who can stand in this sin-polluted age? Only he who has been born again, regenerated by the [S]pirit and kept by the power of Almighty God. He, it is, that shall be able to stand. Within my heart the proposition is fixed and settled to be the servant God is calling for, regardless of the cost. In the dawning of the rapture morning, when the bridegroom in midair shall appear, who shall be able to stand? ... Let us humble ourselves and pray and God will destroy sin that we in the great day of judgment receive a righteous reward.[15]

---

14 The desire for novelty plays into a consumerist mindset that is rampant in the 21st-century Church. The "successful" ministry model was described by David French as "a Coldplay concert followed by a TED talk" (David French and Curtis Chang, "When Pastors Head for the Exits," *Good Faith* (podcast), January 22, 2022.

15 Ida B. Robinson, "Who Shall Be Able to Stand?" Mt. Sinai Holy Church

Robinson is not peddling new ideas or telling cute stories. She takes Malachi's question at face value and passes it on to the church without apology: Whatever the cost, seek God, and ask him to conquer sin in your life.

Preaching the Prophets takes grit. Say it again, and again, and again. We are in covenant with God. He has covenant demands and covenant consequences. God will discipline, and God will restore.

Strategy 16.3 Recognize Your Own Boredom

When the consistent nature of the biblical message begins to feel boring, it can indicate a problem in the preacher's soul. Boredom may by evidence that we are just as prone to hardness of heart, fatigue, and despair as our people. As 1 Peter 5:1–4 reminds us, in the church, shepherds are also sheep, awaiting the arrival (and assessment) of the Chief Shepherd. Moreover, we face additional temptation to spiritual lethargy precisely because the sacred has become routine. As Paul David Tripp says,

> You've spent so much time in Scripture that its grand redemptive narrative, with its expansive wisdom, doesn't excite you anymore. You've spent so much time exegeting the atonement that you can stand at the foot of the cross with little weeping and scant rejoicing.... You've spent so much time meditating on what it means to lead others in worship, but you have little private awe. It's all become so regular and normal that it fails to move you anymore.[16]

The preaching life forms one part of the grind of parish ministry: the relentless, difficult, draining work of discipling people who are great at not being discipled. It wears on us. And we can add to that

---

of America, May 6, 1934, in Bettye Collier-Thomas, ed., *Daughters of Thunder: Black Women Preachers and Their Sermons, 1850-1979* (Jossey-Bass Publishers, 1998), 200.

16 Paul David Tripp, *Dangerous Calling: Confronting the Unique Challenges of Pastoral Ministry* (Crossway, 2012), 114–115.

weariness by our own habits of self-isolation, legalistic posturing, reliance on professionalism, over- or underworking, and dysfunctional leadership.

At times when we are sliding into dark places like this, boredom can be our Father's gift to us: a gracious indicator that all is not well in our hearts, that the gospel message of life and death that used to sear our minds and hearts now elicits a yawn. When the Prophets bore us—when the impending doom of God's people or the grand promises of worldwide redemption fail to move us—we need to pay attention. We can do so in three ways.

First, we can care for our souls. We can reprioritize Sabbath rest each week. We can keep track of our hours and commit to stay within set limits. We can block off time on the schedule for family. We can refuse to let sermon study substitute for personal worship at the feet of Jesus. We can seek out safe peer relationships—which take years to develop and are nonetheless worth it—with pastors in our town or denomination or network. Sometimes what we need to do is just sleep eight hours each night and drink more water. All these practices remind our bodies and souls that we are not God, that our frame is humble for a reason, that the actions of our ministry are not what really moves the kingdom forward. The kingdom grows even when we are sleeping (Mark 4:26–29).

Second, we can care for our minds. Sometimes we are bored because we have ceased to dig deeply into the wonders of the gospel, of the character of God, and of the rich biblical text. As Howard Hendricks said, "If you stop growing today, you stop teaching tomorrow."[17] We need fresh input. The simplest way to do this is to grab that book that has been on your shelf for a few years in the "to be read" pile—maybe the one from that class in Bible college or seminary that you promised yourself you would finish. Take time (at work) and start reading. Or attend a (good, rich, challenging) conference. Or take an enrichment class online or pursue a D.Min or other advanced degree.

Finally, we can care for our people. Sometimes our doctrine is dry because our eyes are, too. If you have let the administrative or academic tasks of your work crowd out pastoral care, then I urge

---

17 Howard G. Hendricks, *Teaching to Change Lives* (Multnomah, 1987), 27.

you to reconsider your priorities. Spend some time with the sick and shut-in; put those counseling hours back on your schedule; invite a parishioner for coffee with no agenda other than to learn about them and pray for them. In other words, pastor. When we acquire a deep concern for the suffering and sin of our people, the words of prophets take on new life.

For the past couple of years, I have visited the staff of our local Emergency Care Center on the same day every week at 6:45am. The work is not difficult: I bring snacks, share a brief word of Scripture, and pray for them as their shift begins. But that simple rhythm is one way that I keep near to those in our town who suffer, and near to those who are there to help. It reminds me that I work with bodies and souls who love, who hurt, and who will not live forever. I find it terribly difficult to get bored in that room.

This book is in large part technical and homiletical. But we must not forget that our Lord cares for sermons only as a means to much greater ends. We ignore those ends at our peril.

Preaching Through a Major Prophet

If your church preaches through books passage-by-passage, the Major Prophets (Isaiah, Jeremiah, and Ezekiel) present a special challenge. Jeremiah, for instance, is the longest book in the Bible by word count. Even tackling a chapter each Sunday would take at least a year. Some chapters (like Jer 4) would force preachers to cover multiple topics, while other sections (like Jer 46–51) would cover the same ground week after week. And all the while the gloom of judgment would be broken only occasionally by the light of hope.

Before suggesting some methods for preaching through Major Prophets, it may help to recall that prophetic books are best viewed as anthologies. What we have in the Prophets is not a chronological record of their weekly preaching, but a "greatest hits album," organized by topic and delivered over the course of years. The exiles from Jerusalem did not listen to Ezekiel's oracles seriatim. So even if your church has quite a high regard for the canon and normally preaches straight through books, it may be a mercy for the church to know that not even Ezekiel subjected his people to a verse-by-verse preach-a-thon. The book of Haggai is helpful in this regard: Haggai's four oracles are all precisely dated and were delivered over a period of four months to those who returned from Babylonian exile under the emperor Darius. That's one oracle every month.[18] We must be careful not to impose modern church habits imaginatively on ancient prophets, or to suppose that their words can be expounded only by a forced march straight through the text.

If the thought of starting in Isaiah 1:1 and settling in for the long haul makes you shudder, you can find other ways to skin that cat. Here are five.

Strategy 17.1 Preach in Themes

Consider grouping oracles thematically and preaching from a representative text for each theme. For instance, if preaching through Isaiah, gather all the oracles against foreign nations in Isa 13–24 and choose one; collect historical texts about Hezekiah and the coming Assyrian invasion; cluster passages that talk about injustice; and so on. This gives the preacher freedom to use wide or narrow categories, making the sermon series as long or as short as will be helpful.

Strategy 17.2 Preach as You Read

Preachers can take the entire church on a reading tour of a prophet. Giving your people plenty of advance notice, the church can read a chapter each day of the week of (for example) Ezekiel.[19] Then the preacher can either pick one of the week's oracles to preach from on Sunday or just preach from the reading assigned to Sunday. Ezekiel can be covered like this in eight to ten weeks.

---

18 His final two oracles were delivered on the same day, so the frequency of his preaching is actually less than that.

19 It helps to assign only five or six days each week to give people a chance to catch up on missed days.

Strategy 17.3 Take Breaks

Churches can intersperse the prophetic text with other material. Preachers can take every first Sunday to preach on Jeremiah, and then return to whatever else is on the schedule. Alternatively, it can be interesting and enlightening to alternate weeks between Jeremiah and, say, the Gospel of Matthew. This not only breaks up the Jeremiah readings but will probably also spark connections between the Testaments.

Strategy 17.4 Take Laps

Consider taking laps. That is, preach from Isaiah every week, but just for a season; then leave Isaiah until the same time each year. As I write this, for instance, our church is preaching through Luke each Lent. We pick up each year where we left off, and we will finish it, Lord willing, some day. Your congregation can get the feel for a prophetic book for a few weeks but does not have to stay there for months on end.

Strategy 17.5 Spend Time on Titles

Finally, when walking through Prophets in any of these ways (or straight through from beginning to end), try using creative big ideas. "Judgment against Ammon," followed by "Judgment against Moab," followed by "Judgment against Tyre," is not to going to whet anyone's appetite. A few years ago, I preached through Isaiah 1–6, and used the following big ideas:

1:1–20	Snow isn't scarlet[20]
2:1–5	Live to be lifted
2:6–22	Look up to let go
3:1–15	Leaders are crucial
3:16–4:1	Followers are called

---

20 Apparently, I skipped Isa 1:21–31. Looking back, I cannot recall why!

4:2–6	It's still on
5:1–7	Faith bears fruit
5:8–24	The favor of focus
5:25–30	The gift of terror
6:1–7	The only remedy for the presence of God is the presence of God
6:8–13	We are a sign opposed

Most of these oracles are judgment oracles. But Isaiah is a brilliant orator, and his stylistic variety helped me label the sermons in ways that explored the topics of sin and judgment with creativity.

In any case, when preaching through Major Prophets, consider beforehand how you will structure the series so that people can hear the same themes time and time again with freshness and power.

Conclusion

The prophets knew that they had a tough assignment, and that part of the challenge would be to take the old familiar covenant demands, threats, and promises and bring them to life in the minds of Israel. We have the same challenge they did, with the same tools of grit and creativity. Refuse to fear monotony, and your people will reap the rewards of your courage.

For Further Study

Arthurs, Jeffrey D. *Preaching as Reminding: Stirring Memory in an Age of Forgetfulness.* IVP Academic, 2017.

Books that can stir us to passion and perseverance in the great task of preaching and pastoral ministry:

Hansen, David. *Loving the Church You Lead: Pastoring with Acceptance and Grace.* Baker Books, 1998.

Peterson, Eugene. *The Contemplative Pastor: Returning to the Art of Spiritual Direction.* Eerdmans, 1989.

Piper, John. *The Supremacy of GOD in Preaching.* Revised and expanded edition. Crossway, 2021.

Tripp, Paul David. *Dangerous Calling: Confronting the Unique Challenges of Pastoral Ministry.* Crossway, 2012.

Talk about It

Is there a difference between monotonous and boring? Talk about a conversation, sermon, or experience that fits into each section of this Venn diagram:

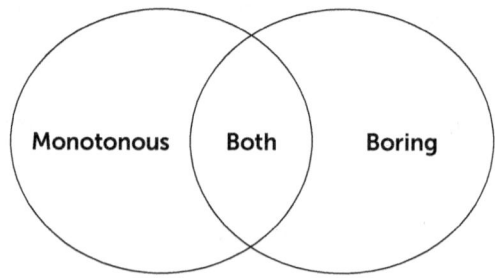

Dig Deeper

Take a close look at Micah. In each oracle, he points forward to disaster or restoration. Make an outline of the oracles, and for each one, note the devices that Micah uses to engage his hearers. How does he handle monotony? How might that inspire you if you were preaching through his book?

Practice

Practice separating monotony from boredom. Have the same conversation with the same person five times in one day. That is, think of something you want to communicate to someone specific: anything from "What lousy weather we're having!" to "I love you so much." See if you can restate it in ways that are varied, interesting, and build on one another rather than just repeating. If they stay engaged, you win. If they say something like, "All right already, you just keep going on about it," you lose.

Conclusion

BY ONE COUNT, the New Testament authors cite or allude to the Prophets over 1,200 times.[1] They write with the assumption that the gospel of Jesus Christ is deeply rooted in the Prophets' words—that it cannot be understood without them. We do not take too great a leap to suppose that those authors would feel the same about preaching the gospel today.

Hence this book. As I stated at the outset, its aim has been to equip readers to preach biblically faithful, theologically sound, and rhetorically effective sermons from prophetic oracles. That can be quite a journey, especially if one has not made a habit of reading and preaching the Prophets heretofore.

To that end, Part I sought to help preachers get their bearings before hitting the trail. It introduced the prophets and their mission, surveyed their body of work, and made a case for continued preaching from the Prophets. It also proposed a theological framework for interpreting and preaching from prophetic oracles based on parallel covenants that enfold Israel and the church.

Part II covered much of the terrain by outlining the major literary features found in the prophets, explaining their theological purpose in its context, and offering strategies for replicating the effect of the form when preaching. Genres like poetry, parable, epistle, and apocalyptic appear in the prophets. They also use images and emotions to powerful effect and are not afraid of creating confusion and even shock in their hearers. Throughout Part II we examined these features and provided a series of strategies for

---

1 NA^{27}, 772-808.

proclamation that aimed at being faithful to the text by recreating similar effects (where possible and advisable) in the pulpit.

Part III rounded out the journey by paying special attention to obstacles that can make preachers want to turn back and go home. We explored the prophets' intense focus on justice, discussed the several forms of distance between their world and our own, and described prophetic monotony, its purposes, and its homiletical possibilities.

Finally, the Appendix below presents two complete sermons on prophetic texts. I chose them because they showcase some of the interpretive and homiletical strategies offered in the text.

Throughout Parts II and III, strategies were numbered and labeled intentionally to facilitate future reference. A book like this can be read once with pleasure (it may be hoped), but without an expectation that all 17 strategies will be absorbed and applied. Instead, my wish is that this book will collect dust on your shelf (or take up storage on your device) until the next time you choose to preach from the prophets and can refer to the appropriate section(s). How well the book has succeeded in those aims may be measured by how soon the day comes when you reach for it because you've decided to preach the Prophets.

May that day come quickly, preacher, and may the Spirit of the Lord guide, teach, encourage, and empower you to deliver his word to his people.

Appendix 1

Sample Sermon

The Favor of Focus (Isaiah 5:8–24)
Andrew Thompson

I preached this sermon as part of a series through Isaiah 1–6.[1] *The passage is a sequence of three woe oracles to different groups within Judah with predictions of judgment. The sermon uses the strategies covered in this text in three ways: First, the interpretive framework operates with continuity, tying old covenant warnings to new covenant warnings in a direct line. I interpret this passage such that OT judgment is not transmuted into NT grace so that we as believers are spared the bite of Isaiah's words. Rather, both the passage and the sermon issue genuine warnings that call hearers to repentance. Second, the rhetorical strategies of Scripture and sermon are similar: the exaggerated depictions in the passage keep their exaggerated forms in the sermon. As Isaiah distorted to shock, so does the sermon. Finally, the imagery in the passage is rich and varied, and the sermon both uses the existing images but also updates many of them to modern equivalents. Each of these homiletical choices shapes the sermon with the goal of making Isaiah's songs ring out with their original clarity and power.*

Introduction

Let me ask you a question: What makes a Christian different than any other kind of person? What sets apart the Jesus community from every other community? One of the things that makes us different has to be our capacity to wonder. Our capacity to stand in awe. As Christians we believe that when we look at the world and

---
[1] Preached at The Chapel, Brunswick, GA, November 1, 2015.

our circumstances, we know that we cannot see the full picture. We believe realities exist that are invisible to us but that are absolutely real. So, we have the capability to look at this world not as a familiar object, but as something that is in the hands of the One who made it and who made us and who loves us. We are able to listen to the voice of God speak to us things we have not known and cannot be aware of. To speak to us, and if needed, to shatter us and re-make us.

One of the ways that we access that—that we hear his voice—is through this book. We believe that when we read this book that somehow, the One that we cannot see is speaking to us. Speaking truth to us in a way that can change us, stretch us, comfort us, transform us, build us up.

That's exactly what Isaiah is doing. Isaiah is an OT prophet who lives in Judah. A prophet is someone who stands in the counsel of God, hears what God says (his warnings and judgments, his promises and comforts), and then turns around and speaks those words to us.

When prophets speak like this, they help us to put things into focus. Often, we don't see very clearly; we think we have perfect vision, but we don't see things the way they really are. We don't see our circumstances in the way they really are; we don't see ourselves the way we really are; we don't see relationships; we don't see promises and possibilities and tragedies and pain and joy—we don't see those things accurately. And what prophets do for us is to clarify those things, to bring them into focus. That is what we are talking about this morning: the favor of focus. Through Isaiah, God does us a favor by putting things in focus.

Today Isaiah is going to put some things in very crisp focus for us. But here's the trick: the way that he is going to put things in focus is by distorting them. He's going to make things clearer by stretching them out of proportion. He's going to take pictures of people and bend and exaggerate them to help us see what he is pointing out.

It will be a little like a funhouse mirror. You've seen these mirrors that stretch your face? There's an app called Photo Booth that does this. [Here I showed comical Photo Booth pictures of me, my wife, and other people in the church]. When you look at a distorted picture of yourself, you know it's not real, but you still walk away wondering, "Is my mouth really that big? Do my ears look like that?" That is what Isaiah is doing. He's going to magnify different parts of who we are, so that we will walk away and say, "Is that what I'm really like?"

And he's going to do it not with pictures but with words, with something called a "woe oracle." (The word "woe" is not "woah," as in, "slow down," but "woe," meaning sadness or grief). These are laments, songs of sadness sung over different kinds of people. In Isaiah chapter 5 the prophet brings different types of people into focus by exaggerating them in woe oracles.

1. Woe to the Hoarders

He begins by singing **woe to the hoarders**, to the people who collect and gather and hog—to the greedy. Now, no one ever thinks they're a hoarder. You've seen the show "Hoarders," right? These people's houses are jammed full; you can't even open the door because inside is a stack of newspapers from 1975, and there are three dead cats in the kitchen. But when they are asked, "Are you a hoarder?" they say "No, these are just things I might need later." They don't see it, they don't feel like hoarders. And yet they are. So, Isaiah is going to sing this song not over people who hoard newspapers but over people who hoard land:

> Isaiah 5:8
> Woe to those who join house to house,
> who add field to field,
> until there is no more room,
> and you are made to dwell alone
> in the midst of the land.

These hoarders are buying up property. Now, in Israel when you go broke you can sell your land and then sell yourself as a laborer. Isaiah is singing about the land buyers: instead of helping the people who are stuck in poverty to get them back on their feet, they're snatching up the property at a discount rate from widows and orphans and people down on their luck and turning these little plots of land into massive farms, until there's no room left in the land.

Now, come on. That's an exaggeration. Who buys *all* the land around, so that they're the only ones left? Who says, "I'm going to buy this whole neighborhood and my house will be the only house here, and I'm going to knock everything down, and make their plots into a decorative lake"? Who does that? No one sees themselves that way. No one says, "Oh man, I hate orphans, and I can't wait to steal from widows!" Isaiah is putting up a distorted, stretched picture of these people. They don't think of themselves as land grabbers.

They think of themselves as savvy businesspeople. They hear about a foreclosure next door; this is a good opportunity. "Someone's going to buy it, it's going at a great price. I might as well take advantage of this chance." This is kind of how we think. Without seeing it, we begin to make this kind of grasping a habit in our lives.

But of course, we don't see it that way. We don't describe it that way. We say things like, "I earned it. I worked hard for this. It's not like I'm not robbing banks or anything, it's my money." (Of course we neglect to mention the fact that all of the natural talents we have come from God, and we were born into a family that supported us and nurtured us and sent us to the right schools, and we had teachers who invested in us, and about that one time when we vandalized that building and someone called in a favor and the judge let us do community service so we got out of that, and then someone gave us a job out of college and gave us a leg up... Of course, we neglect to mention that to whom much is given, of him much will be required. We neglect to mention that everything we have belongs to him and is meant as an instrument to bring about his justice and righteousness, that we will be held to account for the return on God's investment that we make in our lives, that justice and mercy are core parts of being a disciple.)

We forget all the ways that God enabled us to have what we have, and what having those things is all about. We say, I'm just going after the American dream. I don't need to be the richest guy around, but this is what our country is about. (You know what the American dream is, right? Whatever you're making, add 20%. That's the standard. You're almost there. The goal keeps moving.)

So, without knowing it we can end up as hoarders. We don't see ourselves like this. So, Isaiah paints this weird, distorted picture to get us to ask, Do I really look like this? I don't feel like this, but maybe…is that me? Am I a hoarder?

Then he sings grief over the hoarder because this is what happens to them:

> vv. 9–10
> The LORD of hosts has sworn in my hearing:
> "Surely many houses shall be desolate,
> large and beautiful houses, without inhabitant.
> For ten acres of vineyard shall yield but one bath,
> and a homer of seed shall yield but an ephah."

If you want lots of room, you'll get it. If you want empty houses, I'll give you empty houses. They will be empty because I will cut off the food and produce from the land. A vineyard should produce way more than one bath (a couple of liters); a homer of seed should produce about ten ephahs of flour, but it only produces one. If you're so intent on hoarding, I'm going to make sure it doesn't work. Hoarding will not end up well—for them or for us. Isaiah sings woe to the hoarders. In doing so he gives us the favor of focus.

2. Woe to the Hedonists

The next song Isaiah sings is **Woe to the hedonists**. A hedonist is someone who pursues pleasure at the expense of everything else. Pleasure is their number one goal. Whatever their particular form of pleasure might be, that is what they live for.

> vv. 11–12
> Woe to those who rise early in the morning,

> that they may run after strong drink,
> who tarry late into the evening
> as wine inflames them!
> They have lyre and harp,
> tambourine and flute and wine at their feasts,
> but they do not regard the deeds of the LORD,
> or see the work of his hands.

To rise early and stay up late is an expression of hard work. Isaiah twists this to say yes, they rise early—to get drunk. And they stay up late—to drink more wine. It's almost like their occupation, their calling, and vocation is pleasure. They are so caught up with pleasure that they can't see anymore what God is doing.

Now come on. That's ridiculous. Of course, *alcoholics* drink beer at 6am. Some people live the daytime movie special plot of drunkenness and dysfunction. But not me. That's an exaggeration. That's not what I look like. I don't think of myself that way. I'm just having fun. Blowing off a little steam on the weekends. I work hard, you know?

But what if there is some truth to that? What if while we spend our time working or being with family or going to church, our mind is constantly on X—whatever that activity or pleasure or drink or food or person is? Maybe your whole year is built around one week or one weekend, maybe a family vacation or a big trip (which by the way, never goes as well as you think it's going to, especially if you have kids). Or you have this hobby, this thing that you're into, and everyone know when it's hunting season or football season or March Madness, don't even talk to Dad. He's out. He's gone. Or you're just grinding on to retirement. Retirement is the dream, the finish line, because you equate heaven with South Florida, and you cannot wait to get there.

Could it be that we fill up our life with so much stuff that we can't see what God might be doing around us? We can't see the doors that are open around us, because we look a little more like this than we are comfortable admitting?

This is the woe song that Isaiah sings over the hedonists:

The Favor of Focus (Isaiah 5:8–24)

v. 13
Therefore my people go into exile
for lack of knowledge;
their honored men go hungry,
and their multitude is parched with thirst.

The hedonists are going into exile and ruin because they do not know what God is doing. And instead of being full, when you spend all your time trying to get, get, get, you end up empty, you end up parched, you end up starving, you are a husk. The consequences of hedonism are not fullness and fatness, but in the ironic and wise judgment of God, never having your appetite satisfied, never finding what you sold your soul to get.

In fact, others will be full in the end:

vv. 14–17
Therefore Sheol has enlarged its appetite
and opened its mouth beyond measure,
and the nobility of Jerusalem and her multitude will go down,
her revelers and he who exults in her.
Man is humbled, and each one is brought low,
and the eyes of the haughty are brought low.
But the LORD of hosts is exalted in justice,
and the Holy God shows himself holy in righteousness.
Then shall the lambs graze as in their pasture,
and nomads shall eat among the ruins of the rich.

Sheol—the grave—like a yawning pit in the ground opens its mouth to swallow the hedonists. And Isaiah says that the only ones who are going to eat their fill in your house are the wandering animals that walk through the ruins of your home and graze on the grass growing in the cracks of the tiles of your kitchen.

Woe to the hedonists; woe to those who pursue pleasure. This is the favor of focus.

And if you haven't felt blessed yet this morning, if you haven't felt encouraged, then buckle up! Here we go with the final oracle:

3. Woe to the Hypocrites

Woe to the hypocrites. Woe to those who say one thing and live another way. Now no one calls themselves a hypocrite. No one thinks of themselves this way.

But Isaiah sings woe over these people. Listen to his extended description of them:

> v. 18
> Woe to those who draw iniquity with cords of falsehood,
> who draw sin as with cart ropes...

Instead of wearing their brokenness and mess and sin all over themselves so that people can see it, these people look nice. But in fact, they draw all that stuff after them. Have you ever known someone who blows through your life looking great, and it's not until they're gone that you realize how they've poisoned you and ruined everything they touched? After they leave the fallout and the truth of who they are and the damage they have done becomes apparent. Hypocrites: hiding their sin and pretending to be righteous. There is more:

> v. 19
> ...who say: "Let him be quick,
> let him speed his work
> that we may see it;
> let the counsel of the Holy One of Israel draw near,
> and let it come, that we may know it!"

In other words, this is someone who sits in church and shouts, "Amen! Yes, that right! Come on Lord!" They really don't think that God is going to do anything—answer prayers or build his kingdom or chastise the disobedient. But they look good saying it, and so they do.

> v. 20
> Woe to those who call evil good and good evil,

who put darkness for light and light for darkness,
who put bitter for sweet and sweet for bitter!

They switch evil and good; they call things the wrong name. They reverse moral poles.

v. 21
Woe to those who are wise in their own eyes,
and shrewd in their own sight!

They know it all, they've seen it all, they can't be told anything.

v. 22
Woe to those who are heroes at drinking wine,
and valiant men in mixing strong drink…

Heroes and mighty men are strong people in the community who are honored. But the only thing they are really doing, the only thing they are strong at is pleasing themselves.

v. 23
…who acquit the guilty for a bribe,
and deprive the innocent of his right!

They even convict the innocent and free the guilty for money. Woe to the hypocrites.

Now come on. That's a funhouse-mirror distortion. Who sits around and says, "I can't wait to get another bribe so I can convict another innocent person!" We wouldn't say that about ourselves. We wouldn't say we're hypocrites. We would say, "I'm a pragmatist. I mean, who wants to see all my flaws and foibles? No one would enjoy that. I don't talk about it because it's not relevant. And of course, I would *love* to see God answer prayers! But be realistic. We live in the 21st century. Religion is nice for crying old ladies and innocent kids, and it can make you feel better…but come on. God is not going to do anything. I'm not a hypocrite, I'm a realist. You can be an idealist when you're 20 and talk in black and white, but the world is grey. I'm a realist, and the real question is what is going to get the job done. I've been around the block a time or two. I know people, I know how things work, I know how to get things done. I'm a doer, I accomplish things. I'm a person of standing in my community and people know that I know how to get it done. And you know what? A lot of people don't like to see how the sausage is made but they sure do love it when it lands on their plate. I get things done."

We don't like the word "hypocrite." But what if that exaggerated picture describes us better than we think? Do we really look like that? Because here is what happens to hypocrites:

> v. 24
> Therefore, as the tongue of fire devours the stubble,
> and as dry grass sinks down in the flame,
> so their root will be as rottenness,
> and their blossom go up like dust;
> for they have rejected the law of the LORD of hosts,
> and have despised the word of the Holy One of Israel.

Have you ever put hay or grass into a campfire and watch it shrivel up? That is what is going to happen. That is the irony: these people who have never been whole, who have never had integrity, who have lived two lives, they will finally find wholeness: from the root to the tip of the bud, they will be destroyed. And they will finally find the integrity that they have been running from. They will be altogether ruined.

Woe to the hoarders. Woe to the hedonists. Woe to the hypocrites. **This is the favor of focus.**

Now I don't know about you, but when I read that, it doesn't feel like a favor. It feels like a punch in the mouth. Who likes seeing this bloated, distorted picture of our flaws?

4. But focus is a favor.

Focus is a manifestation of the grace of God. Let me explain.

When Isaiah sings these woe songs, the point is not that God

The Favor of Focus (Isaiah 5:8–24)

hates Israel, but that he loves her. He is inviting her to come home so that she will avoid disaster. "Woe" songs are sung *before* the disaster falls, so that listeners can see the end of the path they are on and have the chance to reconsider. Jesus sings the same sort of woe songs to the Pharisees in Matthew 23, and in the very next breath he weeps over Jerusalem's ruin. Woe songs are a tearful plea to hard hearts sung out of covenant love.

It's the same with us. When God points out something ugly in your soul, the next thing he says is never, "Now straighten up." That is never the next word. Instead, when he shines a spotlight on us and we don't like what we see, the next thing he says is always, "Come to me. Let me help. Let me hold you while you while you weep over this. Let me forgive you. Let me help you to be different. Let me transform you, let me teach you to walk differently so that this part of you that was darkness will be light. Come to me." In the gospel, focus is always a favor.

So, when Isaiah says, "Woe to the hoarders," he is inviting us to learn a repentant generosity. God is inviting us to experience his own gracious generosity, to remember everything he has given to us, to bask in his goodness over us, until we become convinced that we have enough, and that he is enough. And then to begin to live generously, to give, to begin to separate the American dream from the kingdom of heaven, and to prefer the latter. It's an invitation to live into generosity, to live into the gospel.

And when the prophet sings out, "Woe to the hedonists," he is inviting us to examine our values and to reorder them. God is inviting us to worship Himself rather than pleasure. God knows that you like the thing that you like because you have not yet tasted deeply of Jesus. And when you have tasted him deeply and when you know who he is more fully, you can turn away from the empty promises of pleasure. The answer is not to get mad at yourself because you like beer. The answer is to ask yourself how you can engage more fully in who God is and see if he cannot satisfy you in deeper ways.

And when we hear "Woe to the hypocrites," that makes us uncomfortable. But that song is an invitation to genuineness, to integrity of heart. God is inviting you to community where you know and are known. God is inviting you to a renewed wonder in him and his kingdom. To drop the pretense and come to him as you really are.

Conclusion

Focus is always a favor. God puts funhouse mirrors in front of our faces not to mock us, but to help us to notice what we would otherwise excuse and overlook. And when God shines that spotlight on your heart, it always becomes a question of trust. It's a question of whether we trust him enough to know that he is for us in Christ, that he is calling us home to him, that his focus is a favor.

Do you trust that when Jesus makes you uncomfortable, he still loves you enough to die for you? And if you trust him, maybe instead of turning away from the mirror, you can step into that discomfort and say, "God, I didn't see myself this way, but maybe I am. Can we talk about it?"

Appendix 2

Sample Sermon

Walking in the Ruins (Micah 4:1–5)
Heather Joy Zimmerman

Heather Joy Zimmerman preached this sermon at the Wheaton College Graduate Chapel (which is why you'll find several references to school buildings, exams, and to Chicago).[1] *She unpacks the astounding promise in Micah of the cosmic restoration that God will one day bring. The central idea is, "Until God rebuilds the ruins, walk in the name of the LORD."*

Four features of this sermon connect to the material in the present book and make it a wonderful model for learners. First, Zimmerman interprets the promises in the oracle from within a progressive dispensational framework. The promise in Micah to restore true worship will be fulfilled in the future for Israel. Note how that framework orients listeners to God's future work (via the Davidic covenant), then forges connection between that work and the present lives of God's people. Second, she handles the historical and cultural distance effectively and briefly. Most of the sermon is focused on here and now, but when needed she gives quick sketches of the literary context or of items relevant to the culture like plowshares and pruning hooks.

Third, Zimmerman's sermon is deeply engaged with issues of justice. She does not hesitate to raise issues of abuse of power, racism,

---

1 Sermon Delivery at: Wheaton College "Walking in the Ruins," *YouTube*, March 24, 2022, https://www.youtube.com/watch?v=S7gjG_qktcM. This sermon was delivered one week after the Asian American murders in spas near Atlanta. Note: This sermon intentionally weaves in lyrics from songs throughout the musical *Les Misérables*. Tom Hooper, Stephen Brooker, Catherine Greaves Becky Bentham, and Rael Jones Anne Dudley. *LES MISÉRABLES. USA/UK//Japan*, 2012. Those lyrics will be italicized, and the source songs will be footnoted.

misogyny, economic inequality, and abortion. She uses real-time examples from the news, the church, and her own life. Micah was concerned for justice; this sermon reverberates with that passion.

Finally, the sermon is a fine example of using creativity to deal with prophetic monotony. Zimmerman weaves in phrases and lines from Les Misérables throughout. For those familiar with the musical, the powerful longing, sadness, and joy of the songs forms a refrain of sorts, making an emotional through-line for the sermon.

There is a song that stirs both a fire and an ache in my heart. It's a song from the musical *Les Misérables*. It's set during the Paris Uprising of 1832 and traces a powerful but painful story of grace through the lives of various characters who are suffering in the ruins of injustice: a man imprisoned for 19 years for stealing a loaf of bread, a woman who wrongfully lost her job and was forced into prostitution to feed her daughter, unrequited love, young boys killed because they challenged the political system, an orphan girl. The people were in ruin, crying out for change, for justice, for hope. And in their brokenness, they begged God and government to *look down*,[2] singing, "*Do you hear the people sing? Singing the songs of angry men? It is the music of a people who will not be slaves again...*"[3]

Perhaps you're a *Les Mis* fan and know the tune. You might pick up on a few more references in this message. But it is a song that has been a rallying cry for those suffering from oppression. In light of the events of this last year and even last week, I want to spend extra time before we get into this passage to give us space to lament what has happened in our world, in our country, and in our community.

Around the world, we see the devastation of injustice, immorality, infection. And we pray, "*God on High, look down*"[4] Do you see what's going on in our world? Do you see the massacres in Ethiopia? Did you hear the cries of those in Yemen, who last summer had a 25% mortality rate from COVID due to the war? Yes, there's a global pandemic. As Stephen Colbert said, it's been a year

---

2 "Look Down," *Les Misérables*, 2012.
3 "Do You Hear the People Sing?" *Les Misérables*, 2012.
4 "Bring Him Home," *Les Misérables*, 2012.

"that took 100 years but was also somehow one long day."[5] There's a global sense of suffering. Most of us have lost something. We're all *in* this, but we can't be trite and say that we're all in this *together*. Some have shared sweet family time, while Native Americans last summer in New Mexico had a COVID mortality rate 23 times higher than their white counterparts.[6] While some were picking up new hobbies like breadmaking, immigrants were hospitalized and dying because meatpacking plant executives resisted protective policies. Some have lost their family business or savings. Celebrities worked from their gorgeous mansions in their sweats, posting funny videos to help us cope with the lockdown. But for others, houses have become prisons, trapping the abused. As horrible as the health crisis has been, we've had a mental health crisis too. I personally know two who have died this year, either by suicide or overdose from an addiction triggered by the pandemic. A friend of a friend has serious PTSD from working as a nurse in a NYC hospital in April.

God on High, look down. Do you see what's going on in our country? *Do you hear the people sing?* Do you hear the desperate cries of those who can't sing because they can't breathe, whether on a ventilator in a hospital or with the knee of racism crushing their neck? Does God on High see the Asian Americans who have been living in fear this last year? Who have been attacked in *our* neighborhoods? Who don't feel safe in *our* grocery stores in the Chicago suburbs? Or specifically our Asian American sisters who have experienced fetishized sexual harassment throughout their lives? There is so much anger in our land. Abortions have not just been allowed in certain circumstances but have been celebrated with applause. Politicians on national television argued like children. Christians questioned another Christian's faith based not on creed but on the circle filled in on a political ballot. "Jesus Saves"

---

5 Stephen Colbert, "The Year That Took 100 Years But Was Also Somehow Also One Long Day," *YouTube*, accessed June 14, 2022, https://www.youtube.com/watch?v=TjSMlj0KRdI.

6 Jens Gould, "Native Americans dying at much higher rate from COVID-19," *SantaFeNewMexican.com*, August 4, 2020, https://www.santafenewmexican.com/news/coronavirus/native-americans-dying-at-much-higher-rate-from-covid-19/article_392ffc22-d66a-11ea-bbd1-8fe3a1929340.html.

signs stood in the shadows of gallows. Prayers in Jesus' name were offered by some thanking the Lord for the success of their trespass, while others cried out for the hanging of a professing Christian.

Fear. Anger. From different viewpoints. But perhaps these emotions are all that unites us these days, aside from Bernie Sanders memes or beloved Christian schools destroying our March Madness brackets. It feels like this is the most divided our country has ever been, our church has ever been. Never mind those who had to pastor churches in the border states after the American Civil War. But I digress.

God on High, look down. Do you see what's going on in our personal lives? Do you see us in the ruins? For some of us, this has been a year of weariness, of heaviness. Maybe you're dealing with rejection—whether related to a relationship, a potential job, another degree program, or a bid on a house. You might have experienced a deep injustice. For others, instead of the COVID baby boom, you experienced a miscarriage. Maybe you lost a loved one and lost the opportunity to process your grief at a funeral. It feels your grief won't end. *What is grief, if not love, persevering?*[7] You don't know if you can handle *one day more.*[8] Whatever it is, for some of you it may feel ages since you *"dreamed a dream of time gone by when hope was high and life worth living."*[9] Others of us are in the ruin of our own sin. Maybe you've felt your *shame inside you like a knife,*[10] as you see the wreckage of your sin—on your children, on your spouse, on your roommates or friends. In the midst of the ruins of our world or our country it can feel our *little lives don't count at all.*[11] We long for a better world beyond the barricades of our brokenness. And we find ourselves helpless and hopeless in the ruins, crying out for God to *look down.* "God, *do you hear the people sing*?"

So, what do we do when we are in the ruins? What do we do when we remain in the ruins, helpless, with little left to rebuild?

---

7 "What is Grief, if Not Love Persevering?" *YouTube*, accessed June 14, 2022. https://www.youtube.com/watch?v=9VATT98uYXk.

8 "One Day More," *Les Misérables*, 2012.

9 "I Dreamed a Dream," *Les Misérables*, 2012.

10 "Valjean's Soliloquy," *Les Misérables*, 2012.

11 "ABC Café/Red and Black," *Les Misérables*, 2012.

Walking in the Ruins (Micah 4:1–5)

There was a time Israel when was walking in the ruins. Economic inequality made oppression rife. Idolatry led to immorality and injustice. The prophet Micah prophesied that Israel would face the consequences of the chaos it chose. But when the storm subsided and the wreckage remained, Micah offered the people of Israel comfort through a picture of paradise *found*. Turn with me in your Bible to Micah 4. Micah 4. In this passage we will see two future promises that will shape how we should respond when we find ourselves in the ruins.

We begin by seeing the promise that **God will restore true worship. God will restore true worship.** Read with me verses 1–2. "It shall come to pass in the latter days that the mountain of the house of the LORD shall be established as the highest of the mountains, and it shall be lifted up above the hills; and peoples shall flow to it, and many nations shall come and say, 'Come, let us go up to the mountain of the LORD, to the house of the God of Jacob, that he may teach us His ways and that we may walk in His paths.' For out of Zion shall go forth the law, and the word of the LORD from Jerusalem" (ESV).

As I mentioned, Micah has already foretold the end Israel will experience. In chapter 3, Micah describes the horrific state of Israel. The wicked go out like the *tigers at night, with their voices soft as thunder to tear hope apart.*[12] The people reject godly leaders. The countryside is *covered in red, the blood of angry men and black, the color of despair.*[13] Israel would eventually be plowed down. But a time will come after the ruin. A time of hope.

Micah begins in 4:1 describing the latter days. I would argue this passage portrays a paradise Israel hasn't experienced yet. And I think there are good reasons to envision this expects a physical fulfillment on the earth when the Lord reigns in Jerusalem, fulfilling the Davidic Covenant. But you don't have to be a dispensationalist or even know what dispensationalism is to appreciate what these "latter days" will look like. Verse 1 then describes how the mountain of the Lord's house will be established as the highest and raised up. If you've been to Jerusalem, you know the temple

---

12 "I Dreamed a Dream," *Les Misérables*, 2012.
13 "ABC Café/Red and Black," *Les Misérables*, 2012.

mount isn't exactly a magnificent mountain... Well, maybe compared to the "Mount Hoy" at Blackwell. Zion is a hill of an elevation of 2,400–2,500 feet, not even as high as the Mount of Olives. But in the latter days, this mountain will be *lifted up*. If we were reading a *Left Behind* book, we'd probably see a cataclysmic earthquake elevate Zion to the height of Everest. But more likely, this is about *establishing* the House of the LORD in Jerusalem as the center of worship. And the peoples of the world will stream to it. This is a powerful image. As the Babylonians floated on the Euphrates to ritually worship, so the masses of people from various nations would flow to worship God. Friends, can you imagine the day a mass of people will flow to anything again? Like they flooded the streets in Chicago during the Cubs championship parade. One day, we'll not only be able to flow in large crowds, but the nations will flow to *worship the LORD*. In Verse 2 the people call each other to the mountain of the LORD to worship Him, using the same summons of the psalmist, and for the purpose "that he may teach us his ways and that we may walk in his paths."

We see here the promise that the Lord will restore true worship in two ways—a missiological way and an ecclesiological way. The Lord will restore orthodoxy and orthopraxy. Simply put, right worship will lead to right practice. We desperately need this hope today.

First, in Billy Graham Hall, we must never forget the countless unreached peoples. People who despite technology have never even heard of the hope of Jesus. One day, the nations will stare into the void, to the whirlpool of their sin and reach for the only One who can pull them out. The world will see how their own evil has destroyed their communities, and the Lord is the only way out. On their journey to worship the LORD, they will say, "This is the Way."

Not only will the nations worship the true God, but they will follow the LORD. Like the Psalmists, we will see that right worship will lead to right living. This promise is so timely. In the last year, we've seen the 'fall' of powerful Christian leaders we thought were faithful. Those who taught others to *"follow the way of the Law"*[14] weren't keeping watch over their own conduct in the night.

---

14 "Javert's Suicide," *Les Misérables*, 2012.

We've heard the disillusionment of the deconstructed. And it's no wonder so many are in a crisis of faith, if we truly believe right worship leads to right living. Christian leaders have been enabled to abuse power for decades. On one day, pastors might say that words don't really matter. On the next, they care more about the language someone uses to categorize their pain rather than leaning into lament. Women have been sexualized and treated as temptations to be feared rather than coworkers in the kingdom.

This is not the first time the people of God have faced a reckoning in their religion. And here, Micah doesn't offer a sentimentalized spirituality but a real hope that one day, God will restore true worship. As we wait for that day, we pray for the peoples who don't know Jesus. I use the Joshua project App on my phone to pray for an unreached people group every day. We befriend those who are not yet friends of God. And we repent of how we have knowingly and unknowingly perverted true worship, trusting that God will not only restore us but will one day restore all things.

And the next verses provide another promise: **God will restore true peace. God will restore true peace.**

Read with me verses 3-4. "He shall judge between many peoples and shall decide for strong nations afar off; and they shall beat their swords into plowshares, and their spears into pruning hooks. Nation shall not lift up sword against nation, neither shall they learn war anymore; but they shall sit every man under his vine and under his fig tree, and no one shall make them afraid, for the mouth of the LORD of hosts has spoken" (ESV).

Oh what a day when not only will relationships with God be reconciled but relationships with each other! *For to love another person is to see the face of God.*[15] The LORD God will be judge. Let's just pause on that. The Hebrew word *shaphat* carries connotations of both "judging" and "ruling." Some scholars believe this word choice is strategic, emphasizing the *just* nature of the LORD's rule.

When He comes to rule and judge, we will never have to worry about a scandal coming out. We will not EVER have to question the justice of systems and situations, to wonder if wrong had been

---

15 "Epilogue," *Les Misérables*, 2012.

done on the basis of: race, gender, social status, economic status, bias, favoritism, or corruption. Can you imagine? The more I experience injustice the more I long for and appreciate God as Judge. Maybe you've personally experienced the pain of injustice—whether missing a promotion you deserved or suffering discrimination. I first wrote and preached this sermon several years ago to process the profound pain of a situation where I had been wronged—not intentionally but by passivity. It was one of the events that led me to believe the lie that as a woman, I was a liability to the Church. Because of the sensitivity of what happened, I had to suffer in silence. I was utterly "*on my own.*"[16] I still wonder sometimes if that pain was in vain.

But one day... we will never have to question justice. Because we will have true peace. Peace, as Dr. King said, that's not merely the absence of tension but the presence of justice.[17]

Not only will God rule as Judge, but we see a beautiful hope for human flourishing in verse 3: "they shall beat their swords into plowshares, and their spears into pruning hooks. Nation shall not lift up sword against nation, neither shall they learn war any more..." (ESV).

Do you hear the people sing? One day, their songs will no more mourn broken relationships. Peace will be more than *a castle on a cloud.*[18] We will see *no more empty chairs and empty tables* from lives lost in battle or from illness.[19] Our military bases will close. West Point will have a major curriculum revision. And not because the UN has this inscribed on the building. Not because of shrewd diplomacy. But because the LORD will reign.

The imagery here is beautiful. Now most of us can conceive of a sword, but in the suburbs, we may not know what a plowshare is. A plow is what stirs up the ground to make it ready for planting. The plowshare specifically refers to that metal part of the plow that cuts into the ground. Instead of metal cutting up other people to bring death, it will be refitted to cut up the ground to bring forth

---

16 "On My Own," *Les Misérables*, 2012.

17 Dr. Martin Luther King Jr., "Letter from a Birmingham Jail," April 16, 1963, in *Why We Can't Wait* (Signet Classic, 2000), 64-84.

18 "Castle on a Cloud," *Les Misérables*, 2012.

19 "Empty Chairs and Empty Tables," *Les Misérables*, 2012.

life. Similarly, the metal on spears used to stab and cut others will be repurposed to clear away brush or to cut off fruit from the vine.

Then every person will sit under his or her own fig tree—the fig tree is so often a symbol of peace and prosperity in Israel. Today, we might say each person will sit under his or her coconut tree on the beach drinking a glass of water turned to wine. The people will sit in peace with no more fear.

Do you remember that time gone by when you were *young and unafraid*?[20] Can you imagine a world where you will never fear? No fear of comprehensive exams. No fear of getting a job to use your degree. No fear of a virus. No fear of losing jobs or freedoms. No fear of racism. No fear of sexual harassment or exploitation. No fear of cancer diagnoses, of car accidents, of losing a home. There will be no more fear. Brothers and sisters, this is a real promise from our real God. One day, when a promised Prince of Peace will reign justly in Jerusalem, we will have true peace. And this will all happen because the word of the LORD. As the nations come in, His Word will go out.

But nations still study war today. North Korea keeps testing missiles. Domestic violence destroys families. Too many people suffer from a grief that can't be spoken. *Pain goes on and on.*[21] Our Churches and families seem helplessly divided with no path forward. So, what do we do in this meanwhile? We get on our knees. Pray for the peace of Jerusalem, of Wheaton, of Chicago. We can read the news with prayer. Each morning, I try to read and pray through two international, two national, and two local news stories specifically. And as members of the already-not yet kingdom, we give our communities a taste of the day when God will restore true peace. Where might God be calling you today to be an ambassador of reconciliation and peace?

Micah gives us two promises: in verses 1–2—that God will restore true worship; in verses 3–4, that God will restore true peace. Since God will restore true worship, and since God will restore true peace, Micah offers a resolution of how to live until we experience that day:

---

20 "I Dreamed a Dream," *Les Misérables*, 2012.
21 "Empty Chairs and Empty Tables," *Les Misérables*, 2012.

Until God rebuilds the ruins, walk in the Name of the Lord. Until God rebuilds the ruins, walk in the Name of the Lord. Read with me in verse 5: "For all the peoples walk, each in the name of its God, but we will walk in the name of the LORD our God forever and ever."

So what does this actually look like to walk in his Name? That's a lot of spiritualized language. It makes me think of a terrific book by Wheaton PhD grad Carmen Imes called *Bearing God's Name: Why Sinai Still Matters*.[22] In it she re-evaluates how we perceive the second commandment: "Do not take the Name of the Lord your God in vain." Literally, the verse reads to "carry" or "bear" God's Name in vain. We don't think in that imagery in English, so we often translate or teach it in terms of not swearing or using God's name as a cuss word. But the imagery is so much stronger than that. It's the idea of a nation of priests who *wear* and *bear* the name of Yahweh *as His representatives* among the nations. We carry the reputation of Christ.

The idea of *walking* as mentioned earlier is to put something into practice, obedience. It can refer to one's lifestyle. Thus, in this verse, Micah is picking up on the motif throughout Scripture of bearing God's Name as His representatives. The nations around us still "walk"—live—according to their own gods—whether the gods of established religions or the gods of greed, hedonism, or immorality.

We have not yet reached the promises of verses 1–4. Micah doesn't give us those promises so we can live in denial but so that we can know our faithfulness is not in vain. Until the LORD rebuilds the ruins, we represent Him faithfully. Whether in studying, in being patient with our clients, in deciding to take a lower grade on a paper if we need to spend time with our kids. We become quick to listen, slow to tweet, and slow to rant on Facebook. We take the time to think outside our own concerns to weep with those who are weeping—whether our housemate or with those across the country or world who are suffering. We prayerfully take courage to love our neighbor both individually and on a corporate

---

22 Carmen Imes, *Bearing God's Name: Why Sinai Still Matters* (IVP Academic, 2019).

level. We recognize that we bear the label "Follower of Jesus" and determine each day: "God, how can I represent You in what's on my schedule today? How do I leave room for where your Spirit may lead me today?" We choose to be faithful, recognizing it may feel utterly in vain here but our hope in the "latter days" is real.

Friends, we are in a world that is groaning. But since we have the promise that God will restore true worship and since we have the promise that God will restore true peace, in the midst of the ruins we walk in the way of the Lord. The musical *Les Mis* ends with a powerful epilogue in which the hope for a new world begins to overcome the ruins. The ensemble sings:

> *Do you hear the people sing?*
> *Lost in the valley of the night*
> *It is the music of a people*
> *Who are climbing to the light*
> *For the wretched of the earth*
> *There is a flame that never dies*
> *Even the darkest night will end and the sun will rise.*
> *They will live again in freedom*
> *In the garden of the Lord*
> *We will walk behind the ploughshare;*
> *We will put away the sword.*
> *The chain will be broken*
> *And all men will have their reward."*
> *Will you join in our crusade?*
> *Who will be strong and stand with me*
> *Somewhere beyond the barricade,*
> *Is there a world you long to see?*
> *Do you hear the people sing?*
> *Say, do you hear the distant drums?*
> *It is the future that they bring when tomorrow comes.*[23]

Friends ... until tomorrow comes ... until God restores our ruins, walk in the Name of the Lord.

---

23 "Epilogue," *Les Misérables*, 2012.

Bibliography

Achtemeier, Elizabeth. *Preaching From the Old Testament*. Westminster John Knox, 1989.

Ackland, Donald F. "Preaching from Hosea to a Nation in Crisis." *SJT* 18 (1975): 43–55.

Alcántara, Jared E. *Learning from a Legend: What Gardner C. Taylor Can Teach Us about Preaching*. Cascade, 2016.

Alexander, T. D. *From Paradise to Promised Land: An Introduction to the Pentateuch*. 2nd ed. Baker Academic, 2002.

Anderson, Kenton C. "In the Eye of the Hearer: Visuals that Support Rather than Distract from the Word." Pages 607-609 *The Art and Craft of Biblical Preaching*. Edited by Haddon Robinson and Craig Larson. Zondervan, 2005.

Aristotle. *Nichomachean Ethics*. In *Aristotle Collection*. Edited by Jefferson Cabell Douglas. Translated by D. P. Chase. Annotated Classics. Kindle edition.

Aristotle. *Rhetoric*. Translated by W. Rhys Roberts. Dover, 2004. Kindle edition.

Arthurs, Jeffrey D. *Devote Yourself to the Public Reading of Scripture: The Transforming Power of the Well-Spoken Word*. Kregel, 2012.

———. "The Place of Pathos in Preaching." *JEHS* 1 (December 2001): 15-21.

———. *Preaching as Reminding: Stirring Memory in an Age of Forgetfulness*. IVP, 2017.

———. *Preaching with Variety: How to Re-create the Dynamics of Biblical Genres*. Kregel, 2007.

———. "What to Do When Your Fig Tree Doesn't Blossom." *PT* (November 2011). https://www.preachingtoday.com/sermons/sermons/2011/november/figtreeblossom.html.

Augustine. *On Christian Teaching*. Translated by R. P. H. Green. Oxford, 1997.

Austin, J. L. *How to Do Things with Words*. 2nd ed. Harvard University Press, 1975.

Bartholomew, Craig G. *Introducing Biblical Hermeneutics: A Comprehensive Framework for Hearing God in Scripture*. Baker Academic, 2015.

Barton, Casey. *Preaching Through Time: Anachronism as a Way Forward in Preaching*. Cascade: 2017.

Barton, John. *Joel and Obadiah*. TOTL. Westminster John Knox, 2001.

Baucham, Voddie T., Jr. *Fault Lines: The Social Justice Movement and Evangelicalism's Looming Catastrophe*. Salem Books, 2021.

Baumbach, Noah, director. *Marriage Story*. Netflix, 2019.

Beach, Lee, and Joel Barker. "Springing the Trap: The Rhetoric of Amos as a Strategy for Preaching Justice and Judgment." *JEHS* 12 (2012): 4–10.

Beale, G. K., ed. *The Right Doctrine from the Wrong Text? Essays on the Use of the Old Testament in the New.* Baker Academic, 1994.

Berlin, Adele. "Introduction to Hebrew Poetry." *NIB* 4:301-315. Abingdon Press, 1996.

Berry, Wendell. "The Wild." In *The Selected Poems of Wendell Berry.* Counterpoint, 2009. Kindle edition.

Blackmon, Douglas. *Slavery by Another Name: The Re-Enslavement of Black Americans from the Civil War to World War II.* Repr. ed. Anchor, 2008.

Blackwood, Andrew Watterson. "Servants of the Word: How to Preach from the Prophets." *Int* 2 (1948): 158–71.

Block, Daniel I. *The Book of Ezekiel Chapters 1–24.* NICOT. Eerdmans, 1997.

Block, Daniel I. *The Book of Ezekiel Chapters 25–48.* NICOT. Eerdmans, 1998.

Bosma, Carl J. "The Challenges of Reading the 'Gospel' of Isaiah for Preaching." *CTJ* 39 (2004): 11–53.

Brown, Michael L. "Jeremiah." Pages 23-572 in *Jeremiah–Ezekiel*. Edited by Tremper Longman III and David E. Garland. EBC 7. Zondervan Academic, 2010.

Brueggemann, Walter. "Bragging About the Right Stuff." *JP* 26 (2003): 27-32.

———. *Hopeful Imagination: Prophetic Voices in Exile.* Fortress, 1986.

———. *The Prophetic Imagination.* 2nd ed. Fortress Press, 2001.

———. "The Secret of Survival: Jeremiah 20:7–13, Matthew 6:1–8," *JP* 26 (2003): 42–47.

Buechner, Frederick. *Telling the Truth: The Gospel as Comedy, Tragedy, and Fairy Tale.* Harper & Row, 1977.

Burke, Kenneth. *Counter–Statement.* University of California Press, 1968.

Burnett, John. "Christian Nationalism is Still Thriving—and Is a Force for Returning Trump to Power." *National Public Radio.* January 23, 2022. https://www.npr.org/2022/01/14/1073215412/christian-nationalism-donald-trump.

Buttrick, David. *Homiletic: Moves and Structures.* Fortress, 1987.

Calvin, John. *Institutes of the Christian Religion.* Edited by John T. McNeill. Translated by Ford Lewis Battles. 2 vols. Westminster John Knox, 1960.

Carlson, Robert A. *Preaching Like the Prophets: The Hebrew Prophets as Examples for the Practice of Pastoral Preaching.* Wipf & Stock, 2017.

Chesterton, Gilbert K. *Orthodoxy*. Doubleday, 1959.
Childs, Brevard S. *Biblical Theology of the Old and New Testaments: Theological Reflection on the Christian Bible*. Fortress Press, 1992.
Chisholm, Robert B, Jr. "Wordplay in the Eighth-Century Prophets." *BS* 144 (1987): 44–52.
Ciampa, Roy E. "The History of Redemption." Pages 254-308 in *Central Themes in Biblical Theology: Mapping Unity in Diversity*. Edited by Scott J. Hafemann and Paul R. House. Baker Academic, 2007.
Cicero. *De Inventione*. Translated by C. D. Yonge. In *Cicero Complete Works*. Delphi Classics, 2014. Kindle edition.
Clements, Ronald E. "Deuteronomy." *NIB*, 2:269-538. Abingdon Press, 1998.
Colbert, Stephen. "The Year That Took 100 Years But Was Also Somehow Also One Long Day." March 12, 2021. https://www.youtube.com/watch?v=TjSMlj0KRdI.
Collier-Thomas, Bettye, ed. *Daughters of Thunder: Black Women Preachers and Their Sermons, 1850-1979*. Jossey-Bass Publishers, 1998.
Collins, John J. *The Apocalyptic Imagination*. 2nd ed. Eerdmans, 1998.
―――. "From Prophecy to Apocalypticism." Pages 129-161 in vol. 1 of *The Encyclopedia of Apocalypticism*. Edited by John J. Collins, Bernard McGinn, and Stephen J. Stein. Continuum, 1998.
―――. "Towards the Morphology of a Genre," *Semeia* 14 (1979): 1-20.
Common Hymnal. *Praise and Protest*. Common Exchange, January 2021.
―――. *Unproduced*. Common Exchange, November 2018.
Craddock, Fred B. *As One Without Authority*. Rev. ed. Chalice Press, 2001.
Culver, Robert Duncan. "Isaiah 1:18—Declaration, Exclamation, or Interrogation?" *JETS* 12 (1969): 133–141.
cummings, e. e. "in-Just." Poetry Foundation. Accessed January 23, 2022. https://www.poetryfoundation.org/poems/47247/in-just.
Currie, David A. *The Big Idea of Biblical Worship: The Development and Leadership of Expository Services*. Hendrickson, 2017.
Dion, Paul E. *Hebrew Poetics*. 2nd ed. Benben Publications, 1992.
Dodd, C. H. *The Parables of the Kingdom*. Rev. ed. Scribner's, 1961.
Ebeling, Gerhard. *God and Word*. Fortress, 1967.
Edwards, J. Kent. *Deep Preaching: Creating Sermons that Go Beyond the Superficial*. B&H, 2009.
―――. *Effective First-Person Biblical Preaching: The Steps from Text to Narrative to Sermon*. Zondervan, 2005.
Edwards, Jonathan. *The Works of Jonathan Edwards*. Volume 2. Edited by John E. Smith. Yale University Press, 2009.
Eichrodt, Walther. *Theology of the Old Testament*. Volume 1. Translated by J. A. Baker. TOTL. The Westminster Press, 1961.

Elliger, Karl, and Wilhelm Rudolph, ed. *Biblia Hebraica Stuttgartensia*. Stuttgart: Deutsche Bibelgesellschaft, 1983.

Emerson, Michael O., and Christian Smith. *Divided by Faith: Evangelical Religion and the Problem of Race in America*. Oxford, 2000.

Fanning, Buist M. *Revelation*. ECNT. Zondervan, 2020.

Fasol, Al. "Preaching from Malachi." *SJT* 30 (1987): 32-34.

Feinberg, John S., ed. *Continuity and Discontinuity: Perspectives on the Relationship Between the Old and New Testaments*. Crossway, 1988.

Fernandez, Tony. "Hope When It's Hard: Habakkuk 1." Broward Church, July 8, 2019. https://www.youtube.com/watch?v=8Imn1sJjNdg.

Fitch, David. "Tim Keller, David Fitch, and Justice." *CT* (August 2020).

France, R. T. *The Gospel of Mark*. NIGTC. Eerdmans, 2002.

French, David, and Curtis Chang. "When Pastors Head for the Exits." *Good Faith*, (podcast) January 22, 2022.

Fry Brown, Teresa. "Surviving Justice Fatigue." Candler School of Theology Fall Convocation, Atlanta, GA, August 25, 2016. https://vimeo.com/180328468.

Fusco, Daniel. "Our Forever Home (Isaiah 65:17–25)." August 9, 2017. https://www.youtube.com/watch?v=Y2IzkLP_Qpo.

Gadamer, Hans-Georg. *Truth and Method*. 2nd rev. ed. Translated by Joel Weinsheimer and Donald G. Marshall. Continuum, 1996.

Gaffin, Richard B., Jr. *Perspectives on Pentecost: New Testament Teaching on the Gifts of the Holy Spirit*. P&R, 1979.

Galli, Mark, and Craig Brian Larson. *Preaching that Connects: Using Journalistic Techniques to Add Impact*. Zondervan, 1994.

Gardner, Susan K. "Equity vs. Equality." Accessed July 2, 2022. https://www.youtube.com/watch?v=nCS7Rus4_-Y.

Gentry, Peter J., and Stephen J. Wellum. *Kingdom Through Covenant*. Crossway, 2012.

Gibson, Scott, ed. *Preaching the Old Testament*. Baker, 2006.

Glass, Philip. "Philip Glass: Complex Minimalist." Interview by Renee Montagne. *Morning Edition*, October 3, 2008.

Gorman, Amanda. "The Hill We Climb." Washington, D.C., January 20, 2021. https://www.youtube.com/watch?v=LZ055ilIiN4.

Gould, Jens. "Native Americans dying at much higher rate from COVID-19." *SantaFeNewMexican.com* (August 4, 2020).

Gregory the Great. *The Book of the Pastoral Rule*. Fig books, 2013. Kindle.

Greidanus, Sidney. *The Modern Preacher and the Ancient Text*. Eerdmans, 1988.

———. *Preaching Christ from the Old Testament: A Contemporary Hermeneutical Method*. Eerdmans, 1999.

Grudem, Wayne. *The Gift of Prophecy in the New Testament and Today*. Rev. ed. Crossway, 2000.

Guthrie, William Norman. "The Poet as Prophet." *SR* 6 no. 4 (Oct 1898): 402-412.

Habel, Norman C. "Deuteronomy 18—God's Chosen Prophet." *CTM* 35 (1964): 575-582.

Hamilton, Andrew. *How to Preach the Prophets for All Their Worth: A Hermeneutical, Homiletical, and Theological Guide to Unleash the Power of the Prophets.* Wipf & Stock, 2022.

Hansen, David. *Loving the Church You Lead: Pastoring with Acceptance and Grace.* Baker Books, 1998.

Hanson, Paul D. *The Dawn of Apocalyptic.* Rev. ed. Fortress Press, 1979.

Harrison, R. K. *Introduction to the Old Testament.* Hendrickson, 2004.

Haugen, Gary. *Good News About Injustice.* 10th anniversary edition. IVP Books, 2009.

Hayes, John H. "The Usage of Oracles Against Foreign Nations in Ancient Israel." *JBL* 87 (March 1968): 81-92.

Hays, Richard B. *Echoes of Scripture in the Letters of Paul.* Yale University Press, 1989.

Heath, Chip, and Dan Heath. *Made to Stick: Why Some Ideas Survive and Others Die.* Random House, 2008.

———. *The Power of Moments.* Bantam Press, 2017.

Hendricks, Howard G. *Teaching to Change Lives.* Multnomah, 1987.

Herando, Caroline, and Efthymios Constantinides. "Emotional Contagion: A Brief Overview and Future Directions." *Frontiers in Psychology* 2021. https://doi.org/10.3389/fpsyg.2021.712606.

Heschel, Abraham. *The Prophets.* Harper Colophon Books, 1962.

Hoekema, Anthony A. *Created in God's Image.* Eerdmans, 1986.

Holmes, Michael W., ed. and trans. *Apostolic Fathers.* 3rd ed. Baker, 2007.

Hooper, Tom, Stephen Brooker, Catherine Greaves Becky Bentham, and Rael Jones Anne Dudley. *Les Misérables.* USA/UK/Japan, 2012.

Hopper, Andrew. "The Sun of Righteousness (Malachi 4)." February 6, 2018. https://www.youtube.com/watch?v=wifO4aND6-M.

House, Paul R. *The Unity of the Twelve.* Almond Press, 1990.

Hughes, Beau. "Into the Storm," The Village Church (podcast), June 22, 2008.

Hughes, Langston. "The Negro Speaks of Rivers," in *Vintage Hughes.* 2nd ed. Vintage, 2004.

Hunter, James Davison. *To Change the World: The Irony, Tragedy, and Possibility of Christianity in the Late Modern World.* Oxford University Press, 2010. Kindle edition.

Imes, Carmen. *Bearing God's Name: Why Sinai Still Matters.* IVP Academic, 2019.

Iser, Wolfgang. *The Act of Reading: A Theory of Aesthetic Response.* Johns Hopkins University Press, 1978.

Jackson, Shirley. "The Lottery." *The New Yorker* (June 1948).

Jacobsen, David Schnasa. *Preaching in the New Creation: The Promise of New Testament Apocalyptic Texts.* Westminster John Knox Press, 1999.

Jiang, Yuwei, Gerald J. Gorn, Maria Galli, and Amitava Chattopadhyay. "Does Your Company Have the Right Logo? How and Why Circular- and Angular-Logo Shapes Influence Brand Attribute Judgments." *Journal of Consumer Research* 42:5 (February 2016), 709–726.

Jobes, Karen H., and Moises Silva. *Invitation to the Septuagint.* Baker Academic, 2000.

Johnson, Bret. "Worship in Justice." Valley Bible Church, March 21, 2021. https://vimeo.com/526178997.

Jonker, Peter. *Preaching in Pictures: Using Images for Sermons that Connect.* Abingdon, 2015.

Kaiser, Walter C. *Exodus.* EBC. Zondervan, 1990.

Keller, Timothy. "A Biblical Critique of Secular Justice and Critical Theory." *GL* (August 2020).

———. *Generous Justice: How God's Grace Makes Us Just.* Viking, 2010.

Kenaston, Denny. "The Approaching Wave of Persecution." Accessed October 29, 2020. https://www.sermonindex.net/modules/mydownloads/scr_index.php?act=bookSermons&book=Habakkuk&page=0.

Kendi, Ibram X. *How to Be an Antiracist.* One World, 2019.

Kim, Chang Hoon. "Prophetic Preaching as Social Preaching." *ERT* 30 (2006): 141–151.

King, Martin Luther, Jr. "Birth of a New Nation." Dexter Avenue Baptist Church, April 7, 1957. http://www.mlkonline.net/nation.html.

———. "Letter from a Birmingham Jail." April 16, 1963. Pages 64-84 in *Why We Can't Wait.* Signet Classics, 2000.

Kline, Meredith G. *Images of the Spirit.* Wipf & Stock, 1999.

Koehler, Ludwig, and Walter Baumgartner. *The Hebrew and Aramaic Lexicon of the Old Testament.* Translated by M. E. J. Richardson. Brill, 2000.

Kolowich, Steve. "Confuse Students to Help Them Learn." *Chronicle of Higher Education,* August 14, 2014.

Korniotes, Matt. "The Parable of Two Eagles and a Vine." August 5, 2020. https://www.youtube.com/watch?v=Vr2KAhkKVtI.

Kuruvilla, Abraham. *Privilege the Text! A Theological Hermeneutic for Preaching.* Moody Publishers, 2013.

———. *Text to Praxis: Hermeneutics and Homiletics in Dialogue.* LNTS 393. T&T Clark, 2009.

Labberton, Mark. *The Dangerous Act of Worship: Living God's Call to Justice*. IVP Books, 2007.

Laja, Peep. "First Impressions Matter: Why Great Visual Design Is Essential." (Blog), April 2019. https://cxl.com/blog/first-impressions-matter-the-importance-of-great-visual-design.

Langley, Kenneth. *How to Preach the Psalms*. Fontes, 2021.

Larson, Craig Brian, ed. *Prophetic Preaching*. Hendrickson, 2012.

LaRue, Cleophus J. "It Will Surely Come." February, 2002. https://www.youtube.com/watch?v=thUNubGmO4E.

Lee, R. G. "Payday Someday." https://www.youtube.com/watch?v=0mstq4QTyrQ.

Leggett, Donald A. *Loving God and Disturbing Men: Preaching from the Prophets*. Clements Publishing, 1990.

Lessing, R Reed. "Orality in the Prophets." *CJ* 29 (2003): 152–65.

LitCharts. "in Just- Summary and Analysis." Accessed June 5, 2022. https://www.litcharts.com/poetry/e-e-cummings/in-just.

Litfin, Duane. *Paul's Theology of Preaching*. IVP Academic, 2015.

Long, Thomas G. *Preaching and the Literary Forms of the Bible*. Fortress, 1989.

———. *The Witness of Preaching*. 2nd ed. Westminster John Knox, 2005.

Longman, Tremper, III. "Nahum." In *The Minor Prophets*. Volume 2. Edited by Thomas Edward McComiskey. Baker, 1993.

Loritts, Bryan. "2020: The Year we Must never Forget." One Community Church, January 4, 2021. The Bryan Loritts Podcast.

Lowry, Eugene L. *The Homiletical Plot: The Sermon as Narrative Art Form*. Exp. ed. Westminster John Knox, 2001.

Luther, Martin. "The True Light." In *The Sermons of Martin Luther*. Accessed October 9, 2020. https://www.monergism.com/sermons-martin-luther-8-volumes.

MacIntyre, Alasdair. *After Virtue*. 3rd ed. University of Notre Dame Press, 2007.

———. *Whose Justice? Which Rationality?* University of Notre Dame Press, 1988.

Manning, Brennan. *Abba's Child: The Cry of the Heart for Intimate Belonging*. NavPress, 2015.

Mason, Eric. "Fresh Expectations," Epiphany Fellowship, December 9, 2020. https://www.youtube.com/watch?v=1QE_dtF1R0U.

Mathews, Ashley. "Isaiah 61:1-4." Trinity Anglican Church, December 13, 2020. https://podcast.atltrinity.org/episodes/isaiah-61-1-4-westside.

———. "Isaiah 9:1-7." Trinity Anglican Church, December 20, 2020. https://podcast.atltrinity.org/episodes/isaiah-9-1-7-westside.

Mathews, Jeanette. "Preaching from the Minor Prophets." *SMR* 223 (February 2013): 1–12.

Mathewson, Steven D. *The Art of Preaching Old Testament Narrative.* Baker Academic, 2002.

McRoberts, Justin, and Scott Erickson. *Prayer: Forty Days of Practice.* Waterbrook, 2019.

Mitchell, Henry. *Black Preaching: The Recovery of a Powerful Art.* Abingdon Press, 1990.

Moberg, David O. *The Great Reversal: Evangelism and Social Concern.* Rev. ed. J.B. Lippincott Company, 1977.

Murray, Pauli. "The Dilemma of the Minority Christian." May 19, 1974. Pages 257-262 in *Daughters of Thunder: Black Women Preachers and Their Sermons, 1850-1979.* Edited by Bettye Collier-Thomas. Jossey-Bass Publishers, 1998.

National Public Radio. "When Emotions Are Contagious." *Invisibilia* (podcast), July 21, 2019.

Nelson, Jesse L. "Barriers: The Challenge for Evangelical Homiletics in the African American Church and Community." Paper presented at the Annual Conference of the Evangelical Homiletics Society. October 19–21, 2019.

Nelson, Tom "*Lord of the Nations.*" Denton Bible Church (podcast), December 14, 2008.

Nestle, Erwin, Barbara Aland, and Kurt Aland, eds. *Novum Testamentum Graece.* 27th ed. Deutsche Bibelgesellschaft, 2001.

North, Robert. "Prophecy to Apocalyptic via Zechariah." Pages 47–71 in *Congress Volume Uppsala 1971.* Brill, 1972.

Nwigwe, Toby. "Fye Fye Fye," (Lanell Grant, 2022).

Olsen, Ted. "The Positive Prophet." *CT* January 1, 2003.

Orlowski, Jeff, director. *The Social Dilemma.* Netflix, 2020.

Orr, Christopher. "How Pixar Lost Its Way." *The Atlantic,* June 2017.

Ortberg, John. "Resisting God." Menlo Park Presbyterian Church (podcast), November 8, 2008.

Ortlund, Dane. *Gentle and Lowly: The Heart of Christ for Sinners and Sufferers.* Crossway, 2020.

Park, Sangyil. "Speaking of Hope: Prophetic Preaching." *RevExp* 109 (2012): 413–28.

Paul, Shalom M. *Amos.* Hermeneia. Fortress, 1991.

Peterson, Eugene H. *The Contemplative Pastor: Returning to the Art of Spiritual Direction.* Eerdmans, 1993.

Phillips, Richard D. "My Strength and My Stronghold." Second Presbyterian Church, Greenville, SC, February 6, 2022. https://sermons.spcgreenville.org/sermons/27221556164843/.

Pierce, Timothy M. "Micah as a Case Study for Preaching and Teaching the Prophets." *SJT* 46 (2003): 77-94.
Piper, John. "Persevering in God-Centered Missions." September 8, 2013. https://www.desiringgod.org/messages/perseverance-in-god-centered-missions.
———. "When I Fall, I Will Rise." July 24, 1988. https://www.desiringgod.org/messages/when-i-fall-i-will-rise#brokenness-contrition-and-remorse.
———. *The Supremacy of GOD in Preaching*. Rev. and exp. ed. Crossway, 2021.
Pollard, Edward B. "The Prophet as a Poet." *BW* 12 no. 5 (1898): 327-32.
Porter, Stanley E., and Jason C. Robinson. *Hermeneutics: An Introduction to Interpretive Theory*. Eerdmans, 2011.
Postman, Neil. *Amusing Ourselves to Death*. 20th anniv. ed. Penguin, 2006.
Price, Eric. "Situating Black Evangelical Preaching Within Scholarship on Black Homiletics: William E Pannell as a Case Study." Paper presented at the annual meeting of the Evangelical Homiletics Society, October 15, 2020.
Rauschenbusch, Walter. *Christianity and the Social Crisis*. Rev. ed. Harper & Row, 1964.
Ravenhill, Leonard. "I Will Work a Work Not Believed." Accessed October 29, 2020. http://ia800301.us.archive.org/27/items/SERMON-INDEX_SID20816/SID20816.mp3.
Rawls, John. *A Theory of Justice*. Rev. ed. Belknap Press, 1999.
Ricoeur, Paul. *Interpretation Theory: Discourse and the Surplus of Meaning*. The Texas Christian University Press, 1976.
Robertson, O. Palmer. *The Christ of the Covenants*. P&R, 1980.
———. *The Christ of the Prophets*. P&R, 2004.
———. *The Israel of God: Yesterday, Today, and Tomorrow*. P&R, 2000.
Robinson, Haddon. *Biblical Preaching: The Development and Delivery of Expository Messages*. 3rd ed. Baker Academic, 2014.
———. "The Heresy of Application: An Interview with Haddon Robinson." *Leadership* 18 (Fall 1997): 20-27.
Rothstein, Richard. *The Color of Law: A Forgotten History of How Our Government Segregated America*. Liveright, 2018.
Russell Howard. "Unboxing Amos." October 7, 2020. https://www.youtube.com/watch?v=0gI_HcS4bZI.
Sailhamer, John H. "Preaching from the Prophets." Pages 115-36 in *Preaching the Old Testament*. Edited by Scott M. Gibson. Baker, 2006.
Sandel, Michael J. *Justice: What's the Right Thing to Do?* Farrar, Straus and Giroux, 2009.

Scazzero, Peter. *Emotionally Healthy Spirituality*. Updated ed. Zondervan, 2017.

Schade, Leah D., and Jerry L. Sumney. *Apocalypse When? A Guide to Interpreting and Preaching Apocalyptic Texts*. Cascade: 2020.

Schorn, Daniel. "The New Beirut." *60 Minutes*, December 22, 2005. https://www.cbsnews.com/news/the-new-beirut/.

Seitz, Christopher R. *The Goodly Fellowship of the Prophets: The Achievement of Association in Canon Formation*. Baker Academic, 2009.

Seitz, Christopher R. *Isaiah 1-39. Interpretation*. Westminster John Knox, 1993.

———. *Prophecy and Hermeneutics: Toward a New Introduction to the Prophets*. Grand Rapids: Baker Academic, 2007.

———. *Word Without End: The Old Testament as Abiding Theological Witness*. Eerdmans, 1998.

Sensing, Timothy R. "A Call to Prophetic Preaching." *ResQ* 41 (1999): 139–54.

Sider, Ronald J. *Rich Christians in an Age of Hunger*. New ed. Thomas Nelson, 2005.

Smith, Gary V. *Amos*. Mentor, 1998.

———. *The Prophets as Preachers: An Introduction to the Hebrew Prophets*. Broadman & Holman, 1994.

Snodgrass, Klyne. *Stories with Intent: A Comprehensive Guide to the Parables of Jesus*. Eerdmans, 2008.

Spurgeon, Charles Haddon. "The Carnal Mind Enmity Against God." April 2, 1855. https://www.spurgeon.org/resource-library/sermons/the-carnal-mind-enmity-against-god/#flipbook/.

———. *Lectures to My Students*. CreateSpace, 2018.

"Statement of Faith of the National Association of Evangelicals." Accessed June 12, 2022. https://www.nae.org/statement-of-faith.

"The Statement on Social Justice and the Gospel." Accessed June 12, 2022. https://statementonsocialjustice.com.

Stearns, Richard. *The Hole in our Gospel*. Thomas Nelson, 2010.

Steiner, Lee. "Isaiah 59:14-15, Justice Demands the Truth." Trinity Baptist Church, Shreveport, LA, October 4, 2020. https://www.youtube.com/watch?v=oH_kUrCNoQo.

Sternberg, Meir. *The Poetics of Biblical Narrative: Ideological Literature and the Drama of Reading*. Indiana University Press, 1987.

Stott, John. *The Preacher's Portrait*. Eerdmans, 1961.

Stuart, Douglas. *Hosea-Jonah*. WBC. Word Books, 1987.

———. *Old Testament Exegesis*. 3rd ed. Westminster John Knox, 2001.

———. *Studies in Early Hebrew Meter*. Scholars Press, 1976.

Sunukjian, Donald R. *Invitation to Biblical Preaching: Proclaiming Truth with Clarity and Relevance*. Kregel, 2007.

Sunukjian, Don. "My Name is Harbona." *PT* (September 2006).
Swan, James. "Luther: Every Week I Preach Justification by Faith to My People, Because Every Week They Forget It." (Blog), August 3, 2020. https://beggarsallreformation.blogspot.com/2020/08/luther-every-week-i-preach.html.
Sweeney, Marvin A. *Isaiah 1-39*. FOTL. Eerdmans 1996.
Taylor, Barbara Brown. *An Altar in the World: A Geography of Faith*. HarperOne, 2010.
The (Online) Book of Common Prayer. The Church Hymnal Corporation, 2007. https://www.bcponline.org.
Thiselton, Anthony. "Reader-Response Hermeneutics, Action Models, and the Parables of Jesus." Pages 79-113 in Roger Lundin, Anthony C. Thiselton, and Clarence Walhout, eds. *The Responsibility of Hermeneutics*. Eerdmans, 1985.
Thompson, Andrew C. "Community Oracles: A Model for Applying and Preaching the Old Testament Prophets," *JEHS* 10 (March 2010): 31-57.
———. "Projection Interpretation: Toward a Hermeneutic for Homiletics." PhD diss., London School of Theology, 2020.
———. "The Favor of Focus (Isaiah 5:8-24)." The Chapel, Brunswick, GA, November 1, 2015.
Thompson, Rebekah. "Social Justice and Biblical Justice are Actually the Same." *CT* (October 2021).
Tisby, Jemar. *How to Fight Racism: Courageous Christianity and the Journey Toward Racial Justice*. Zondervan, 2021.
Tripp, Paul David. *Dangerous Calling: Confronting the Unique Challenges of Pastoral Ministry*. Crossway, 2012.
VanGemeren, Willem A. *Interpreting the Prophetic Word*. Zondervan, 1990.
———., ed. *New International Dictionary of Old Testament Theology and Exegesis*. Zondervan, 1997.
Vanguard Church. "God's Love Never Gives Up." February 7, 2016. https://vimeo.com/154492339.
Verhoef, P.A. "Prophecy." *NIDOTTE* 4: 1067-1079.
Vroegop, Mark. *Dark Clouds, Deep Mercy: Discovering the Grace of Lament*. Crossway, 2019.
Walton, John H., Victor H. Mathews, and Mark W. Chavalas. *The IVP Bible Background Commentary: Old Testament*. IVP, 2000.
Wells, David F. *No Place for Truth: Or Whatever Happened to Evangelical Theology?* Eerdmans, 1993.
Westermann, Claus. *Basic Forms of Prophetic Speech*. Translated by Hugh Clayton White. Westminster John Knox, 1991.
"What is Grief, if Not Love Persevering?" Accessed June 14, 2022. https://www.youtube.com/watch?v=9VATT98uYXk.

Whisenat, Edgar C. "88 Reasons Why the Rapture Will Be in 1988: The Feast of Trumpets (Rosh Hash-Ana) September 11-12-13." World Bible Society, 1988.
Williams, Thaddeus J. *Confronting Injustice Without Compromising Truth*. Zondervan Academic, 2020.
Willis, John T. "On the Interpretation of Isaiah 1:18." *JSOT* 25 (1983): 35-54.
Wilson, Paul Scott. *The Practice of Preaching*. Rev. ed. Abingdom, 1995.
Wittig, Susan. "A Theory of Multiple Meanings." *Semeia* 9 (1977): 75-103.
Wolterstorff, Nicholas. *Divine Discourse: Philosophical Reflections on the Claim that God Speaks*. Cambridge University Press, 1995.
———. *Justice: Rights and Wrongs*. Princeton University Press, 2008.
Wredberg, Josh. "The Gospel and Those People." Southeastern Seminary, October 19, 2018. https://www.youtube.com/watch?v=RgzlotbHkRA.
Wright, N. T. *Jesus and the Victory of God*. Fortress, 1996.
———. *The New Testament and the People of God*. Fortress, 1992.
Yancey, George. *Beyond Racial Gridlock. Embracing Mutual Responsibility*. IVP Books, 2006.
Yui, Lin, Roslin J. Ng, and Hiran Perera. "Concrete vs. Abstract Words – What Do You Recall Better? A Study on Dual Coding Theory." *PeerJ Preprints*, January 2017. https://doi.org/10.7287/peerj.preprints.2719v1.
Zamchiya, Muboso. "Repent (Joel 1)." Anacostia River Church, 2020. https://soundcloud.com/archurch/worship-in-preaching-the-message-of-joel-repent.
Zimmerman, Heather Joy. "Walking in the Ruins (Micah 4:1-5)." Wheaton College, March 24, 2022. https://www.youtube.com/watch?v=S7gjG_qktcM.

Scripture Index

Genesis	
1:26–27	109
8:22	42
12:1–3	53
15:18–21	22
20:7	16

Exodus	
15	3 n. 5
20:3–6	21
20:4–7	109
20:25	109
21:1–32	22
22:25	44 n. 30

Leviticus	
11:44	44
25:10–24	20
26	21
26–27	230
26:3–5	32

Numbers	
12:6–8	15 n. 16, 17
23–24	4

Deuteronomy	
1:34–40	22
5:2–3	22
18:15–22	16 n. 20, 17
19:14	20
27:1–8	22
28:7–10	53
28–30	21, 230
28:36	22
28:49	32
28:63	20
29:15	22
30:6	231
30:7	53

Judges	
5	3 n. 5
6:8	16
9	88
14	88

1 Samuel	
2	3 n. 5
3	17
7:1–3	18
9:9	15 n. 16

2 Samuel	
12	88

1 Kings	
9:3	155
13	16
21	121
22:17	96
22:19–23	21

2 Kings	
17–19	18
21:7	223
22	3 n. 5

1 Chronicles	
9:22	17
26:28	17
29:29	17 n. 24

2 Chronicles	
13:22	16
35:18	17 n. 24

Psalms	
87:4	212 n. 4

Proverbs		13–24	241
1:1	88 n. 7	13:2	119
15:23	75	14:4–21	90
18:8	75	16:11	140
28:5	193	18:3	119
		19:16–25	225
Isaiah		20:1–4	171
1	125	22:4	130
1:1–6:13	242–243	23	212
1:2–20	131	25–27	99
1:15–17	182	25:7–8	96 n. 19
1:19–20	31, 33, 125	25:10–11	181
1:20	121	28	182
2	47, 69, 71	28:7–13	233
2:8	33	28:17	33
2:10–11	69	30:7	212
3:5, 12	33	30:17	120
3:16–4:1	171, 176, 211	30:19–21	222
3:24–26	211	31	19
4:2–6	84	32:2	76
5:1–7	14, 88, 93	32:16	206
5:2	81	35:1	230
5:7	81	40	2, 178
5:8–25	207, 247–258	40–55	232–233
5:26	119	40:3–5	230
6	29, 147	40:12–31	41
6:1	212	43:1–7	46
6:1–8	123	43:2	115
6:8–13	106, 156, 214 n. 6	43:7	109
6:13	110	44:6–8	31
7–8	4	46:1–4	159–160
9	82, 140, 144	46:8	19
9:1–7	218	48:1	33
9:8–10:21	67, 70	49:22	119
10:5–19	89	51:1–3	32
11:1–2	110	51:9	212 n. 4
11:1–9	118	53:3–6	161
11:6–7	118	54:10	36
11:10	120	55:3	19
12	144	55:10–11	121

Scripture Index

56–59	204	15:18	120
56:3	141	16:1–21	220
56:7	142	19:1–13	95, 126
57:5, 17	33	21–23	229
58	190	22:13–30	44
58:13–14	19	23	4 n. 8
60:1–6	1	23:1–8	71–72, 225
61	190	23:14	19
61:1–2	51	25:9	229
61:1–4	143	29:10	230
62:2	39	30:12	120
62:10	119	31	230
65:17	96 n. 19	31:31	19, 36
65:17 25	104	31:31–34	51
66:20–24	102–103	31:35–36	19
66:24	171	33:20–22	42
		34:13	32
Jeremiah		36:1–32	126
1:10	213	38	233
2:12–13	113	43	233
2:13	110	45:1–5	33
3:1–4:2	68	46–51	240
4	240		
5:28	204	**Ezekiel**	
6:14–15	120	1	5, 172
6:16	19	1:3	18
7:4	223	1:4–28	154
7:11	142	3:1–3	112
7:30–8:3	216	3:18	199
8:11–12	120	4	89, 172
8:22–9:2	133	8	172, 181
9:1	130	9	110
10:19	120	9:4	127
12:1–13	72	10	154
12:4	231	12	172
13	88	12:1–6	107
13:1–11	125	14:14	178
13:12–14	91	15:1–8	94
14:7	120	16	172
15:2	52	16:30	90

16:60	19	**Joel**	
17:1–24	92	1	122
18	89	1:1–20	50
18:2–29	214–215	1:2–12	153
20:49	233	1:6	153
21:10–17	63	1:12	64
23	95, 172, 185	1:13–20	153
24	185	2	71, 117, 164
34:1–24	56–57	2:1–27	50
34:20–24	19	2:2–9	153
34:25–31	32	2:8–9	67
36:22–23	172	2:10	155
36:25	19	2:12–17	154
36:25–27	155	2:14	100
37	155, 210, 230	2:28–32	47, 50, 51
37:26	35	2:30–32	230
38	210	2:31	12, 96 n. 19, 155
40–44	110	3:1–16	50
40–48	98	3:3	202
47	83	3:11	98
47:1–12	107	3:14	99
48:35	155	3:15	155
		3:16	78–79
Daniel		3:17–21	50
7–9	99	3:18	61
Hosea		**Amos**	
1–2	83	1:1	18, 235
2:9–13	172	1:2	176
2:14–15	142, 172, 180	1:3–2:16	162–163, 235
4:1–14	44	2:10	31
6:1	163	2:13	115
6:1–6	110	3:1–8	235
6:3–4	114	3:11–15	46
8:1–12	75–76	5:4–24	235
11:1	56	5:18–20	140, 222
11:1–4	43	6:1–7	137, 182, 235
11:2	231	7:3	171
11:7	44	7:9	171
14:8	31	7:10–13	233

Scripture Index

7:14	18	2:8	153
8:4–6	19	**Habakkuk**	
8:4–14	235	1–2	99
9:11–15	37, 235	1:1–11	164
9:12	24	1:2	78, 79
9:13	179	1:2–4	177
9:13–15	230	1:5	2
Obadiah		1:5–11	32
10–15	53	1:12–17	177
16	82	2:1	177
18	12	2:1–4	3, 234
		2:9–11	113
Jonah		3:16	177, 178
2:2–10	4 n. 10	3:17–19	111–112
3:4	4 n. 10		
4	131	**Zephaniah**	
4:10–11	95	1:1–18	131
		1:2–18	68
Micah		1:4–14	18
1:8–9	130	1:10–12	112
2:1–5	20	2:1–3	44
2:6	233	2:1–3:8	131
2:6–11	14	3:1–13	48
4:1–5	259–269	3:9–20	131–132
5	46–47	3:17	222
6:3–16	31		
6:6–8	45	**Haggai**	
6:8	19, 21, 44, 183, 190	1:6	117
		2:9	137
7:8–9	221	2:10–14	211
7:10–17	20		
7:11	223	**Zechariah**	
7:18–20	42	1:1–17	100–101
7:20	19	1:3	103
		2–6	211
Nahum		3:10	190
1:2–12	153	5:5–11	12
1:15	153	9:9–17	131
2	5	13:1–6	103

14:1–5	96 n. 19, 230	Luke	
14:20	48	1	3 n. 5
		2	175
Malachi		4:18–19	190 n. 5
1	5	8:26–39	82
1:6–14	19	11:49–51	16
1:1–10	141	16:7	218
2:3	181	17:32	29
2:10–11	31	24:19	16 n. 20
3:1–4	110		
3:2	115, 237	John	
3:16–18	127	2:18–21	45
4	101–102	3:16	216
4:1–3	96 n. 19, 155, 230	4:1–45	12
4:5–6	17 n. 26	4:35	126
4:6	83	6:14	16 n. 20
		10:10	214
Matthew			
2:15	56	Acts	
3:4	17 n. 26	2:1–41	164
5:17	13	2:40	103
9:13	13	3:24	17 n. 24
10:37	217	13:20	17 n. 24
11:5	13	15	37
11:9–11	17	21:8–9	16
13:10–17	52 n. 39, 106	21:10	16
13:14–15	13		
16:14	16 n. 20	Romans	
16:18–19	224	1:13	214 n. 6
23:1–36	173	2:24	13
		5:20	43
Mark		9–10	52 n. 39
4:10–20	214 n. 6	9:1–13	137
4:26–29	239	11:25	214 n. 6
8:29	151	15:16	237
8:31–38	151		
9:12–13	17 n. 26	1 Corinthians	
11:15–19	142	3:16	45
13	173, 214 n. 6	10:1	214 n. 6
16:1	151	11:17–22	137

12:10	16	4:1–2	156
14	166	4:2	1
14:20–25	52 n. 39		
14:21	13	Hebrews	
14:26	213	8:1–13	51
		11:32	17 n. 24
2 Corinthians		12:3–11	214
1:8	214 n. 6	12:28	42
4:2	139		
6:14–18	45	1 Peter	
8	45	1:14–16	44
12:1–10	214	2:4–5	45
13:10	138, 163, 213	5:1–4	238
Galatians		Jude	
3:29	43 n. 29	4	16
4:27	13		
5:12	137, 173	Revelation	
		1:3	4
Ephesians		2:5	213
2:20	213	3:2	185
4:29	174 n. 7	3:19	138
5:14	2	5:6	173
6:12	214	6:4	173
		6:14	173
Philippians		9:1–11	173
4	137	10:1–4	173
		11:13	173
1 Thessalonians		13:1–8	173
1:9	217–218	13:10	51
2:7	137	14:20	173
		19:15	173
1 Timothy			
4:12	174 n. 7		
4:15	203		
2 Timothy			
1:3–7	137		
2:24–25	174		
3:16	13, 185		

www.ingramcontent.com/pod-product-compliance
Lightning Source LLC
Chambersburg PA
CBHW070129080526
44586CB00015B/1614